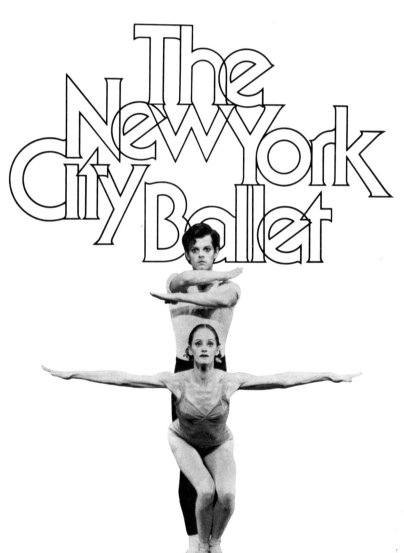

The New York City Ballet

ALSO BY LINCOLN KIRSTEIN
FOKINE (1934)
DANCE (1935)
BLAST AT BALLET (1938)
BALLET ALPHABET (1939)
TCHELITCHEW DRAWINGS (1947)
ELIE NADELMAN DRAWINGS (1949)
THE CLASSIC BALLET (1952)
WHAT BALLET IS ABOUT (1959)
RHYMES OF A PFC (1964)
MOVEMENTS AND METAPHOR (1971)

ALSO BY MARTHA SWOPE
MOURKA: THE AUTOBIOGRAPHY OF A CAT
(with text by Tanaquil LeClercq) (1964)
MARTHA GRAHAM: PORTRAIT OF THE LADY AS AN ARTIST
(with text by LeRoy Leatherman) (1966)

The New York City Ballet

TEXT BY LINCOLN KIRSTEIN
PHOTOGRAPHS BY MARTHA SWOPE
AND GEORGE PLATT LYNES
ALFRED A. KNOPF, NEW YORK, 1973

THIS IS A BORZOI BOOK PUBLISHED BY ALFRED A. KNOPF, INC.

Copyright © 1973 by Alfred A. Knopf, Inc.
All rights reserved under International and Pan-American Copyright Conventions.
Published in the United States by Alfred A. Knopf, Inc., New York, and
simultaneously in Canada by Random House of Canada Limited, Toronto.
Distributed by Random House, Inc., New York.

Library of Congress Cataloging in Publication Data
Kirstein, Lincoln, (date) The New York City Ballet.
Includes bibliographical references. 1. New York City Ballet. 2. Kirstein, Lincoln, (date)
GV1786.N4K57   792.8'09747'1   70-79331   ISBN 0-394-46652-7

Manufactured in the United States of America
First Edition

Grateful acknowledgment is made to the following for permission to reprint
previously published material:

Robert Craft and The Estate of Igor Stravinsky: For excerpts from *Dialogues
and a Diary* by Robert Craft and Igor Stravinsky (Doubleday & Company, Inc.,
1963).

Doubleday & Company, Inc.: For excerpts from *Balanchine's New Complete
Stories of the Great Ballets*, by George Balanchine, edited by Francis Mason,
copyright © 1954, 1968 by Doubleday & Company, Inc. Reprinted by permission
of the publisher.

Alfred A. Knopf, Inc.: For excerpts from pages 24–5 and 117 of *Themes and
Episodes*,by Robert Craft and Igor Stravinsky. Copyright © 1965, 1966 by
Robert Craft and Igor Stravinsky. Reprinted by permission of the publisher.

Liveright Publishing Corp.: For an excerpt of text material and 8 lines of poetry
(from "The Dance—Powhatan's Daughter") from *The Collected Poems and
Selected Letters and Prose of Hart Crane*, by Hart Crane. Copyright © 1933,
1958, 1966 by Liveright Publishing Corp. Reprinted by permission of the
publisher.

Newsweek: For an excerpt from an article by Emily Coleman, October 25, 1948.
Copyright Newsweek, Inc., 1948. Reprinted by permission.

The New York Times: For excerpts from two reviews by John Martin which
appeared in *The New York Times*, March 6, 1935, and November 22, 1950.
Copyright 1935/1950 by The New York Times Company. Reprinted by
permission.

CONTENTS

For Edward M. M. Warburg and
in memory of A. Everett Austin, Jr.
and Morton Baum—L. K.

And, of course, for Mr. B—M. S.

FOREWORD

Theatrical memoirs are always frustrating. Vividness in performance is based on a fast-evaporating amalgam of color and electricity, of physicality approaching hysteria that is impossible to reconstitute or render impressively in words. Shock, surprise, amazement, all fade in retelling. No matter what is described—stage action, song, or dance—it all sounds as if one has read it somewhere before. In the present recital, however, there is aid from photographs, which to some extent suggest a lost immediacy and compensate for inevitable failure in reconstruction. In the case of many photographs taken in George Platt Lynes's studio, Balanchine, guided by Lynes's taste and skill and using his approximation of theatrical lighting, actually snapped the lens of a stroboscopic camera. When Lynes died, far too early, his function was assumed by Martha Swope, who had been trained as a dancer and whose interest, preoccupation, and passion triumphantly won the confidence of intransigent stagehands, diffident performers, harried rehearsalists, and irritable ballet masters. She has accumulated an enormous file of documentary material, almost unique in this country in this century. Hers is a visual record invaluable not only to our company but to the entire range of the performing arts.

Words accompanying the pictures can't attempt to compete with them. Instead, the text makes suggestions by way of reviving key occasions that contributed variously to the development of an organism which, after nearly forty years, presents itself as the New York City Ballet. These suggestions take the form of quotations from an imaginary diary, such as might have been kept but in fact was not, paired with a running commentary on the diary's telegraphic accounts of historical fact. Many ballets whose antecedent elements are indicated remain in repertory and may be presently seen at the State Theater in New York City from season to season. Many more have been ploughed under, sometime to reappear in subsequent if much altered forms. The emphasis, however, is on extratheatrical factors which furnished background, springboard, or occasion for organization, and on mechanisms which produced dancers and dance works.

It has been noted, not always with approbation, that from its inception our company has held an attitude, indeed a metaphysic, which differs from others not only in philosophy but also in kind. To explain this difference, it has been necessary to penetrate the inscape and morality of those who were chiefly responsible for its birth, maintenance, and achievement. Its development has been eccentric and haphazard but, at the same time, continuous and possibly rational. Hence there

may be a temptation to eliminate accidental factors, to attempt to straitjacket chance into a logic of conscious contrivance. And yet, when the normal increment of accident is admitted or even accentuated, there remain principles that were clear from the beginning, points of departure which determined the kind and quality of school and company.

This vein of independence has been interpreted as arrogance; it presupposed assurance in direction even when the means to achieve it were in doubt. From the start it disavowed personalism, the projection of vaunted stars to sell a product. It insisted on erecting a new repertory instead of borrowing prestige from established personalities and known works. It persisted in collaborating with the progressive musicians of the epoch, notably Stravinsky; in using unfamiliar scores, old and new; as far as possible, in commissioning new music to fit current needs and tastes. From the first there was a trinity of aims: the foundation of a school as basis for a company; the creation of a repertory to accommodate an academic style particular to our climate and continent; the construction of a theater which would house such a company and the development of an audience which would maintain it. Initially this might have seemed to be, on the basis of historic precedent, an ambition to found a native school for a national company. As years passed, and several tentative experiments foundered, it grew clear that our country was far too large to be served by a single representative company, and that any audience which would be practical and desirable was less than a national constituency though rather more than a provincial or parochial one. Later, economic considerations intervened; the format of the resultant repertory enlarged to demand a frame too big for much mobility in touring. It became necessary to depend on a stable, localized subscription public. This was possible only in the single largest available metropolitan area which had a geographical center or focus. Hence what began as the American Ballet and toured as the Ballet Caravan resolved itself into Ballet Society and then the New York City Ballet. Deliberate identification with the cultural if not political capital of a nation justified many elements which led to continuity, stability; the elimination of improvisation and the establishment of a family audience.

In the process of building school, company, and theater, a considerable number of persons were involved, many of whose individual contributions were preponderant at the moment but ephemeral over a long run. It is impossible to be just to many. Some emerge in snapshots; their aid was often far greater than the space given them here suggests. Others—for example, Balanchine himself, whose school, company, and theater it

has been, is, and will be, and whose contribution and position are self-evident—may seem slighted in favor of less familiar figures.

The form of a synthetic, factitious "diary" was assumed for compactness and symbolic value. Entries indicate key memories that, never isolated, were steps contributing to the sequence of formation and growth. Memorable premieres, brilliant diplomatic galas, are scanted because the preparations which made them possible were more relevant and instructive. Performances are rarely described but only suggested through the atmosphere which surrounded them. In "diary" entries, a frank artificiality extends to present tense and personal pronoun, in an effort to suggest the air of a particular moment and the diarist's age, rather than displaying all in the diffused glow of hindsight. Total honest recall, absolute frankness, is impermissible. Any complete cast of characters reads mostly as dull names printed on a blank page, hardly even applicable to photographs which might identify them. Small or large, they cannot be seen as characters in the dimension of film or novel. The most one can hope for from the "diary" device is that it confers more vitality than statistics or the conscientious amplitude of specialized theatrical histories.

If and when a time comes that it may appear useful or interesting to compile a more complete history of our company, the present synopsis could serve as spine. If every proper name mentioned here were followed to its logical conclusion (involving twice as many persons and places), something approaching fullness might result. This would include a dizzy financial record which might have some value, though its special nature would be unlikely to interest many readers. However, since money occupied somewhat more than half our waking hours, at least a few words must acknowledge the economic factor, as tedious and awkward as it was to consider in our perennial crises. There was never enough money; unlike the situation in socialist states, there never will be. We rationalized this capital realization into something approaching advantage, although it produced constant serious modifications in our planning—notably regarding stage decoration. We have capitalized on a meager decorative style in a dimension which is importantly visual. Two prime considerations have always been music and plasticity, maps of motion based on piano or orchestral scores. Balanchine's ambition has ever been to make audiences see sound and hear dancing. It is a peculiar conjuring act which requires a particular set of conditions. It is not intended to please as many people as are captivated by ball games. The ensuing "diary" is a shorthand chart of a process which still proceeds.

LINCOLN KIRSTEIN
NEW YORK CITY
JULY, 1973

ACKNOWLEDGMENTS

This book contains no mention of many persons who, unknown to an audience, have made and still make possible the continuing activity of the New York City Ballet. Since it has no pretensions to any completeness, the introduction of perfunctory paragraphs as token tribute could only irritate those who are not mentioned but surely not forgotten. Thirty-eight years is a long time; many whose work was primary and capital are no longer here. Only the smallest measure of justice has been paid in print (although I hope not in the pictures) to dozens of individual dancers. This is not from lack of appreciation but from want of skill in translating the impact of performances into lively language with the tone of family pride. The ambiguities of praise or lack of it, affection, or a seeming slight, make one helpless to detail innumerable occasions which have given personal delight. However, it became necessary to record a few names so that, if or when a comprehensive history is undertaken, those most responsible may receive proper due.

Edward Bigelow has become, after Betty Cage, key administrator and functionary—at home, on tour, in so many capacities from his early seasons as a dancer and from stage to desk that his duties are too encompassing, various, and intricate to be precisely described. But they have been and are indispensable. Barbara Horgan has served not only as personal aide to Balanchine in his international commitments, but organizes his time so that the home team gets most benefit, without denying his repertory to the domestic and foreign institutions that seek it out. Rosemary Dunleavy stopped dancing to become ballet mistress, coordinator, rehearsalist. It is she who is to be thanked when an evening shoots along seemingly under its own power; the trigger is hers. Carole Deschamps has been invisibly onstage most nights in the last ten years, picking up pieces when anything in the mechanism momentarily cracks.

Mary Porter made sense of an impossible manuscript, full of tiresome emendations and gaffes, so that printers might read it. Mary Barnett, after everyone else, including the author, had abandoned it, put a cold eye on the text and thereby salvaged it for style and sense. Robert Gottlieb of Alfred A. Knopf, Inc., proposed this book. As a boy he was a devoted member of the audience at City Center's old Mecca Temple, where he paid his pennies to sit at the top of a balcony to applaud many of our early programs.—L. K.

PREFACE

Many people have photographed the New York City Ballet over the years, but two have been associated closely with the company for a long period of time as official photographers, George Platt Lynes in the thirties, forties, and early fifties, and myself from the late fifties until the present time.

I never knew George Platt Lynes, but I always admired his wonderful photographs with their beautifully lighted, somehow timeless quality and perfection. When the company was younger and there was more time, often whole evenings were spent in his studio with Balanchine himself setting poses and occasionally even taking action photos. George Platt Lynes was an artist in many ways: he himself often painted the backgrounds for his photographs—such as those of SWAN LAKE after the Eugene Berman stage set, and the sky for JONES BEACH which, inverted, became an impressionist scene for THE PRODIGAL SON. And certainly he sculpted with light.

When I began to think of this book, it seemed a splendid idea to combine two very different styles of photography reflecting, in a way, two different periods of the New York City Ballet as well as of our culture. Today the company has grown to great size, dancing and rehearsing throughout the entire year—the pace is faster, our vision more fleeting and candid. Most of my work has been an instant recording of what happens in rehearsal or onstage—not a careful distillation of an essence but rather the ephemeral moment caught and held.

I started out as a student at the School of American Ballet and progressed from taking pictures with a Brownie of my teachers and classmates to my first published photo, a rehearsal shot of Jerome Robbins and WEST SIDE STORY in *Life* magazine. I can never forget the day when Lincoln Kirstein, after seeing that picture, strode across the big dance studio on upper Broadway and asked me to work with the New York City Ballet. It was the beginning of a difficult and rewarding association—difficult because I was extremely limited in equipment and knowledge of photographic techniques, and had literally to learn as I worked, and with the world's greatest dancers in front of my lens! Difficult also because there was never time or money for photocalls on stage, as is the case on Broadway or in Europe, thus necessitating shooting during performances either from the audience or from the wings. At City Center, in the mezzanine, one had a front view of the work; at the State Theater, the only really feasible locations are the side rings and the wings, an altered viewpoint. However, despite the problems of point of view and of irritated audiences (one lady hit me over the head with her handbag while I was snapping away), there are an excitement and immediacy to candid photography that I think are appropriate to today.

And rewarding because of the association with these three great men who dominate the dance world—George Balanchine, Lincoln Kirstein, and Jerome Robbins—who gave me a most wonderful new career and the opportunity to work in a field of incredible beauty and meaning. I owe them much.

So here is the collaboration. George Platt Lynes is not alive to make his own choices, so I can only hope that we have served him well. Our ambition was not to amass a complete historical chronicle, which would have entailed unending research and a much more confining form, but rather to present from the two files what we found most interesting, representative, and beautiful. In the process, my editor, Robert Gottlieb, and I looked at every single frame on some 5,000 contact sheets of mine, and prints from every George Platt Lynes negative available in the Library Museum of Performing Arts. Much credit also goes to Robert Scudellari, whose taste and creativity in design contributed so much. It was a labor of love, and I hope it will be received with love.

MARTHA SWOPE
NEW YORK CITY
JULY, 1973

The New York City Ballet

APRIL, 1912: ROCHESTER, NEW YORK

Ma took us to the Lyceum. We sat in Uncle Mart's box. Red and gold; everything, red and gold. Drapes on this box, the front curtain; red. Gold fringe flopped when the curtain went up and down. Hundreds of people singing, whirling. One man in a black moustache, red-and-gold uniform, sang; not very funny. A lot of girls kicked very high in black garters. They were fast. Ma says I should say rapid, or quick. "Fast" is wrong. They moved faster than any bodies I've ever seen.

An uncle, Martin Woolf, controlled the Lyceum Theater, a provincial opera house built in the Teutonic taste of the sixties, a not too distant cousin of the San Carlo, Fenice, Maryinsky, as well as my ideal for a State Theater which Philip Johnson would build us fifty years later. THE MERRY WIDOW was performed by amateurs for charity; its cancan was a shocker. "Fast" then implied loose behavior. My first contact with stage dancing introduced me to a preoccupation, commitment, or addiction. Cocteau named it the "red-and-gold disease." The malady, obsession, advanced state of unease, indeed disease, was compounded of passion for the preposterous, the tease of perfection which was an impersonation of grandeur, or in exalted cases, the superhuman and heroic. Sex, also, is an expression of intense physicality; the restraint, release, and control of mind and muscle. At the Lyceum I also saw Otis Skinner in THE GARDEN OF ALLAH, but my sister's fingers clamped across my eyes while Haji, the beggar, was drowned in a small octangular pool bubbling with real water. The gurgling was acoustically perfect; the sound was more horrible than any sight might have been.

JUNE, 1916: BOSTON

Ma has gone to the Russian Ballet at the Opera House and would not take me. I am too young. I am nearly ten. I would not understand. I would, too! Miss Prescott explained everything. Scenery is painted like a signboard; it's not supposed to be real. A blob on the wall means: a fly. Russians are the best dancers in the world. Their best dancer is Nijinsky. He flies because he has bones like a bird. I will never forgive Mother.

I've never known exactly why I was not allowed to see Diaghilev's company on tour. Later I suspected it was because Nijinsky, in blackface as the golden slave in SCHÉ-HÉRAZADE, made love to a white harem queen. Miss Prescott was my teacher in public grade school. She wrote children's books and explained the basis of post-Impressionist painting from colored illustrations in the ballet's souvenir program which I *was* given to look at. Nijinsky's feet were, of course, no different from mine, except that he was a trained acrobat, among other important capacities. Fifteen years later, when I was working on his biography with his wife, I learned that in all probability Nijinsky never appeared in Boston at all because of a sudden indisposition which was an ominous warning of his increasing illness. His stand-in, Alexander Gavrilov, substituted for him unannounced. However, an image of him, fleshed out by colored reproductions of Bakst's costume sketches, was a spark that set me off. For years I tried to find onstage the magic which I was robbed of here.

JULY, 1919: LAKE SEBAGO, MAINE

Chris says I could be a dancer if I worked. She is a very good dancer, but she says not as good as her teacher, Isadora Duncan. I work out with her each morning before diving class. Some boys think I'm silly, fooling with Chris. I'm serious. Dancing is not hard; you have to feel free and keep time. Chris says it's by breathing, not by counting. Anyway, I'm chosen to be Pipe Bearer. I don't dance; I just hold the pipe. Then Cap lights it and hands it to the Chief Cub. It looks silly practicing walking and handing over, but it's not as hard as half gainers or jackknives.

At a boys' camp, a girl friend of the director had been one of the first Isadorables. She taught rhythmic exercises disguised to look as little as possible like dancing. Marking my interest, she confessed that actually a few steps further on would almost amount to "real dancing," and that if I truly wished, I could be a dancer. This seemed like admittance to a secret society. She also prepared me as hierophant in a ceremony, around a campfire, in which younger boys were admitted to a higher order. From this I recognized something of the ritual essence of bodily movement—designed for repetition, hence: repertory. Also that there was a superior element in spectacular performance even without a red-and-gold interior—that it could happen equally well in a clearing around a pinecone fire in Maine woods. Later the meaning of the cant theatrical term "camp" would be clarified. It may have derived from induced hysteria of congregations at evangelical camp meetings on the banks of middle-American rivers in the nineteenth century. "Camp" applied to a quality of impersonation, an imitation of heroic gesture, a parody of sacred mad behavior, an ironic or sarcastic criticism of advanced narcissism; the recognition of which would be a kind of antibody diminishing the more humorless sepsis of the red-and-gold disease.

Lincoln Kirstein, first standing
figure right of center

APRIL, 1920: BOSTON

Nat Woolf called; Ma let me go with him; he's seen Pavlova in New York; she is the greatest dancer who ever lived. And Nijinsky? Nat says great dancers are women. Symphony Hall was full; lots of applause, but it was not a real theater. A rigged-up gray curtain; no red and gold. Pavlova in her SYRIAN DANCE; trousers and a tall hat; she moved fast but couldn't jump. Nat says this number is a miniature version of SCHÉHÉRAZADE; made for concert halls, not opera houses. Ma is letting me go tomorrow night too. As for her DYING SWAN, Nat says it is "grotesque."

Dr. Nathaniel Woolf was the son of that uncle who owned the Lyceum in Rochester, and my first cousin. A junior at Harvard, he became my aesthetic mentor. Enthusiastic, in love with theater and poetry, an excellent student, he took a medical degree but hardly practiced. His childhood was tragic, his career aborted; he was able to exile himself in Europe, where he touched fringes of the backstage world. He appears fleetingly in the published diaries of Harry, Count Kessler, the German patron of Diaghilev and Gordon Craig. In my European vacations from college he fed me gossip of the Ballet Russe and gave me a relish for fashion and novelty, as well as a certain skeptical attitude toward accepted models. Once my mother took us both to L'AFRICAINE at the old Metropolitan Opera. There was an elaborate ballet in the house's Italian tradition, which he pronounced appalling. Heretofore I had no notion that anything in a format so splendiferous could be in "bad taste." My mother scolded him for spoiling my "pleasure," but this gave me much to think about. His assumption of proprietary interest in theater rubbed off on me; he presupposed he had the right to say what he liked and do as he pleased. Licensed or not, he suggested that participation in the production of art was possible, even by such alien amateurs as we were. From him I realized that theater was not simply a "pleasure" but a matter of appreciating, making, and performing. His inherent interests and kindness, ambiguous existence, and inconsequential end had a cautionary effect. Dilettantism could be attended by mortal danger from the red-and-gold disease, and was a depressing symptom of some of that malady's fringe benefits.

I watched Pavlova with Nat Woolf in Symphony Hall five nights running. Before this exposure, I had a vague idea that dances were somehow improvised according to the "mood" of dancers on their every hearing of the music, and took "inspiration" for method. But on watching the professional repetition of identical figurations night after night, I began to realize that there was something like design in dance, comparable to musical notation or a rationally laid out palette. Structure was as important as personality or expression. "Soul" was a word then uttered far more than now; it began to have a specious sound. Craft, skill, pattern supporting the dance began to suggest themselves, and "personality" seemed a suspicious ingredient.

JUNE, 1922: LONDON

My brother and I were in bed; it must have been around one or two. David woke us up. He gave us some of the girls' yellow-and-orange pyjamas. We went downstairs; Lydia made us do some easy steps in the garden. In the studio, lots of people. George was rather disagreeable but too sleepy to mind. We got through the dance more or less, thanks to Lydia. It was embarrassing but I enjoyed it. Lytton gave me a drink. Maynard is going to marry Lydia; no one seems surprised.

My sister, Mina, had taken a house in London, together with Henrietta Bingham, daughter of Judge Robert Bingham, owner of the Louisville *Courier-Journal* and later ambassador to Great Britain. The two girls, some ten years older than I, were involved with the Bloomsbury group, among whom was the masterful economist and architect of artistic patronage, Maynard Keynes. Lydia Lopokova, the most brilliant of Diaghilev's soubrettes, had become a star of the post–World War I seasons. I could not know that at this very moment, in Leningrad,

Lydia Lopokova

her brother Feodor Lopukhov was rehearsing with a young fellow student, Georgei Balanchivadze, for an experimental program of revolutionary ballets. Although there were a number of well-known characters in and out of our house, they were taken for granted. Lytton Strachey meant more to me as the model of his huge, lanky portrait by Henry Lamb than as a writer. David Garnett had dedicated his second book to my sister. "Bloomsbury" never seemed to me special or snobbish; rather it was the shifting site of an endless party taking place at various houses all over London and in the country. Art, gossip, or opinions about art seemed its main occupation.

Maynard Keynes showed me an exhibition of Gauguin at the Leicester Galleries and demonstrated the difference between a "good" Gauguin and a "bad" one. Or at least, he made it clear that he considered there was this difference. Heretofore I had assumed that any and every Gauguin was per se of prime importance. He disconcerted me by saying that pictures were also negotiable securities, signed like banknotes or bills of sale. To him the fact that they had other values besides aesthetic or romantic ones accentuated their primacy as historical, social, and economic properties. Any appreciation of art became more complex than the simple acceptance of a personal talent. Gauguin, whom I'd been given as an advance-guard champion, now retired to the status of some minor old master.

Later I would take rooms in Russell Square, and come to know a number of the personages who were for their epoch a concentration of opinion makers and taste masters. Those I knew best were minor members, but these, and one in particular, had a major effect. He was a sculptor, son of a Lord Chief Justice who disapproved of his sculpture. Stephen Tomlin gave me the run of his studio, let me watch him draw from the nude, work with his clay, and play at being serious, disinherited, and in the vanguard. He also let me put gold studs in his boiled shirt when he went into another world of formal "society"; from him I learned the polarized compatibility of High and Low Bohemia. Intimacy with studios gave me a certain security when I later dealt with artists.

JUNE, 1926: LONDON

Diaghilev is bankrupt; Lord Rothermere will put up no more money; he must play in a vaudeville theater; Stravinsky has deserted to Ida Rubinstein. Anyway, the present theater is dreary and smaller than the Lyceum in Rochester. I expected more. Not much dancing; not enough dancers. But one exciting moment. In FIREBIRD the magician Kastchei was made up as Ghenghis Khan; Mongolian, with long fingernails like gilded claws, a frightful vulture. In a fantastically evil way he manipulated the others. Afterward, to a restaurant; there he was, among other dancers. I wanted to ask him for a drink, but didn't dare.

I entered Harvard as a freshman in 1926, having worked for a year in a stained-glass factory, since it was thought I should learn something concrete before college. Because my father was self-educated, he was both respectful and suspicious of "higher" education unless it had some practical basis. The stained-glass shop taught me something about technical method and expert execution which applied to other forms of expression. I came to consider familiarity with digital mastery, combined with instruction in the materials of painting and the means of rendering, as the basis of critical judgment.

My parents let me spend most summer vacations in Europe; attendance at Diaghilev's seasons, mainly in London, became increasingly the focus of my interest. In most ways I was uncertain of any vocation. I wished to be at once painter, poet, and professional horseman. My models were traditional rather than progressive, although I was involved with Edward Warburg and John Walker in the Harvard Society for Contemporary Art. It took me some time to realize that "being a painter" was not painting, nor did "being a poet" produce good verse. It was roles or impersonation rather than the lodged activity which attracted me.

I attached myself to the fringes of ballet and Bloomsbury without real contact. The dancer who had appeared as Kastchei was George Balanchine. When I asked about him I was told that he was an excellent dancer with bad lungs, that Diaghilev had confidence in him as ballet master and choreographer, that he lived with Alexandra Danilova, that he had a personal life apart from Diaghilev's intimate court.

I spoke bad French, accumulated a smattering of gossip that serves as a key to superficial entry into closed worlds. Then, curious and energetic Americans were something of a curiosity to Europeans. We could penetrate shut circles with reasonable ease. I was fascinated by what I could not decipher of the ballet world. What I discovered was neither reassuring nor interesting. There must be something beyond personal tension, jealousies, financial insecurity which made what I saw onstage as dancing come to life, although this would elude me for years.

Meanwhile the vague figure named Balanchine gradually assumed more definite shape as his responsibilities and reputation grew. But he was never starred as a performer and infrequently appeared. However, I was not much interested in star personalities. They seemed to have only a single limited self to sell. There were no canonized ballerinas and at that time Massine, Dolin, and Lifar represented star values to the exclusion of everyone else—except Parisian painters, upon whom Diaghilev was forced to depend since he had no strong company of dancers in depth. Deprived of a Russian source or seedbed, Diaghilev enlisted Picasso, Matisse, Derain, Rouault, de Chirico, Tchelitchev, Max Ernst to produce designs that were more impressive than much choreography. But the combination of painted cloths and theatrical movement igniting the final Diaghilev seasons was a disturbing ferment, a delicious torture, which upset all my anticipatory speculation in the months when I could not see them. I complained in the borrowed fashionable formula, but I was addicted, as in a love affair.

DECEMBER, 1927: NEW YORK

Tony's speakeasy, West 52nd Street, the first I've been in. Seems like the cozy back room of an Italian restaurant. You're let in by being inspected through a hole in the door; perfunctory gesture; no danger. The whole place, the cabin of a pirate ship, like Treasure Island. Everyone knew each other. I felt like the cabin boy in the barrel, overhearing a conspiracy. Gin confused the picture. Muriel Draper, the most extraordinary female I've ever met. In London she was known as the White Negress. She wore a gold turban and sat with a powerful black man, Taylor Gordon, a singer. She looked me up and down as if judging a horse. She was shameless; immediately intimate, but did not try to scare me. Taylor Gordon gave me a drink, and left for Harlem. Mrs. Draper told me to sit in his chair; asked me what I wanted to be? Be? Rather than do. I tried thinking this through: I, well, I wanted —to be, a dancer. She said: Well, you won't; you're too old, too tall, too rich.

Muriel Draper, whose papers repose in the Collection of American Literature at Yale, awaits a biographer who will do justice to a capricious, flamboyant, influential, and forgotten American woman. An ardent feminist, she liberated herself past the wildest dreams of any Unitarian suffragette. A New Englander from Haverhill, Massachusetts, her father was allied with Alexander Graham Bell in early inventions. Before the First World War she grew up in Italy and England, and married Paul Draper, who had an exquisite tenor voice and sang *Lieder* better than any other American. They were parents to one of the best dancers in the most musical idiom of tap. Muriel's memoirs, *Music at Midnight*, have not half the quality of her conversation but tell much of her years as hostess before she lost fortune and husband and found Marxism. She returned to New York, supported two small sons as an interior decorator, and wrote weekly about house decoration for the *New Yorker*. Although she was well-connected socially, independence was her main concern. She made consequential theater out of her poverty and, in a mad decor of furniture and objects salvaged from thrift shop and warehouse, for twenty years conducted what may have been the last valuable intellectual salon in New York.

Muriel Draper

NOVEMBER, 1928: CAMBRIDGE

Muriel up for the Harvard-Yale game, staying with Mother in Boston. Worried; after all, she's twenty years older than I, but marvelous with Father. We got as far as the stadium; Muriel decided she'd seen enough football. To Concord; Walden Pond; we put a big stone on the cairn. To Lexington. Mrs. Ames was in; she lives in Hawthorne's Old Manse, was resting on a laying-out couch. Hawthorne's grave in the late afternoon. Muriel spoke of Nijinsky, whom she knew at Bar Harbor when he was working on a ballet to Bach. She knew Diaghilev. She knew everybody.

I learned more from Muriel Draper about art and life than from five years in Cambridge and London. Before knowing her I had contact with the Big World at one remove; she seemed the Big World itself. There was hardly anyone, from Samuel Courtauld and Bernard Baruch, Lady Rothermere and Lady Cunard, Anne Morgan and Mrs. Willy Vanderbilt, to Jacques Rigaud and Marcel Duchamp, Elie Nadelman and Carl Van Vechten, Gilbert Seldes and A. R. Orage, Henry James and Charles Demuth, Edmund Wilson and e. e. cummings, whom she had not known or did not know—intimately. She was also close to anonymous characters whose histories were equally fabulous for me and even more preposterous, since their provenance was more exotic, their habit less familiar. I was a conventional product of class-conditioned, so-called higher education, knowing nothing but Cambridge, Concord, Boston, and a self-exclusive fraction of London. Now I found myself immersed in Manhattan with a passkey to boroughs as fascinating as Balzac's or Proust's *faubourgs*, which in many ways I felt that New York in the late twenties resembled. It was the site of a continuous educational holiday which stretched from Oyster Bay and Tuxedo Park to Harlem, from Robert Chanler's house on 19th Street to Robert Locher's on Staten Island.

Muriel told hard truths: I would never be a painter, professional writer, dancer. My gifts, such as they were, applied to organization; my talent, if any, was toward tasty management. Puritan New England gave her a conscience in the line of Margaret Fuller, Harriet Beecher Stowe, and Jane Addams. For a decade from 1927, she was a dominant companion and influence. Later she sloughed off such nugatory matters as the life of art, the warmth of friends, or intoxication in music. She became a passionate Communist, with or without a party card, involved in international congresses, traveling to France and the Soviet Union in awkward and perilous times. Although she came to watch ballets we produced, after I married just before the Second World War we saw each other less. But it was she who led me in my directions of most possibility, who gave focus and meaning to my dissipation and inconsistency. She indicated not what I thought I wanted to do, but finally what I wanted to be.

AUGUST, 1929: VENICE

Agnes Mongan disagrees about El Greco. She thinks his elongations derive from conventions of Byzantine painting learned as a boy in shops of Cretan ikon painters. I'm sure it's myopia or astigmatism, but, after spending a morning with San Marco's mosaics, perhaps she's right. Tried to get into San Giorgio dei Greci, where Greek merchants worshipped, and Greco must have too, but its front was draped in black and silver for a funeral. Sun dazzling; impossible to see inside except candle flames against the ikonostasis. A sacristan assumed we were mourners. He would have let us in but we felt shy. A basso intoned the service, like a solo from BORIS GODUNOV.

For my junior year at college I had what amounted to a vacation in Florence. I had been working on El Greco for my senior dissertation. Previously I had traveled through Spain, visiting every church in which he'd worked. Now I tried to retrace his steps from Venice to Rome before he was employed at the Escorial. My two "favorite" artists (or personalities from the past) were Domenikos Theotokopoulos, the Greek, and William Blake. My two favorite paintings were Greco's *St. Maurice and the Theban Legion* and Blake's *Glad Day*. The first incorporated a big corps de ballet of male dancers in skin armor. The second was a sunburst emanating from a youth who proclaimed the Creator's eternal dawn.

Lincoln Kirstein at Harvard

My choice of two philosophical painters was neither conscious nor exactly accidental. My tutor in college was S. Foster Damon, a vastly erudite Blake expert, whose knowledge of metaphysical literature excited me more than any other teaching at college. I would learn to rationalize my choice of two mystical artists, one in the tradition of Greek Orthodox Holy Wisdom, the other an inheritance from Jakob Böhme and Swedenborg, but what essentially attracted me was the Mannerist elegance of the male nude. It was more about style than sexuality, although polo players, fencers, and acrobats were more concrete models than any ballerina I had so far seen. I could not make much of El Greco as a person; the pallor of his historical presence never became flesh in my mind; but Mannerism, a tension of opposites, I recognized as the quintessential style of academic ballet. The impersonation of grandeur, the reduction of Michelangelo's grand manner, or *maniera*, to a possibly humane theatrical scale, indeed, Giovanni da Bologna's *Mercury* itself, incarnated the essence of what was most focused for me in stage dancing.

In 1929, I considered the ballet as a province apart and closed to me, particularly after a Covent Garden season of Diaghilev's ballet which was distinguished by a reprise of Balanchine's APOLLON MUSAGÈTE and the premiere of his PRODIGAL SON, with collaborations from Prokofiev and Rouault. Whatever direction I was to take, it would be in the line of painting, possibly in art history. Also, I loved horses and learned to box badly; and somewhere in my fantasy still loomed the idiotic notion that dancing was not excluded.

The day following our failure to enter the Greek church, Agnes Mongan, my tutor in Italian painting at the Fogg Museum (and recently its director), and I took the train to Padua to inspect Giottos and Mantegnas, returning by way of the Brenta Canal. Here among other Palladian villas lay La Malcontenta, filled with frescoes by a painter who may have had connections with El Greco. Agnes had bought a London *Times* at the station and we learned to our amazement that yesterday in Venice we had all but attended the obsequies of Sergei Pavlovich Diaghilev, who had died on the Lido some days before. At La Malcontenta, the owner, Alberto Landsberg, was extremely courteous, if abstracted. He had not known of our coming but showed us the villa, let us inspect the frescoes, left us alone to look. However, we had broken into a situation of private distress, and leaving, we sought to apologize. As we walked down the stairs of Palladio's portico, we encountered the Russians who had gathered for Diaghilev's funeral. I had never before seen Lifar or Dolin offstage. The silence of personal grief was almost audible; there was no more splendid background possible for the immediacy of this end of an epoch. The positive absence of a princely presence from this palatial yet domestic decor was intensely poignant. Here was a fusion of life, death, and theater, which elevated one afternoon into the sunset celebration of an era. Returning to the Venetian skyline and seascape, the monumental combination of man-made architecture and the Adriatic, we felt the wizardry of imagination and humane capacity.

FEBRUARY, 1932: NEW YORK

I know Fokine thinks it's ridiculous. I only want to learn the structure of his teaching, but he thinks I'm some sort of mad millionaire (like Ida Rubinstein) who dreams of dancing. Do I want to start an "American ballet"? I do, but of course this sounds crazy. I am incapable of lifting a leg. However, as an exercise in free will (the most recent Muriel Draper has given me), I persist. Also, I write down exactly what Fokine says; it will be a book, if he gives me an hour a day.

I broke away from Beacon Hill, Cambridge, and Concord largely because of Muriel Draper's magnetism. Harvard, for me, was a summation of the lively residue of the nineteenth century. There I learned how to look hard at pictures and objects, to use a library, to sense the proximity of powerful minds. Dante with Charles Grandgent, French romanticism with Irving Babbitt, metaphysics with Whitehead, Coleridge with J. L. Lowes seemed to tap the long sequence of a living tradition at its source. I also helped edit a literary quarterly called *Hound & Horn*, which enjoyed the patronage of both T. S. Eliot and Ezra Pound. Our Harvard Society for Contemporary Art introduced Picasso as well as Buckminster Fuller, Sandy Calder, and Isamu Noguchi to Harvard. A great influence was John Brooks Wheelwright, son of Boston's last civic architect, a truly properly improper Bostonian, an odd combination of devout Anglican and active proto-Marxist. He was a philosophical poet of power, an exciting adviser to me and other young men.

Beacon Hill was historically attractive, but Murray Hill opened possibilities which made home tame. I explored New York as a foreign country, and through Muriel Draper gained insight into high life, night life, and low life. While directing such postgraduate studies, she heightened and focused my purpose; she made clear what I wanted to be and do—something connected with dancing. I realized that ballet for me as a performer was out of the question, but two aspects of the human body in action and repose seemed open. I continued to draw from the nude model, and I learned to box at the West Side Y.M.C.A. from an ex-lightweight who was a fireman at a nearby firehouse. Sometimes I spelled him when he needed a night off. Through him I met a galaxy of exotic characters who preserved me somewhat from the dangers of class conditioning and too shy a life. Also, I became involved with Muriel Draper's nascent Marxism and flirted with a number of passive Communist theorists and active organizers.

But my main interest was dancing, and painfully I placed myself under Fokine as the most eminent practitioner of the art and skill in America. It was he who, early in our century, precipitated the original choreographic revolution which Diaghilev framed to show the West. Although he was repudiated by the advance guard, I found him a living monument and talked to him for hours. This resulted in a small book published in England which did not entirely displease him, although he was a vain, resentful, disappointed veteran who could see nothing in any work save his own, and whose restricted taste was that of his early youth. He thought I was wasting his and my time. Nevertheless, my opuscule on Fokine served as a passport, legitimizing my dilettante pre-dilections. It showed I had some, however borrowed, authority in an area which was largely closed to aliens and in which authority seemed to descend by physical apostolic succession alone. By birth, training, or merit I could never belong, but by association with Fokine, something might rub off on me. Indeed, at first I had a notion of an "American" ballet centered around Fokine. Since 1917 he had enjoyed numerous chances of his own; apart from sporadic commercial success on Broadway, he had done little after breaking with Diaghilev except teach two generations of American dancers. Also, there was Madame Vera Fokine, an imperious beldam who emerged from time to time to register disdain, which Fokine himself kept in restraint at least while he talked to me. Yet I absorbed from his *barre* exercises a modicum of what is necessary in the schooling of professionals. I learned the consummate logic in the progression of academic exercises from first steps to ultimate virtuosity.

DECEMBER, 1932: NEW YORK

Difficulties with Romola Nijinsky. Legal problems over her passport. Spent the day at Ellis Island. No more money. Tea with Mrs. Vanderbilt; she will help again, but for absolutely the last time. Romola is desperate. Took Vaslav's notation theory and had it photographed. Gave her back his manuscript and a copy. She says I am a thief and will sue. I apologize; we are reconciled. Privately I think I did right. Anyway, we got plastered with Ma Garrett. Another séance. Romola asked certain questions through Little Blue Bell. Whole morning in dictation. To the cemetery. In spite of everything we laughed a lot; Romola is great fun and very brave.

Having served a brief, modest, and anxious apprenticeship as amateur chronicler of Michel Fokine, I soon became attached to the wife of Vaslav Nijinsky. She came to America to support her husband (then in a Swiss sanatorium), and enthusiasm landed me as her amanuensis. For the next three years I was occupied trying to adapt her memoirs as a book and a film. I had not been permitted to see the original Russian Ballet on a stage, or Nijinsky in the flesh. But now, in service of some private personal and public historical necessity, I was able to relive in its immediate dimension the whole saga of Diaghilev's early seasons through the eyes of a principal participant.

Quite apart from ballet, the epic of Romola Nijinsky's unique, fantastic survival makes a marvelous recital. In the first days of her American adventures she met the influential agent Elizabeth Marbury, as well as Anne Morgan and Mrs. W. K. Vanderbilt. Her life was a succession of desperate ploys, built on persistence, imagination, thin air, and spiritualism. She arrived in New York with the coffin of a friend who had died in Indonesia, and saw that it was placed in a receiving vault in Woodlawn. A notable trance medium, Mrs. Aileen Garrett, was Romola's constant and intimate companion. Psychic research was an adjunct in preparing the biography of

Nijinsky. Various lacunae in documentation, or anecdotes where memory failed, were filled out capaciously by consultation with an ancient Persian and his control, Little Blue Bell.

During all this my life became so trying that death held no terror. I grew increasingly fearful that Romola would precipitate herself past our terrestrial plane onto another that she deemed more promising. A part of me was living by proxy in the aura of the initial Paris seasons of the Russian Ballet. Another part was attending peculiar séances which chilled me because the tangential or fragmentary truths they even seemed (often enough) to hit upon were moderately impressive, but had no relation whatever to my own interest or experience. Hence I took the manuscript of Nijinsky's unpublished book on dance notation, which seemed to me to contain the key to unimaginable treasure, and had it secretly photographed against her continual threats to destroy it and herself. There followed a procession of lady lawyers who made me seem like a criminal ingrate, when I felt I had acted like a knight in shining armor.

Behind *all* this was the benevolent patronage of Mrs. Willy Vanderbilt, with whom I had become friends. She did not then appear so ancient, although she could easily have been my great-grandmother. She had adored Vaslav Nijinsky and relished observing late developments in his drama. I knew nothing of her own story and little about New York "society," so I later read Dixon Wecter's history for background. In her lovely house on Sutton Place, with its China-export wallpaper and a broad view of the East River, she encouraged my dreams for an "American" ballet. Later she gave us money. I gave her Wecter's book, and reading it, she told me she discovered in a footnote something she'd quite forgotten: in her youth she had been briefly engaged to Franklin Roosevelt's father.

Vaslav Nijinsky by Frank Haviland

MARCH, 1933: NEW YORK

To see Fred King for his scrapbooks; to Mr. Bernays for his. Reports that Hurok has bought Diaghilev's properties, and is reconstituting the Ballets Russes under de Basil's management. Depressing. This means no chance for an American ballet; all money will be siphoned off for the Russians. Fokine produced his BACCHANAL (TANNHÄUSER) in a Brooklyn state armory for a benefit for White Russian charities. Scenery: a huge howitzer covered by tarpaulin. This is what ballet in America comes to.

Frederick King had been the theatrical editor of the *Literary Digest* for many years. His collection of clippings, photographs, memorabilia led to my own scavenging. His records of the American tours of the Russian Ballet provided some random accuracy for Romola's romantic portrait of Nijinsky which was finally published. Bernays had been employed by Otto Kahn to publicize the American tours following Diaghilev's appearance at the Metropolitan Opera. The Italian management controlling the Met was terrified lest the Russian somehow might exert control over the Opera, and to prevent this, systematically sabotaged the American tour upon which Diaghilev had counted to maintain his troupe away from Europe during the First World War. Otto Kahn covered the losses. Madame Nijinsky had given me a highly glamorous account of Diaghilev's world; Bernays provided a succinct record of infighting and sharp dealing which was quite another side of historical actuality. A sharper picture of what actually occurred prepared me, to a degree, for my own imminent involvement.

Following Diaghilev's death, in the early thirties succession fell upon various companies, commencing with the foundation in 1931 of Les Ballets de Théâtre Monte Carlo. The company was under the patronage of the Princess of Monaco and the direction of René Blum and Baron de Guinzbourg. Balanchine and Boris Kochno, the artistic directors, then invited Léonide Massine to join them. Portions of the former repertory were inherited and the debut season, sparked by the triumph of Balanchine's COTILLON and CONCURRENCE, was a resounding success. The collapse of ballet, which Diaghilev's disappearance in 1929 had at first promised, had not come to pass. Resurrection was achieved. I had no notion that there was already schism in the organization of the revived company in Monte Carlo, that Balanchine and Kochno, who to a large degree were responsible for its inception, would be leaving. Friends who had been in Paris told me of the excitement aroused by the renascent activity. I was torn between curiosity and disappointment. While I had no right to any sort of proprietary resentment, the Russians had scored again and the chances for an "American" ballet seemed to me that much further off.

JULY, 1933: PARIS

Pavel Tchelitchev's studio. A working model for his new ballet, ERRANTE, for Balanchine; seven strips of white paper. Costumes, magnificent; bodies alone, as if designed by a Renaissance draftsman, merest indication of decoration; overall nudity. He treated me like an idiot child, but was encouraging, since I was enthusiastic. He brought out recent pictures; as he said, serious work. Theater is only a game. As for Balanchine —certainly gifted, but essentially a musician. No visual sense; can't tell red from green. Diaghilev took him to a museum once—but it was hopeless. Theater is not dancing, not music, but a mad salade russe, which ends up where all food ends up; an amusement. It relaxes him, but not as activity for serious artists.

I was taken to Tchelitchev's studio by Monroe Wheeler, who had known him for years, from the time Gertrude Stein first interested herself in his painting, before they inevitably came to quarrel. For Diaghilev, Tchelitchev had designed the ballet ODE by Massine in 1928, with Nicolas Nabokov's score, in a decor which for the first time used light instead of paint, with the addition of projected films. He had survived his exile, first in Kiev and then for more years working in theater from Constantinople to Berlin, where Diaghilev first saw his work. Despite his disdain of theater, he was the theatrical wizard of his time. He used the stage as a laboratory for preparing his canvases; yet his reputation as a scenic artist would overwhelm his prestige as a painter, causing him to abandon ballet and all theater in disgust.

At our first meeting he asked me what I wanted; I told him: to create an American ballet. This was idiotic; Russian ballet has not been Russian for twenty years; there's been no French ballet for fifty; nationalism in any form is nonsense. He spoke excellent idiomatic English, laced with a heady amalgam of current slang and casual obscenity. When I exposed my big hopes and small experience, he told me not to get mixed up with Fokine or Massine; they were part of a past. If I was to persist in such folly, Balanchine was the only possible choreographer; at least he was not brainless; simply—tasteless. Tchelitchev would supply enough taste for all; this was his speciality. Balanchine had no fixed taste. Good and bad taste were equally reprehensible. Everyone had *le bon goût;* the French worst of all. They are starving from good taste, which is simply the good taste of cooks or dressmakers; *comestibilité.* It's what ruined French art: eatable taste; everything for the stomach; nothing for the mind. He invited, or rather commanded, me to come to the Champs-Élysées Theater, where Balanchine's new company was rehearsing.

Pavel Tchelitchev

Virgil Thomson tried to explain the wars that exist here. At the Châtelet, the Ballets Russes de Monte Carlo (under Massine) are having a big vulgar success. At the Champs-Élysées, Les Ballets 1933 under Balanchine are enjoying little popular success, but great prestige. Massine thinks Diaghilev is still alive and lives off Diaghilev's old formulae. Balanchine is musically oriented and, at the moment, music is indeed more interesting than painting; except for two stage designers who prefer to be considered as painters, Tchelitchev and Christian Bérard, both appropriated by Balanchine. Also, he's latched on to Bert Brecht and Kurt Weill, fashionable German exiles with Communist leanings now supported by Parisian society. Virgil knows of my interest in an "American" ballet, but he made clear the importance of money: whose money? how much? how certain? Balanchine, for example, seems currently to have an unlimited amount and throws it around like a drunken sailor, but his source is English and they never patronize anything for long. There is no future for him; for Massine there's a big financial future—not alone in Europe; more so in America.

No one has understood the politics of lyric theater, painting, or musical institutions as well as Virgil Thomson. His intelligence is analytical, surgical, cheerful, realistic; it is optimistic in spite of an unsentimental manner which is the passionate reverse of enthusiastic. Instruction from him let me see many factors in depth; his portraits of persons were objective and unromantic; his attitude toward the plans for a company I hoped one day to form, helpful and cautious. He paid me the compliment of assuming that what I declared I wished to do could be done. In Paris I was dazzled by theatrical activity which for the first time I saw at first hand. He undazzled me. He revealed the skull beneath the skin of personages whom I tended to take on trust from their reputation. He showed me many ways to do what I wanted.

I did not have enough cash of my own to do much but travel. My father had humored me in providing partial support for *Hound & Horn*, a magazine with which I was no longer involved, since it had been largely taken over by men with a more genuine interest in abstract ideas than I would ever possess. I never thought of myself as an intellectual, but as an artist or athlete. Virgil's insistence on money gave me the opportunity to decide whether I was serious like him, or silly like my cousin Nat Woolf.

Actually, I had an ally as far as money went—an ambivalent, unwilling, but generous friend, also my classmate in college. It was he who made my presence in Paris and my conversations with Thomson and Tchelitchev not entirely irrelevant. Edward Warburg was the youngest son of Felix Warburg, an old friend of my father's and a business associate of Otto Kahn's. Felix, himself a distinguished amateur and patron of the arts, had a particular interest in Italian tempera panels, Rembrandt etchings, German *Lieder*, and chamber music. In our freshman year of college Eddie and I found ourselves living in the same dormitory, on different floors of Gore Hall. His friends were flashier than mine—boys who made good clubs and good grades. Lacking a vocation, he early found one, that of clown. Overshadowed by powerful parents and three older brothers, he discounted his own genuine qualities, playing at mimic and jester in the theater of his own life. Later he would teach for a while, but his true genius was for the organization and implementation of charity and philanthropy.

Eddie Warburg commenced generously with me on a small scale, which was then an enormous help. His later large support permitted us to make promises that led to first steps without which nothing could have followed. Forcing him as hard as I could, and gaining five years' support, I finally exhausted his patience and interest. Thirty years later on the few occasions when we met, we would greet each other effusively, even apologetically, as if we had both been involved in a mutual disaster which good manners alone could patch up by forgetfulness of what had actually happened. And much of the first years of our joint venture was indeed disaster. Eddie endured failure with grace; he was bullied, abused, ridiculed; he was made unhappy, not willfully by either Balanchine or me, but rather by circumstances in the historical process of our venture. In any case, when I had nowhere near enough money of my own, he let me use much of his. This made it easier to think of approaching George Balanchine with a bit of conviction.

But how was I to get to Balanchine? What, concretely, might I offer? There was little to be done before his own season opened, but now I had the good counsel of Virgil Thomson, Monroe Wheeler, and soon enough, Tchelitchev. Also, we had formed a shadow plan which promised some amorphous stability, although it was roughly designed and weakly supported. A. Everett Austin (Chick to his friends) was building a new wing on the Hartford Atheneum, of which he was director, having been appointed as soon as he finished training at the Fogg Museum under Edward Forbes and Paul Sachs. He had a passion for theater, included a charming small stage and auditorium in his new building, and for the gallery, purchased Serge Lifar's collection of sketches for the most important Diaghilev ballets. Chick and I conceived the notion that Hartford—or at least his museum—would be the perfect place to install a ballet school and a ballet company which might eventually serve a nation. Nothing could have been further from actuality, as it happened, but with Eddie Warburg's guarantee of at least two years' help toward putting us on an institutional basis in a respected public museum, I was given two tools powerful (and dangerous) enough to hoist us with our own petard.

The closer I found myself to the furnace of activity, stoked by various characters and situations attached to the immediate production of ballet, the more intoxicated I became. Using the flimsiest support as my strongest arm, I involved or precipitated Warburg, Austin, and myself with a blind conviction and impersonation of authority which should have surprised us all had I retained any objective insight. Both Warburg and Austin were in America; communication was by ship or letter. I took this as an excuse and told myself I had a free hand to act, although there was no condition or principle upon which negotiation could proceed. I had not even spoken to Balanchine, who had absolutely no notion of my existence. I knew that for a meeting I could count on Tchelitchev, who in some occult way seemed to become our third partner. He had been intimate with Gertrude Stein, Virgil Thomson, Monroe Wheeler, and other Americans; he felt his own future would be in New York, and he was right. His judgment was not hasty, and he thought nothing, including my ambitions, impossible. In more ways than one his ardent instinct made them probable.

Dress rehearsal of LES SEPT PÉCHÉS CAPITAUX at the Champs-Élysées Theater. Wonderful scenery by Caspar Neher. Lotte Lenya and Tamara Toumanova in a doubled singing-and-dancing lead. Edward James afraid of anti-Communist (or, Virgil says, anti-Semitic) demonstrations. Tchelitchev furious because rehearsals of ERRANTE are delayed by (needless) elaboration of Neher's decor. Threats of postponement. James is demoralized, only interested in ballets in which Tilly Losch (his wife) appears. If it were not for Dimitriew nothing would be accomplished. Balanchine stays invisible. I never know where he is, since he is never onstage.

After Diaghilev's death, Balanchine worked for films and Sir Charles B. Cochran's popular revues in London, but even Maynard Keynes was unable to obtain a permanent work permit for him. Had he stayed, he might well have been involved in the birth of that company which, with the developed talents and muscle of Marie Rambert, Ninette de Valois, and Frederick Ashton, resulted in the Royal Ballet. Instead, he became ballet master for a season with the Royal Danes in Copenhagen and was then offered the Paris Grand Opéra. There was even talk of his joining Anna Pavlova in America, to invent dances which would somehow be updated versions of THE DYING SWAN.

At the end of 1932 (I had no notion of how it all came about) Balanchine and Boris Kochno, having initiated the Monte Carlo successor to Diaghilev's company, found themselves dismissed. The new power was one Vasily Grigorevich Voskresensky, promoting himself as "Colonel Vasily *de* Basil," an ex-military policeman whose approach to theater combined the ablest features of desk-sergeant and huckster. Not for him a wan career as taxi driver, as it was for many other White Russian émigrés. He parlayed muscular shrewdness into an egregious but solid position as successor to a truly princely impresario. As the poor man's Diaghilev he has his niche in theatrical history through the thirties and forties. Like most policemen he believed control is superior to creation. Balanchine already had his fill of such discipline. Diaghilev's benevolent or malevolent despotism had been, however, a valued education. The young dancer and choreographer had also endured long

12-year-old George Balanchine as Amor

the New York City Ballet

apprenticeship under the strictures of Serge Grigoriev, the ex-dancer who was Diaghilev's regisseur, and whose omnivorous memory held the relics of Diaghilev's repertory for de Basil's manipulation. I could hardly have known it, but my two firmest allies in attracting Balanchine to America were de Basil and Grigoriev. Without them and their insistence on a ferocious commercial policy, I would never have seemed to offer Balanchine that total license which, while wholly meaningless, promised whatever liberty means to an idealist.

When Balanchine and Kochno quit the patronage of Paris and Monte Carlo, they determined to build a proper company of their own, in apostolic succession from their lost leader. They proposed to perpetuate Diaghilev's reckless caprice, passion for novelty, and disdain of failure. Having exhausted what money they first found, they were momentarily rescued by Coco Chanel, Diaghilev's old and generous friend. After spending her money to recruit a company of very young, unknown, and brilliant dancers, Kochno found Edward James. But the kind of venture capital on which investors hardly expected to receive a return, to say nothing of a profit, was forthcoming only for de Basil. However, James enabled Balanchine to bid farewell to Europe—for nearly twenty years—in a style of which Diaghilev might have been proud.

Edward James was the diminutive, supple, and elegant heir of Mrs. Willy James, one of Edward VII's most preferred hostesses. It was he who was now backing Balanchine's Ballets 1933, partly for his wife, Tilly Losch, a lovely Viennese who had been the dancing partner of the mime Harald Kreutzberg. James was in the tradition of monumental English eccentrics whose manias, taste, and money have enriched the mythology of art patronage since the eighteenth century. He had now come into a fortune derived from his father's collection of worldwide railroad stocks. In West Deane, his Sussex house, the marble entrance hall was hung with a hundred antlers. On one wall was the gold button which King Edward had pressed to release an electrical impulse signaling the completion of the Canadian-Pacific Road.

Vladimir Dimitriew, whose name was new to many, presumably served as Balanchine's "manager." A former secondary basso from the Maryinsky Opera, he had in 1924 organized their common flight from Leningrad. During Diaghilev's life, he had settled for a new career as photographer. More recently he had taken over Balanchine's affairs. Methodical, hard, strong, honest, professional, courageous, he did much to madden Edward James, but also to launch the season. It was clearly indicated that if ever I was to reach Balanchine, it must be through Dimitriew. Tchelitchev hated him, while granting his usefulness. After the Revolution he had been a croupier in a gambling casino. I would come to fear him, to admire him, even to be fond of him. At that time he seemed merely one more, possibly the worst, obstacle.

But the actual performances of the ballets were a parade of brilliant artistic successes, notably Tchelitchev's ERRANTE (for Tilly Losch) and Christian Bérard's MOZARTIANA for Tamara Toumanova, then a sixteen-year-old baby ballerina whom Balanchine had discovered in a White Russian school the year before. In addition to the collaboration of Brecht and Kurt Weill, André Derain made two of his most beautiful scenic investitures for LES SONGES and LES FASTES. Night after night there were premieres which were the epitome of Parisian advance-guard taste of that particular vintage year—1933. The essence of one ephemeral season was distilled and sprayed about, like an expensive, novel, and fastidious scent over a capricious public expressly primed for it. A wholly Parisian phenomenon, it could never have been repeated with anything approaching its original panache in any other town. When the ballets were taken to London, Edward James would be chagrined by their lack of comparable éclat. He would miss Perret's beautiful theater, designed for dancing, as well as a snob public which could be excited to argue about new ideas and unknown dancers.

Les Ballets 1933 was my veritable introduction into Russian ballet. It would be the model for our American venture, and no very logical or sensible one. What the median international audience would pay for was what it remembered or could properly project from Diaghilev seasons; this is precisely what Colonel de Basil, Massine, and the Ballets Russes de Monte Carlo provided for the next two decades. That I then scarcely foresaw. I was too ardent in my enthusiasm for Balanchine, enhanced by concrete examples he now gave night after night of his fantasy and ceaseless invention. Everything he did spoke for the present, of immediacy, by surprise, with brilliance: for 1933. There was a magical transference of private caprice onto a public platform. Studio talk and studio planning were projected in a heroic dimension, far larger than life. Everything was intensified through the physicality of the dancing itself, through the power, athletics, and lyricism of ballet's language. This was where I wanted to live. This was what I wanted to do; here I was learning how it should be done.

JULY, 1933: PARIS

To Tchelitchev's, to tell him how wonderful ERRANTE had been. He cut me short and said that half was Balanchine. No real dancers; no chance for magic, like films could make. But with little, a great deal can be done if analyzed; the chief thing is analysis; relationship of everything visual to earth, air, fire, and water. ERRANTE was made out of air, fire, and light; nothing of earth. As for Balanchine, his is a complex case. A Georgian, half Moslem, half orthodox, essentially oriental. He has TB in one lung, will die in three years, and adores girls; this is important since The Dance is Woman— Terpsichore, La Danse. I said something about Nijinsky. "Pfui, you're another one in love with Nijinsky. He wasn't man, or woman. He was an intelligent bird; not about earth, about air. He couldn't stand earth. He tried. LE SACRE finished him. Too much earthiness. He flew; not a man but an angel; sent for a time. Not sick; he wished to leave. Earth's no place for saints or angels." Much about Diaghilev; I can't repeat it to Romola Nijinsky or use it for her book. Although Balanchine likes girls, his is an angelic vision; dancers are sent (like Toumanova) for his purpose. He has a normal advantage in liking earth (the world). Diaghilev said of all the boys he'd known, Balanchine had imagination most like Nijinsky's; that is, his province was plastic movement, conquest of air in space by time. Did I know any mathematics? I got into college by memorizing the first five books of Euclid. "You are illiterate; you understand nothing without geometry. APOLLON was non-Euclidean geometry. My dee-ar boy; if you want to make ballet—take Balanchine. Only possible with him. No one else—now." But what if he dies in three years? In God's hands. Exhausted, I wanted to leave. "But why you have to go? I have not finished your lesson." I had some sort of rendezvous; some sexy affair? No; only Virgil Thomson promised to take me to Bébé Bérard, whose painting and decor I admired. Tchelitchev produced an approximation of (real?) rage. If I liked Bérard I was not a serious person. Bérard took opium, was a friend of Cocteau's (a disease in itself), an amateur's miscarriage of Aubrey Beardsley, good only for perfume makers and couturieres. If I went to see Bérard, I need not see Tchelitchev again. However, I left and met Bérard; it was worth it.

Pavel Tchelitchev has suffered from an ambiguous reputation. In life and after, he was admired, feared, and envied as a ferocious wit and fantastic decorator. Since he was a sworn enemy of official Surrealism, he never shared in the scandal or prestige of its politics as a clique or academy; yet his free-floating, serious, whimsical rhetoric fatally suggested some likely connection. It accentuated a systematic derangement of the senses, as he said, sur mesure et par commande, fantasy by formula, hysteria on demand; substructures touched the rational and metaphysical, while academic Surrealism "comes out of the tube; lies flat on the brush." His huge allegorical Hide and Seek in New York's Museum of Modern Art is the canvas which (after Picasso's Guernica) is most purchased in reproduction. When young students ask for it, however, they refer to it more often than not as "that picture, you know—about Life," rather than remembering the name of its artist.

Tchelitchev was an aristocrat who had long become a citizen of world capitals, a magician with a phenomenal gift of digital mastery and verbal invention. His sole mistress was, as he said, Mrs. Nature, a metaphor appropriated from him by Wystan Auden, his friend and admirer. In an age of haphazard improvisation, his fantasy fed continually on vividly observed anatomies of animal, vegetal, mineral, and celestial worlds. To be sure, he was "impossible"; he loved impossible colors—the gorgeous chromatics of sunsets, autumn leaves, orchids, jewels, and hummingbirds. He liked dancers and loved to dress them, chiefly by undressing them, but cared little for their dancing once he'd costumed them for the stage. He respected Balanchine but lamented his disinterest in the visual—except for three-dimensional plasticity. He adored the painting of the past; his ideal was the arcane imagery and superrational composition of Andrei Rublev, Piero della Francesca, and Mikhail Vrubel, whom he considered his master.

In spite of personal brilliance, or perhaps due to it, Tchelitchev never promoted his own gift with that seriousness which is a commercial requirement for negotiable success. He was thought to spend too much time on fashionable ladies and handsome young men. He worked like a demon; the boys were his models, students, slaves, and cooks; the ladies his patrons and fashion plates. Also, dressing them relaxed and amused him as well as served him for sketches or research toward his more determined invention. Arriving in New

York, he announced he would find me "the keys of the city," which I certainly lacked. In his view, the keys to that particular citadel were in the custody of Mrs. Pleydell-Bouverie, daughter of Lady Ribblesdale, who had been born Alice Astor. He painted a penetratingly melancholy picture of her, which frightened her so much that it was found only after her death. As in many of his portraits, he saw deeply into character with an uncomfortably prophetic or X-ray eye. In time she became our ballet company's important friend and patron, but by then Tchelitchev had removed himself to more impersonal, private, enigmatic preoccupations, far from theater, fashion, and our world.

JULY, 1933: LONDON

With Romola, from Holland, after failing to finish Nijinsky's biography. Arnold Haskell will help us find a publisher. The opening of Ballets 1933 at the Savoy. Romola says it is like a school performance compared with the best Diaghilev season. Rumors about Edward James suing Balanchine. Romola will bring me to Balanchine. At Hungaria Restaurant, she said it might be a good idea for her to marry Serge Lifar and star him in a film about Nijinsky, which would sell the book and support Vaslav in the sanatorium. Balanchine's in love with Tamara Toumanova; her mother thinks she is too young (16) to marry; besides, Balanchine will not live long. Romola gave me a sealed envelope with the date of his death, provided by Ma Garrett via Little Blue Bell.

The considerable Parisian success of Les Ballets 1933 was not repeated in London. The Savoy Theater did not have either the cachet of historical association or the physical apparatus of Le Théâtre des Champs-Élysées. English audiences were not as coherent socially or as advanced in artistic taste as the French. The tension in management was no help. If anything pleased Edward James more than patronizing artists, it was suing them. He was so aroused by legal excitement that he was quite capable of hiring two sets of lawyers to sue each other in a case for which he would ultimately pay all costs. He scarcely promised much as a stable influence. The very name of his company, attached as it was to a single year's date, guaranteed no succession nor much future. All was not well between his wife and him, and while I could not know half of these factors, they were preponderant in Balanchine's final decision.

I finally met Balanchine, in the kitchen of a house leased for the London season by Kirk Askew, an excellent art dealer whom I knew from Harvard. I made a headlong onslaught; what Balanchine thought of an anonymous youth who in exaggerated desperation proposed an entire future career in half an hour, he did not say, except that he must think it over. I consoled myself that, at the least or most, it was not absolutely impossible. He was not in the best of health and had no personal security whatever. But since we had met, he now knew of another possibility. Also, he owned half the repertory of the 1933 company as his share. I was not then aware that he had a mentor and partner in Vladimir Dimitriew.

LATE JULY, 1933: LONDON

Batts Hotel, Mayfair. Tea, a lively revival of Edwardian life. Three debutantes from the West Riding, with plumes in their hair, dressed for presentation at court, resembling ballerinas in Balanchine's COTILLON, as dressed by Bérard. Waited from four-thirty to six in rising apprehension. He arrived at six, tired. His first dancer was ill; he would have to perform tonight. He was not in practice. He was disarmingly frank. There was little in Europe to hold him. As for the Paris Grand Opéra, this could go to Lifar. As for de Basil's Ballets Russes de Monte Carlo, it was Diaghilev's repertory. He had offers from film and commercial theater; these were not ballet. On my part, I only offered a steamship ticket, and the possibility of the Hartford museum. He was polite and remote; we could meet again. I wrote long letters to Chick Austin and Eddie Warburg, more enthusiastic than honest.

From Warburg I obtained money for steamship fares. From Austin I extracted guarantees ensuring immigration and the legal right for two aliens to be employed in educational capacities. I now met Vladimir Dimitriew, whom I found to be Balanchine's self-appointed agent and manager, twice Balanchine's age. With him was Kyra Blank, a charming ballerina; with Balanchine must come Pierre Vladimirov. (Vladimirov was the eminent dancer who followed Nijinsky at the Maryinsky Theater, and married Felia Doubrovska, one of the last of Diaghilev's soloists, and a graduate, with Alexandra Danilova and Balanchine, of the old Imperial School.) Teachers, after all, were necessary to form a school and company. This was far more than I'd anticipated, although I could see its sense. Balanchine was exhausted after the Paris and London seasons; he needed rest. Dimitriew had little confidence that I would do much; with these additions to our roster, my initial enthusiasm somewhat declined.

Dimitriew gave me the name of a town in France where they had been invited to spend a vacation: Nègrepelisse. The name took on an occult significance. I was to return to America; if I could manage something effective, he would proceed with local legalities. Nègrepelisse? What could it mean? A moor's fur cape? In the next weeks, waking in the middle of the night, I would try to decode the name as if it held the clue to our future.

I took Romola Nijinsky to the seashore, delivered her to Arnold Haskell, who, having completed her biography, arranged for its English publication. In New York, I went straight to White Plains, where, on a tract of land as large as a duchy, the Warburgs held state in considerable grandeur. Armed with photographs of the 1933 dancers, I tried to sell Eddie on the absolute necessity of Balanchine's immediate importation. His father, a sympathetic, urbane, grizzled gentleman, received me courteously. The fantasy of ballet was within the realms of his imaginings, if not of his interest. There were, after all, pretty young girls involved.

In Hartford, I was welcomed with understanding and excitement by Chick Austin, who understood exactly what I was talking about and who promptly devoted himself to making the entire improbable plan come true. He showed me the new wing of his museum, of which he had been the virtual architect. It was at the time one of the most progressive designs in the United States, severe, elegant, with a surprising combination of contemporary rectilinearity and a splendid baroque marble fountain splashing in an open central court. In

his own office each wall and the ceiling were painted in a contrasting color, then a shocking innovation, borrowed from the Bauhaus. He had just purchased excellent examples of those new painters whose work I had seen in Paris, including Bérard, Dali, the brothers Berman, and Tchelitchev. His small theater, with murals by Kristians Tonny, would be (to my eye) perfect for ballet performances. Austin's own house, which he had designed himself, was a delightful Palladian villa set in a site very like a Brenta canalscape. His generosity and excitement made everything seem not only easy but inevitable.

But what was happening in Nègrepelisse? Rumor flew as to the imminent arrival of de Basil's Ballets Russes, as well as Serge Lifar's personal company. When these loomed as threats on our horizon, I did not have the generosity or foresight to recognize that such importations could only familiarize America with an alien art, that only after considerable exposure to ballet as appreciated in Europe could this country be willing to accept any kind of indigenous effort.

With the ostensibly secure backing of Hartford as an institutional anchor, Warburg seemed disposed to guarantee the full amount of money needed. He was willing to head a corporation, which ensured a legal entity. Nègrepelisse was notified. Dimitriew's telegrams were succinct; he insisted on rigorous conditions, but these were not exorbitant. They were mainly about security in the eventuality of failure, and a return trip to Paris.

NOVEMBER, 1933: HARTFORD

Two Italian sisters who keep a dancing school gave an interview to the Courant saying that bread is being snatched from their mouths by Bolsheviks. They attacked Chick Austin for making tax-exempt premises available for a nontaxable enterprise in order to put them out of business. The last straw. Dimitriew and Balanchine announce they're leaving for New York (probably Paris); Chick has spent considerable on lawyers, public relations, etc., all of which might damage his position as director of the museum. Thank God we have money in escrow to ship the Russians back to Paris. Also, Balanchine is coughing badly and only consents to see a wisewoman, who bleeds him with leeches. In despair I called Warburg, who asked me to White Plains. His father was extremely pleasant.

Dimitriew and Balanchine had, between them, decided not to return to Europe come Hell or high water. However, they had hardly left that continent to immure themselves in Hartford, Connecticut. As for myself, I had precipitated a first formal failure and, worse, seemed to betray a friend. I had promised Chick Austin some real issue for all his guarantees of institutional bulwarks. I had never questioned that Balanchine would be anything but content in a provincial American landscape. I had not foreseen the angry reaction which intrusion of foreigners would provoke.

When crisis came, I ran off to New York with my Russians, leaving Austin to endure the consequences of ragged explanations, inconvenience, and humiliation, besides his own genuine disappointment. I acted as if in the military dilemma of *force majeure*. Conventional loyalty may have required another course, but here was an act of God and my historic or objective responsibility lay not to a closed past but a future possibility. Later there would be far more ambiguous and awkward failures, more serious and anxious betrayals. In the great world of power politics, money, and property, convenient legalities accommodate treachery. In the small world of theater, traitors are former friends or lovers. While ruptures seem more piercing, they are also more ephemeral. However, they cost bad nights, shabby reputations, and hard feelings.

JANUARY, 1934: NEW YORK

Opening the School of American Ballet, 637 Madison Avenue. Balanchine had the walls painted a gray-blue he remembers from the Imperial School. Dimitriew furious about nonaligned mirrors. I tried to calm him down; at least, finally, we were opening. Americans don't understand the difference between amateurs and professionals: "Assez de dilettantisme"; Warburg and I are hopeless dilettantes. I anticipated some small celebration; Dimitriew said there was nothing to celebrate but our stupidity. About thirty kids turned up, including three boys. Balanchine's tryout class, which I was wild to watch; Dimitriew insisted I stay in the office and "superintend." Superintend what? His vile temper. Telephoned Father to tell him we had opened; bad connection. Passed Muriel Draper's house; her light was on. She comforted me about the Russians; they know more theater than anyone, pretending it's important, knowing it's only play; objectivity permits expertness. They are saved by essential lack of selfishness, knowing their selves, have a superior sense of identity, but are more interested in the game than in personalities. Cruelty is just another act, like love; everything is impersonation; high camp; they act <u>as if</u> it were true. But since there is no independent, objective truth, they impose one which is their choice of "truth." Lots about "as if"; <u>als ob</u>; she gave me Vaihinger's book. She says Dimitriew is a typical Russian pro and I should learn from him; I was too drunk or tired to listen.

Dimitriew had been singer and soldier, having served his czar onstage and in the field. Personal existence had been harsh; education and orientation were Prussian, in the style of the German-trained bureaucracy which had guided Petersburg policy. He equated order with honesty, disorder with degeneracy and failure. When I knew him he was already confirmed in contempt for mankind as well as theater. Since he was in good health, he intended to make his fortune. This, through the combination of Balanchine, Warburg, and my father, he did, and within five years. Meantime he gave full service, educated me in many ways, laid down governing principles for our school and company. The single most important thing he achieved was to discover in New York a young Russian girl from an eminent family. Eugenie Ouroussow's grandmother conducted one of the famous Parisian salons of the Third Republic. As yet unmarried, Eugenie had hardly worked before. From her difficult apprenticeship as secretary and aide-de-camp to Dimitriew, she would develop into a sagacious educator and administrator who, within a decade, would conduct the most influential academy of dancing in America.

Dimitriew knew that I was drawn to him. He was old enough to have been my father; although we spoke French, he always called me "Boy"—when he liked me. When he didn't, he snarled: "Kirsh-stayn." He resembled a gray-and-white striped tiglon or liger; his method was Blake's: "Damn braces; bless relaxes." Few were ever relaxed around him, except when he judged we had had as much riddling and needling as we could take. He orchestrated or choreographed both explosions and reconciliations; he would take us to excellent Russian restaurants, to get us drunk. Before midnight tolled, Warburg or I would have signed another check, ensuring the school's existence for another few months. My father understood and admired him; since he considered me a financial idiot, there was some security in Dimitriew's unyielding penny-pinching.

What Dimitriew felt for Balanchine was mysterious. Certainly as a basis, there was comprehension and even affection; he had recognized a boy's talent long before Diaghilev. But when Balanchivadze turned into Balanchine, Dimitriew's attitude became ambivalent. Caring nothing for dancing as such, except as a pretext for a paying profession after he had lost wife and voice during and after the First World War, he never envied Balanchine's rising reputation. What he most disliked in anyone, most of all in artists, was the element of disorder, which also comprised their freedom, but which he interpreted as willfulness, irrationality, caprice, and self-indulgence. His taste was retardative, his curiosity restricted; his energy military and exacting; his spirit cynical. He hated humanity; a primitive species. Theater was a ridiculous gloss on life's absurdity. This approach became demoralizing, despite his great abilities. We rid ourselves of each other as soon as we were able. However, he stuck to his, and our, guns and was responsible for much in our beginning which promised permanence. He grafted iron on our spines when we had none.

We found rooms for our school in a loft building where Isadora Duncan once had her studio, paid for by Paris Singer. One iron post stood stubbornly in the center of a splendid open space, but it could not be removed without the collapse of the entire three upper floors. This column assumed an extraordinary metaphorical importance; its implacable challenge to our whole future seemed to be magnetized, in its formidable uprightness and slim mineral solidity, as every possible negative threat. If it could only have been removed we would have

Balanchine

had some eighty square feet of unencumbered floor. This was pine and could easily be patched where walls had been inset. The cost of inserting a steel beam to replace the post was prohibitive. Engineers found no solution; Balanchine was determined that he needed the whole open area. We had put a down payment on the lease of the rooms; letterheads had been printed; we had announced our date of opening. Now we were halted by this single intransigent cast-iron pillar. It was one more in an acceleration of last straws following us since the debacle in Hartford. But a week before we were due to open, Dimitriew went early to the building and tapped the walls. One which we had assumed to be a retainer proved a much later addition. It could be removed, giving us necessary space, although with a slightly different disposition of rooms. Dimitriew installed a movable wall between two studios, so that while one room served as a fairly large performing area, the other could seat a small audience. Thus he would solve various insoluble problems with imagination, efficiency, and dispatch.

I did not pretend to be a ballet student, as formerly with Fokine; however, I took parts of enough classes to understand something of what was required to school a professional. Under Dimitriew's tutelage, I also enrolled as a student of management. When he saw that I subordinated myself to his will and direction, all was well. When Warburg and I felt we were merely being used, and crassly at that, there were tense moments and wounded feelings. These were the times when Dimitriew feasted us and got us tipsy.

Balanchine would tell us Arabian Nights tales of the court of Diaghilev as seen from the slaves' quarters. He had never been as much an intimate as Nijinsky, Massine, or Lifar; he had not been a member of the informal secretariat like Boris Kochno and, earlier, Nouvel, Bakst, and Benois. As for Dimitriew, after bringing Balanchine from Russia to Berlin and superintending his entrance into Les Ballets Russes, he'd become a photographer and led his own life.

Dimitriew was a burden, but among several of his proverbs, he often quoted: "God gives the Cross and strength to bear it." He found in New York the possibility of survival on a scale superior to Paris; he risked a present toward future retirement. He had no money; our parents were rich; we could afford varieties of folly and disorder, ballet being the most insistent. An important aspect of his service was to prevent waste, but we bridled under his yoke. As for Balanchine, he was too occupied with the immediate business of inventing dancers and designing dances to worry much about day-to-day disasters, which were often Dimitriew's didactic exercises. He was making a new life for himself in a new world, feeling independence and possibility. Together we all moved toward some sort of student demonstration, as prelude to the formation of a professional producing company.

SERENADE

MARCH, 1934: NEW YORK

Work started on our first ballet at an evening "rehearsal class." Balanchine said his brain was blank and bid me pray for him. He lined up all the girls and slowly commenced to compose, as he said — "a hymn to ward off sin." He tried two dancers, first in bare feet, then in toe shoes. Gestures of arms and hands already seemed to indicate his special quality. When I reported this to Dimitriew in his office, he growled: "Je ne sais rien du tout," calculated to crush my too ready approval. Did I know how it would turn out? Balanchine also had his failures; it's not the role of a director to license unproven work. Son of a bitch.

SERENADE, to Tchaikovsky's piece for stringed orchestra, was originally devised as an exercise to demonstrate the difference between classwork and theatrical dances for the advanced girls' division in our school. Balanchine's initial choreography in America, it was also an analysis in depth of those elements then available, upon which we might build a company. Later he would invent many plotless works, but he had done nothing like this either for Diaghilev, the Royal Danes, or Edward James. A possible exception was APOLLON, which, however, had a vague narrative pretext and no corps de ballet. SERENADE possessed a loose narrative line embedded in the music, but it was more atmospheric or suggestive than logically narrative. There was a central male figure supporting three girl soloists who involved themselves with each other in a linked series of tender, amorous, fractured, or fatal episodes. Yet, rather than any plot, it evoked an ambience in which passion was expressed, denied, or transcended in rupture or loss. It was, in fact, an "abstract" ballet, the most intensely romantic and architectural of its genre since Fokine evolved LES SYLPHIDES in 1909 from the earlier CHOPINIANA, which itself derived from a situation corresponding to our own — a schoolroom, or an academic recital projected toward repertory theater.

Balanchine commenced by lining up as many girl students as chanced to be in class on March 14, 1934. On that day there were seventeen. These he placed in military order according to height. One more, a tiny but brilliant dancer (Leda Anchutina, later married to André Eglevsky) slipped into the studio late, a few minutes after he had begun to compose. Her tardy entrance was incorporated, framing her as a first dancer, which, an advanced Fokine pupil, she decidedly was, perhaps the most capable of whom we could boast. At the next rehearsal only nine girls appeared; at another, only three. For them he arranged other portions of action, exactly as if they had been especially summoned and scheduled. The ballet was structured piecemeal, with no time wasted and no energy spent lamenting the nonappearance of individual dancers. Rehearsals were as much lessons as sessions toward composition and repetition. While the purpose was certainly eventual performance, no date was set; we were all too occupied with day-to-day maintenance to consider any definite time for public exposure.

SERENADE thus was woven from chance. Given the traditional academic language, which Balanchine employed here in a rare transliteration without inversion, deformation, or parody, he now fitted patterns from his analysis of the music onto a formal sequence largely governed by accident. It was not precisely improvisation, but rather a control or ordering of chance. Recently there has been an aesthetic vogue for an empirical method based on aleatory devices, the throw of dice and coins, the rules of I-Ching. It is a projection of accidental "happenings" intended to seduce audiences into closer identification with fictive acts, or more intimate participation in experiencing them. But this is a reactionary program or polemic, a confusion of art with life. Masters over such ceremonies pretend to act in a godlike capacity, ordaining a "fate" and suspending logical causality, a method which is presupposed as irrelevant, inconsequential, hence presumably piquant. It is not a useful device for those who live by the bloodbank of repertory seasons. In ballet, improvisation, as in SERENADE, may initially push toward invention, but only on a substructure of an established idiom, and only until the choreography is set. After that, brilliant interplay between acrobatic dancers is too hazardous for the intervention of any untimed or unforeseen surprise. In the "modern" dance, aleatory techniques supplement the gamesmanship of unvirtuosic performers who attempt to substitute shock for structure. More often than not this is only a spry and hopeful simulacrum of steady, lasting, and genuine invention.

A girl tripped and fell in rehearsal, close to the end of SERENADE's first movement. This accident Balanchine kept as a climactic collapse by which a genuine minor mishap became a permanently framed controlling excitement, a contribution precipitating but by no means perpetuating chance. At the start no boys were available; when five eventually appeared, three were used. At the start the chief solo role was shared among five girls; parts of it were later combined for a single soloist. There were also numerous novelties of pattern and plastic structure, although the ballet was as much a primer for our pupils as it was a demonstration of economical procedure. In the pas de trois there was a device by which a girl, supported by a crouching boy half hidden by her voluminous skirts, seemed to revolve on point in slow motion, as if balanced by her own extraordinary tension in control. Asymmetrical units of shifting dancers seesawed in contrapuntal accord; a solo dancer, holding a half of the stage, was echoed by a unison group in unlikely opposition. The prime quality of SERENADE from the moment of its inception was cool frankness, a candor that seemed at once lyric and natively athletic; a straightforward yet passionate clarity and freshness suitable to the foundation of a non-European academy. Balanchine had not seen Isadora Duncan in her best days, but she had certainly affected Fokine, and one might detect a strain of her free-flowing motion here.

When the curtain rises, the corps de ballet, in a strictly geometric floor plan, are seen as a unison platoon standing at guard rest — or actually, in the first of the five academic positions which are successively assumed in the initial twenty measures of the music. Hands are curved to shield their eyes, as if facing some intolerable lunar light. At the first rehearsals all arms were stiffly raised, but since Eddie Warburg imagined that this resembled the *Heil, Hitler* arm-thrust salute, Balanchine altered it to a more curvilinear, tentative, and vague fanfare of indeterminate gesture.

At this time I had been instructing myself in the basic principles of three-dimensional plasticity, standing as a model for the sculptor Gaston Lachaise, who had also carved a very fine rose-pink alabaster head of Warburg. Lachaise had chosen the identical annunciatory arm gesture which, quite by accident, seemed to be a visual pun on the Nazi greeting. I did not speak of this, although now it was in my mind, but one morning when I came into Lachaise's studio, I noticed that he had removed the right arm from its socket. Later he revised its angular thrust to the same degree as in the ballet. Certain gestures, their mutants or variants, seem to be inlaid in or summoned from the texture of historic incident. Mussolini's public stance had its precedent in D'Annunzio's operatic Byzantine histrionics. The language of gesture may possess visual metaphors, puns, or correspondences which contain subconscious or unconscious connotations arousing very different reactions — reactions quite apart from the intention of choreographers.

APRIL, 1934: NEW YORK

Dimitriew announced at a "meeting," summarily called, that the School of American Ballet is a total désastre; no publicity; not enough students or enough scholarships to attract whatever good dancers exist. Their training is so various that they look as if they are speaking in different accents. Americans are not accustomed to work. Balanchine is only interested in pianos, automobiles, and girls. Warburg is not serious. I am greedy, interested in something produced onstage which must take years and then may be no good. If he had known what he knows now, he'd never have left Europe. Insists on seeing Eddie's father — and mine. Called him in Boston; too busy to talk. Explained (?) everything to his secretary.

From the start Dimitriew made a clear distinction between *the* school and *a* company. In order to toss two separate bones to two different pups, he began to assign school to me, company to Warburg, although our functions continued to overlap. Whatever a school cost, he knew a company would cost more, and Eddie's father seemed a more solid resource than mine. Also, Dimitriew wished to focus our interests and energies on single definite targets rather than let enthusiasm range widely and result in little. He imposed the school on me; actually, he (with Eugenie Ouroussow) ran it and (with Balanchine) the fledgling troupe. In a few years he withdrew from both; our respective fathers made it possible for us to buy him out. I would see him less. His second wife, Kyra Blank, an excellent teacher and good dancer, died. He became a misogynist, his lonely, immaculate apartment empty of love or interest. Depression was his climate and habit — a heavy drug; yet his integrity was unquestionable. My father believed in him, appreciating his efforts to force me into a simulacrum of a solid businessman. My father was remote; communications were siphoned through secretaries; he kept a file on each of his children; papers referring to us held more meaning for him than what we actually did. Ballet for him hardly promised a necessary future, but perhaps, or largely, through Dimitriew's status *in loco parentis*, instead of withdrawing aid to the school, he increased it.

JUNE, 1934: WHITE PLAINS, NEW YORK

All morning, trying to redeem the stage, after yesterday's washout. Removed tarpaulins; pools of water; everything soaked. Mr. Warburg inspects the catastrophe and makes jokes; light mist until noon; then sun. No notion whether or not anyone would come back tonight. Quite a few turned up; performance went better than I would have expected. Estlin Cummings a big help, morally; he made us laugh. Afterward, a party in the garage. Dimitriew blows up; ghastly scene.

June, 1934, was doubtless no rainier than average. Months before, we had scheduled a demonstration-debut for our putative "American Ballet," to take place on the grounds of the Warburg estate in White Plains. Dimitriew designed a bare pine dancing floor for the open air. Rain drenched the announced first night; the second was no distinguished debut for an ambitious venture. Our one performance was cautiously announced as a "demonstration," yet we could not help hoping it might kindle a brush fire which, in no time, would ignite into a full-fledged company. Three ballets were presented, two from Les Ballets 1933 which had been brought over from Paris as part settlement in the termination of Edward James's venture. MOZARTIANA, handsomely decorated by Christian Bérard, incorporated some of Balanchine's most mysterious and touching psychological ambiguities capitalizing on the fragility of postadolescent performers. LES SONGES borrowed the atmosphere of *Alice in Wonderland* for a series of infantile nightmares. André Derain designed splendid costumes, including an enormous fringed rat in which Balanchine was amused to appear on several occasions. SERENADE opened the program.

I was then seeing much of Estlin Cummings, more widely known as the poet e. e. cummings. My dream was to employ poets as instigators, as had Diaghilev. I felt we needed our own particular Cocteau; cummings was a willing candidate. In Paris the summer before, he had warned me about my flirtation with theater and with those types whom he named "Rooskies." I had published the first chapters of his journal to Sovietland (*EIMI*) in *Hound & Horn*. Now I commissioned him to write a libretto for a choreodrama based on *Uncle Tom's Cabin*, which in ignorance or innocence I decided would make the perfect plot for an "American" ballet. Eddie Warburg paid Ben Shahn, who was then emerging as an easel painter, to make attractive sketches for scenery and costumes.

When I read Balanchine what Estlin had written, translated into demotic French, he said it might well be splendid prose or even poetry, but there were no pretexts therein for dancing. He recalled that Boris Kochno, Diaghilev's secretary, who had pretensions as a poet, used to provide suggestions for choreography or, rather, scenes which might serve as libretti. In these rough schedules there would be always one number labeled *"Promenade."* However, Kochno never specified what would actually take place during this promenading. Ostensibly — "just" plain dancing. In the eighteenth century, professional French ballet composers mastered a craft justifying their abstract music. This was the craft of *faire entrer les danses* — how to introduce pure dancing logically into what preceded and followed mimic action. cummings wrote a prose-poem which has its own interest. Later it was published, accompanied by some of Shahn's designs, with no reference to its blighted birth. How could I ever explain to so eminent an author that what he had written at our command was, for us, quite useless? He convinced himself that this was still another example of atrocious Rooskie behavior. At the start, however, he was amused to watch our tentative first steps and comment on them with feline malice and scabrous slurs.

As for our baptism-by-fire (and rain) in the performance at White Plains, it received its final thunderclap following a straggling reception for a few well-wishers who returned for a second night. A pleasant feast had been prepared for our company following the performance. A clean cinder-block garage was decorated with red, white, and blue bunting; flowers and candles for every table. Dimitriew, already exasperated by the weather, Warburg's family retainers, and my nervousness, permitted himself one of the grandest denunciation scenes since Chaliapin's in BORIS GODUNOV. Were artists to be fed like pigs in a barn? He had known we were dilettantes with no comprehension of art, but were we under the gross illusion that good artists were serfs to be served in a filthy stable? cummings gravely regarded this display, comparing it to other operatic extravaganzas he had witnessed. Here, whatever our amateurishness in performance or production, was professionalism at a high peak. Here was spectacular behavior marvelously sparked by Great Nature (the weather), framed in glory (the Warburg duchy), and projected on a special audience (Eddie, Balanchine, the dancers). Thus empires are born; enunciation of power as rage. Bismarck forged Imperial Germany by uniting it in hate. Dimitriew would merge us in the unity of disaster and a determined will — if he didn't kill us first. Or, as Estlin suggested, if we didn't kill him.

Heidi Vosseler, Charles Laskey

SERENADE

APOLLON MUSAGETE

APOLLO

APOLLO

ERRANTE

ORPHEUS & EURYDICE

Ballet Caravan

Yankee Clipper
Filling Station
Air and Variations
Charade
Encounter
Pocahontas
Show Piece
Promenade
Billy the Kid

Filling
Station

DECEMBER, 1934: HARTFORD

Dress rehearsal. The spiral decor designed for SERENADE impossible to hang. This theater is pretty, but built with no space to hang scenery. Bad dress rehearsals may mean good openings; tonight's was worse than White Plains. The ballets are only echoes of what I saw in Paris. SERENADE seems to fill whatever space it's given. At least there's no hysteria. Warburg was cheerful, delighted with costumes by John Held, Jr., for ALMA MATER. A year ago, we left Hartford in a mess and everything seems to have turned out, if not perfectly, at least promisingly.

The debut of our "American Ballet" took place in Hartford, as we had originally anticipated, but under quite other circumstances. Patchwork and improvisation are methods of salvage; something had been eventually clamped together which roughly resembled a working organism. Chick Austin and his trustees generously forgave and forgot. Our premiere was not a disgrace; Warburg could feel that his contribution, for once, was more on the side of art than of cash. For he had successfully invented a workable pretext upon which Balanchine based dancing.

In 1934, Warburg and I were still essentially undergraduates, our tastes more or less formed by, or against, that of the Fogg Museum and its fine-arts faculty. We were aware of progressive currents in the visual arts, having founded the Harvard Society for Contemporary Art; we had handled and hung artifacts of many of the chief artists of our time, some of whom we came to know well. Through editing *Hound & Horn* I was involved at least in discussion of a number of general ideas, which commanded my awe if not much of my attention. I had few social or political prejudices or preoccupations, but

I was very impressed by two models of behavior— James Cagney and T. E. Lawrence. Much moved by the British tradition of illegitimate or extralegal activity and feudal responsibility, I wrote a short essay on Lawrence's life following the Arab revolt, and received a reply from him in his retirement. Excited by Cagney's films, I wrote another, for *Hound & Horn*. Cagney responded by coming to watch a ballet class; he had been trained as a dancer. I had notions as to which roles he should appropriate—John Paul Jones (following Melville's *Israel Potter*), Billy the Kid, Benvenuto Cellini, Studs Lonigan. Abstract concepts as exemplified by humanist, Marxist, or agrarian symposia meant little to me, but heroic types in personifications of action composed a dramatis personae for a continuous historical drama which I always found exciting. In attempting to project an "American" ballet, our dependence on native mythology may have been naïve but seemed necessary. Diaghilev himself passed through a decade of extracting color and melody from Slavic folklore with an almost scientific attitude.

So, when we first tried to discover a suitable subject for a contemporary work in an initial repertory, Warburg drew on the world he knew best and liked most, that of an Ivy League undergraduate. Just as I was under the spell of Hollywood ganglands, Arab revolt, and Diaghilev's court, he was magicked by rituals of college eating clubs, big football, and Harvard-Yale games. Forty years ago football was not only a spectator sport but, undefiled by television, a participant ceremony involving choirs of noisy partisans, tipsy old grads, orgies of organized cheerleading, song, and bathtub gin from

pocket flasks. Team spirit had no commercial additive, and diminutive halfbacks, shortstops, and strokes were personal champions. While it was acknowledged, particularly by "intellectuals," that the whole athletic mythos was faintly ridiculous, it did provide a genuine and decorative atmosphere. Football formations were, in their way, elementary choreography; a cheerleader was a kind of first dancer, or could be presented as one.

Warburg's notion for a ballet was triggered by turn-of-the-century sepia photographs of football teams posed against sections of the old Yale fence, or grouped pyramidally with the year's captain displaying a pigskin inscribed with the date. We'd all read the inspirational texts of Owen Johnson and Ralph Henry Barbour in prep school. *Stover at Yale, Brown of Harvard* proposed a campy campus silliness ingrained in ritual rivalries solemnly perpetuated by generations of loyal alumni. Eddie's aim was ironic as well as comic—to satirize the synthetic idolatry of athletes and athletics—and he would be disappointed when Balanchine grasped little if any of this special vein of humor, simply resorting to an old bag of European music-hall and circus gags and tricks.

Eddie's inventions for ALMA MATER involved an idiotic demigod quarterback and a Salvation Army lass who turned into a *strip-teaseuse*. John Held, Jr., the Charles Dana Gibson of the Jazz Age, designed various undergraduate types in crew cuts, raccoon coats, helmets and shoulder pads, bell-bottom trousers, and flapper regalia. Balanchine was piloted to the Yale Bowl; the tactics of broken-field running, surprise plays, and dropkicks were offered to his ingenuity. We asked George Gershwin for a score. Already overoccupied with Hollywood, he suggested that his friend Kay Swift would be witty and capable, and her score triumphantly vindicated

MOZARTIANA

THE BAT

his confidence. Balanchine often said he felt like an American even before he left Leningrad, and he had used popular music for revue numbers in London.

ALMA MATER was, at the least, an earnest of pious intentions toward the creation of indigenous repertory. In it we fumbled toward an expression of the male principle as athlete rather than prince or god. Balanchine had already paved the way nearly a decade before with APOLLON, in which the Sun-Dancer played games with his muses rather than making love to them. Girl cheerleaders and baton twirlers were Atlantic City beauty queens—Miss Americas rather than fairy swan-princesses. Balanchine knew that a small-scale domestic frame was all that so slight a pretext could contain, but his carpentry made it viable, and the miniature songless musical comedy lasted for several seasons. At the commencement of his American career, he recognized the coltish virtuosity, professional amateurism, contrived improvisation which distinguished our best popular stylishness. Prime examples were Gershwin and Cole Porter, Fred and Adele Astaire, Jimmy Cagney, and Ginger Rogers.

ALMA MATER had some importance economically and even politically, because it temporarily proved to Eddie that he had uses past signing checks. Also, I imagined I saw signs and portents by which the ballet idiom might be removed from the elite or epicene European atmosphere to gain a public, not equaling but at least approaching a mass audience as something less than a snob attraction. Sooner than we then could know, Balanchine would be working in Hollywood on a film intended for George Gershwin, who would be dead before he could begin it. Thirty-five years later, however, there would be a genuine collaboration in WHO CARES? for in that carefully contrived romp, the orchestra stays silent during a tape of Gershwin at his piano. Gershwin had appeared frequently in Diaghilev's circle abroad. Stravinsky's RAGTIME was an early manifestation of the growing appreciation of Americana. It was Balanchine's unprejudiced catholicity in musical taste which was to give our repertory its special savor; this commenced with ALMA MATER.

From the NEW YORK TIMES, March 6, 1935:

Though totally obscure, it [TRANSCENDENCE] . . . is of far greater interest. . . . It has the quality of phantasmagoria and some of its incidents are of distinct power, but whether for straining for choreographic novelty or again because of its complete unsuitability to the talents of the company, it remains largely incomprehensible. Throughout the performance there was manifest a sense of strain. A young and inexperienced group is being pushed beyond its limits of accomplishment, and thereby the future of a promising enterprise is being seriously jeopardized.

Thus John Martin—practically the first, for four decades the most influential, dance critic in the United States, and historically the best-informed and least self-serving—analyzed our opening in New York. As Warburg had been responsible for ALMA MATER, TRANSCENDENCE was my responsibility, as far as pretext for decor and danced action went. I had read Sacheverell Sitwell's lyrical evocation of the career of Nicolò Paganini, the quasi-diabolical virtuoso who was a variant of, or twin to, E. T. A. Hoffmann and Franz Liszt, as wizard-performer-composer. At

Weimar in 1852 Liszt published his *Études d'exécution transcendante*, in which keyboard acrobacy was pushed to its digital limits. In our early ballet tours we could never be sure of an orchestra; hence we considered music which might be played without too much loss by a two-piano team. I felt sure that Liszt-Paganini, combined as one dancer, was a suitable pretext for unlimited possibility in a musical dance-drama. Pantomime and national dances were genres lacking in our repertory. The fused figure of violinist-pianist might stand as archetype and metaphor for the wizard-performer. A male soloist's whole physique could express the power and control of fingers on ivory keys or bowed strings. In William Dollar, an advanced pupil of Fokine's who was a superb athletic classicist, we had an ideal dancer for this role.

At some central European (Hungarian? Czech? Polish?) peasant gathering, a young girl is bewitched by a wandering minstrel. Fascinated by his mad music making, she deserts her horrified fiancé on her wedding

ALMA MATER: Charles Laskey, Heidi Vosseler

day. Then, appearing as a sinister monk, the mysterious minstrel conducts her through the black rites of a witches' sabbath. In an elaborate *pas de deux* he hypnotizes his virginal victim (a reversal of the hypnotic somnambulism of NIGHT SHADOW a dozen years later). She is saved at the last moment by her fiancé and his friends. The devil—for it is indeed he—is exorcised. However, at a spring festival which follows, the enchanter-minstrel revives himself as the Year-Spirit, a Jack o' the Green; with the returning April sap or energy, creativity or virtuosity is displayed as both good and bad, lucky and unlucky, ephemeral and eternal.

Ingredients were from a mixture of sources, including the Sitwell biography, Sir James Frazer's *Golden Bough*, Jessie L. Weston's *From Ritual to Romance*, T. S. Eliot, and what Romola Nijinsky had told me of MEPHISTO VALSE, a ballet Vaslav prepared with Robert

Edmond Jones at Bar Harbor in 1916. This waltz served as our witches' sabbath. In 1928 Bronislava Nijinska had created LA BIEN-AIMÉE, with music by Liszt, for Ida Rubinstein. Here, a pianist mused over his keyboard, recalling past inspiration, which in turn recalled Fokine's first version of LES SYLPHIDES—the CHOPINIANA of 1908. After the massive onslaught of modernism and a canonization of contemporaneity in the middle and late twenties, radical manifestations in literature and the plastic arts, there had come a definite reaction, drawing on the Gothic, Victorian, and Edwardian neoromantics, in which Edith, Osbert, and Sacheverell Sitwell were prime movers. It coincided with centennial celebrations of Franco-German romanticism, distinguished by exhibitions of Delacroix and Géricault and renewed interest in Berlioz and Victor Hugo. TRANSCENDENCE anticipated several works of similar taste and interest: Frederick Ashton and Cecil Beaton's APPARITIONS to Liszt (1936), Massine and Bérard's SYMPHONIE FANTASTIQUE (Berlioz, 1936), and Fokine's PAGANINI (Rachmaninov, 1939).

TRANSCENDENCE seemed to promise so much that we risked commissioning an orchestration for a small pit band from George Antheil, a young advance-guard composer. He had arrived in 1926 with his "Airplane Sonata" and BALLET MÉCANIQUE, in which propellers and other mechanistic effects were a precedent for much later and more developed electronic devices. He was a protégé of Ezra Pound, who had proclaimed him in a zealous pamphlet entitled "Antheil, or the Future of Harmony." A solid, small, blond, compact, permanent postadolescent, he hardly fulfilled his early heady notoriety. He all but deserted composition for a dubious career in Hollywood, not a career writing film music but one producing newspaper columns on the place of endocrine glands in the human organism. He was a professional musician, a brilliant pianist, an enthusiastic if disappointing collaborator, *bien rusé* in international musical-theater politics, one of the American vanguard, along with Marc Blitzstein, Paul Bowles, Aaron Copland, and Virgil Thomson (all of whom were to write scores for us), educated in Paris, largely under Nadia Boulanger, who would soon return to New York to employ native material.

The beautiful pen and watercolor costume designs for TRANSCENDENCE were by Franklin Watkins (they are now in the Museum of Modern Art). His heroic murals graced the Rodin Museum in Philadelphia, and he had just won the Carnegie International painting prize. His peculiar personal quality of baroque expressionism and a stormy palette recommended itself to the subject. We found that he wished to work with dancers. I was happy with the quality of his collaboration—particularly Balanchine's Hungarian dances, the mesmerizing *pas de deux*, and William Dollar's frenetic pantomime and acrobatic classicism. Those who have seen Balanchine's BRAHMS-SCHOENBERG QUARTET (1966), which Brahms himself could hardly have imagined without the precedence of Liszt, may find a faint echo of TRANSCENDENCE.

In any case, this novelty, such as it was, had been created from scratch in Manhattan, with absolutely no reference to Parisian precedent. I might take satisfaction from the knowledge that it had evolved at my own suggestion, that it embodied a collaborative effort on high poetic principles, and most important, that it had got itself danced on a stage. To be sure, its libretto offered pretexts too overwhelming for our executant potential at this time. But although everyone else (starting with Balanchine) saw our performances as they transparently were, I often managed to see them as perhaps they might have been. TRANSCENDENCE, a firstborn, remained my favorite of dozens of promising short-lived children engendered over the next thirty-five years.

MARCH, 1935: NEW YORK

John Martin writes in the Sunday Times that it might be a good idea for us to send Balanchine back to Paris, where he belongs. He says SERENADE is serviceable rather than inspired, that REMINISCENCE was the "real delight of the evening." Nothing could make me angrier. "Here Mr. Balanchine has taken actual dances from his memories of the Russian Ballet and adapted them to his own uses. Here the real abilities of the company get their first showing. . . . On the basis of such technical discipline as is here evidenced fine things can certainly be expected in the not too distant future."

REMINISCENCE was planned as a ballet to end an evening, an applause-machine concocted after a tested, tasty recipe. Balanchine considers himself a carpenter, plumber, restaurant-keeper, and short-order cook. His professionalism enables him, often with surprising piquancy and variety, to resuscitate démodé music. Here he took a suite of dances by Benjamin Godard, whose "Berceuse" from the opera JOCELYN was for decades a favorite of palm-court tearoom orchestras. John Martin, covering Balanchine's choice of Brahms's LIEBESLIEDER WALZER in 1960, suggested that he might next choreograph pages from a telephone directory. As an accomplished and erudite musician, Balanchine learned musical repertory the way medical students read Gray's *Anatomy*. He has not been deterred by the transient strictures of snobbish good taste. Indeed, if an individual talent, once popular, is currently in disfavor, he has often seized on it for forgotten or unsuspected excellence—as, for example, the piano pieces of Chabrier, lost symphonies of Bizet, Gounod, Ives, and Tchaikovsky; Sousa's marches, Gershwin's songs, and music expressly written for forgotten dances by Bellini, Donizetti, Drigo, and Glazunov.

To me REMINISCENCE represented everything banal, compromising, and retardative in a philosophy of what we should *not* be doing—except its execution by our dancers. It was pastiche, a concession at one remove to the Ballets Russes public, a betrayal of Diaghilev's *avant-gardisme;* ten steps backward. Its success and practical uses were incontestable. As a diploma of technical efficiency, at least, it pleased the managerial powers that would land us, sooner than we might have hoped, at the service of the Metropolitan Opera Association. However, our first New York season had its modicum of prestige success and a recognition of energy and money expended. A Russian impresario was found who agreed to arrange a tour. Warburg allowed himself some natural if unwarranted elation; the tour collapsed in Scranton, Pennsylvania. The matter of picking up pieces, restoring morale, paying bills offered little amusement to a generous, eager, and fun-loving young man.

MAY, 1935: NEW YORK

With Warburg to see Edward Johnson, the Met's new general manager. I hardly believed where I was, or how I was talking. He hadn't heard of our disaster. Balanchine was at least a name to him. I explained he'd been hired by Diaghilev in 1924 to do all the opera ballets for Monte Carlo in ten days; he said this was exactly the sort of man he needed. He has ideas about reviving the Met, with some new notions. He liked the name "American Ballet"; he is a Canadian. I suggested we might give one whole ballet program a week on Sunday nights with no extra cost. He agreed. After Hartford, I thought we were finished. After Scranton, again. Suddenly here we are, serving the Met.

Edward Johnson, an ex-tenor of much grace and warmth, an excellent singing artist, was a sympathetic gentleman. My ambition had always been to represent and be supported by an established institution. I was naïve in thinking that one could be found in a year. The Met's offer was providential. We saw all sorts of possibilities, but as yet had no idea of the nature of a structure logically rooted in the routine of a repertory system, employing international singers. Here, first and last, the voice was supreme, with every other consideration secondary. Also, we had not yet encountered Edward Ziegler, Johnson's adjutant, whose experience and power made him the real master of the Met. An indigenous version of Vladimir Dimitriew, he regarded our intrusion into his precincts with a jaundiced eye. Ziegler, like so many able managers, was undeterred by personal interest in the arts, ballet least of all; his duty was to enable the Met to survive during a serious economic depression. We had hardly forgotten that the management of the Met was dominated by Italian singers, repertory, and producers, and that this family was determined to keep Diaghilev out of any permanent local presence. But we were ourselves "American," and Warburg's father was from olden times an associate of Otto H. Kahn, who with Puccini, Caruso, and Gatti-Casazza before the First World War had led the Met to surpass La Scala as the prime opera house of the world.

I fell promptly in love with the whole dusty fabric of the Met. Here history lived, as it must have for nearly a hundred years, in a genuine nineteenth-century house, a dinosaur in amber, static yet breathing. Racks filled with thousands of costumes, an armorer's shop, a wig room, shoes to fit a crusader's army corps, a carpentry shop that turned out everything from stagecoaches to ships in full sail—a hugely efficient machine to equip and produce the preposterous, merged in a heady potion to poison me further with another serious attack of red-and-gold disease. My experience so far had been in small theaters. The vast scale of the Met made me drunk. As for Balanchine, he proceeded to turn out necessary divertissements for the fourth act of CARMEN, the second act of LA TRAVIATA, the "Bacchanale" from TANNHÄUSER with dispatch and often considerable inventiveness. We were not even a failure immediately. To him it was simply another opera house, bigger than Copenhagen or Leningrad, drearier than Paris, less productive than London, less innovative than German or Austrian theaters. Warburg and I were determined to make the best of our luck in actually being employed under such formidable auspices. We were hardly counting on Ziegler's antagonism, or Balanchine's quite different interests and ambitions. These could scarcely be reconciled; but meantime we'd found a haven which I felt was heaven. I abandoned any idea of innovation for the moment; we must show the Met how useful we could be. Night after night, whenever a ballet was included in an opera, I would be onstage, like Johnson and Ziegler, in tails and white tie, a splendid official uniform.

As a safe and modest start, Balanchine took music from DIE FLEDERMAUS, inserting a big waltz—a sketch, in fact, for the enlarged setting of Ravel's LA VALSE fifteen years later. I was made happy by his acceptance of one notion of my own. The eponymous *Bat* was no single dancer, but rather a girl and boy, each having one huge bat's wing of smoky, spangled China silk which, supported on bamboo armatures, collapsed or expanded, fluttering like proper wings. Balanchine invented pleasant devices; there was a gypsy interlude. A conventional piece had its satisfactory reception. We seemed to be doing what we were there for, and we were being paid as well. What could be better?

ORPHEUS AND EURYDICE: Tchelitchev's design for the final scene

DECEMBER, 1935: NEW YORK

To Tchelitchev's studio, 55th Street and First Avenue. A penthouse turned into a garden. New portraits of Charles Ford and Natalie Paley. Marvelous. He says New York is now ready for him, and for us. Insisted I take him to the Met. Stopped the taxi to buy whiskey. He did not want to meet either Johnson or Ziegler but only the chief carpenter. He said to Carl Steinmetz: "I am a mad Russian; in the spring, we will work together. Drink this whiskey; in April, you remember who I am and what I want." Steinmetz amused; I had no more idea than he what Pavlik was talking about. Later he announced we would produce Gluck's ORFEO ED EURIDICE as ballet-opera in the spring. Does Balanchine know anything about this? "He doesn't, but will."

Tchelitchev's descent on New York was vital and drastic for all of us. He brought a desperate urgency, his own big talent and authority, and stirred up infectious excitement. Immeasurably the most gifted scenic designer of his epoch, he always used the stage as a seedbed for more serious easel pictures. Among young models he found likely aspirants for our school and company. Young painters drawn to his work would be recommended as designers. He had a notion of total lyric theater in which poets, painters, and musicians would be working for dancers. While he was with Balanchine he joined in a few memorable collaborations; those talents, other than his own, which attracted him were rarely congenial to us. What Tchelitchev refused to realize was our particular sphere of dance—also the fact that music required little visual appurtenance beyond the proposal and fulfillment of human plasticity and measured motion. Tchelitchev was so seductive a talker, so apt a wit, so ingenious a diplomat that he could make his most insane project sound normal and possible. Since he abandoned theater in America before we had any chance to give him the resources of a large format, it will never be known what he might have accomplished with his more fantastic schemes.

There was one he called EPISODES, an evening's spectacle involving three archetypes: Don Juan, Don Quixote, Hamlet. Another was MEDEA, a great hill, mountain, or beehive which opened for the perennial battle between Ants and Bees (Fascism against Communism). On one occasion we did have an opportunity to work together on a project which employed the equipment of a big opera house. The result was the most beautiful visual spectacle I have seen on any stage.

The choice of Gluck's ORFEO seemed modest and rational: a two-act work employing only three soloists and dancers. In it there was much music actually written for ballet. It had not been presented in some years; it contained some of the loveliest vocal music in repertory. Eddie Warburg would pay for a visual production, while the opera contributed the musical services. This ensured that Tchelitchev might have a free hand. He was not extravagant at all; he loved to improvise with the poorest materials. Genuine silk and satin were vulgar—worse, these were not legible as richness under stage lighting. ORFEO's scenery was made out of chicken wire, cheesecloth, and dead birch branches. He was distressed because there was no good flying apparatus, since he wanted Orpheus, Eurydice, and Amor to soar up into his marvelous celestial regions at the end of the fourth scene, with wires painted frankly white so they could be read as physical lines of magnetic force.

His splendid drawings, forty of them, are now in the Museum of Modern Art. They appear to be life studies as much as costume design, for he insisted upon as much nudity as was then licensed, with skeletal additions of wings, chains, garlands. His poetics were highly organized around elements of earth, air, fire, and water (mist and clouds). Mineral, animal, vegetable, and aerial; winter, spring, summer, autumn were frames upon which he hung his analysis of the Orphic myth. He was one of the last in the line of High Renaissance artists who used a metaphysical ikonology expressed in alchemy, gnosis, and mythopoetic symbolism.

The noble sobriety of Gluck's score proceeds like an aural mural; only in the Hell scene are there violence and strong turbulent action. The entire production was conceived without an element of paint. Rather, pigment was actually light. All hand-props and scenery were three-dimensional. Backgrounds were impalpable, chosen for their capacity to transmit, reflect, or change light. Everything occurred in air. As far as possible, space was unlimited and the frame itself—two transparent towers of which only the mortar for the masonry seemed solid—would disappear.

When the curtain rose, Orpheus, a big boy in a transparent T-shirt and black trunks, impassive, frozen in grief, watches the construction of Eurydice's memorial monument. Friends and neighbors try to comfort him, bringing reminders of his lost happiness. On crossed beams they drape rags, stack brooms, ladders, pots, ordinary objects of domestic ritual. This homely structure is capped by a cloth with Eurydice's wan portrait on a translucent veil. All except Orpheus himself were covered in gray body makeup, shades of sorrow. Alone, he was presented as both athlete and poet. Across his back was strung a crystal lyre. The groups Balanchine found were reminiscent of pietàs, entombments, depositions, ritual groupings gravely proceeding in flowing plastic sequences.

Hell, the second scene, was a Piranesian prison, crossbars of which were made of braided barbed wire. At that period the reference to concentration camps was not as legible as it would soon become; we were criticized for injecting polemics into spectacle. Orpheus' crystal lyre seemed to draw blood from red-orange silk flames. Demon guards, masked in horse skulls with manes of serpents, brandishing snaky whips, lashed gangs of chained prisoners suggesting a Last Judgment or Doré's engravings for *Paradise Lost* and Dante's *Inferno*. This underworld was composed of stone and fire, chain and bone.

In the third scene, Orpheus' lyre led him through an airless Umbrian landscape in some timeless limbo. Birch trunks, stripped of leaves, hung in midair over a massive mound or burial barrow. A solemn procession of graybeards, vestals, and adolescent youths offered their meager homage of bone-dry laurel. In this anomalous ambience, dancers were swathed in doubled nettings of blue and violet which read as changeable taffeta, revealing naked bodies inside. Among the shadows of a once living world, figures passed in fluid solemnity, vague as forgotten ancestors.

In the final scene, spread across the wide sky, was a self-illuminated Milky Way, thousands of stars superimposed across the traditional diagrams of Lyre, Dipper, Cassiopeia's Chair, standing out against a vibrating mosaic of tiny stars powdering the black velvet night. Within this vast surround, there were only three figures for the entire scene—Orpheus, his regained Eurydice, and an angelic Hermes-Amor, performing a deliberate interlace of knotty figures at once intensely erotic and plastically splendid.

Eurydice was danced by Daphne Vane, a slight girl of doelike sweetness and fragile pathos, sheathed in mother-of-pearl chiffon which barely veiled her. William Dollar as Amor manipulated his goose-feather pinions with astonishing nobility, combining the roles of protector, guide, savior, a permutation of Hermes Psychopompos, the divine messenger who conducts souls to Pluto's realm. Mercury's wings were set on his dancer's feet. Orpheus was danced by Lew Christensen, one of three brothers of Danish-Mormon origin, all with excellent training by Luigi Albertieri, a famous Italian dancing master. Lew was tall, fair, finely proportioned with a noble head, extremely musical, possessing an acrobat's dignity and innate good taste matching his advanced technical security. Balanchine was happy to say there was no male performer outside Russia who could match him as a *danseur noble*. The male principle in America was then sadly lacking.

No singers were onstage; voices rose from the orchestra pit. The opera was presented without an entr'acte, increasing the displeasure of the Metropolitan's subscribers, for whom intermissions are as pleasurable as performance.

In New York, at the only two performances we were granted, the general responses were titters, yawns, or weak, ironic applause. Our audience was totally unprepared for an interpretation which transformed vaguely familiar myth and music into a heroicized domestic tragedy of artist, wife, and work; hell as a forced-labor camp; eternity as no happy heaven, but a paradisiacal planetarium where time and space crossed. Tchelitchev's and Balanchine's marriage of metaphors—Hellenistic, Christian, post-Newtonian—were lost on a public that wanted to listen passively rather than actively look.

To the general audience, the use of allusive imagery, the shimmering incandescence of unfamiliar industrial stuffs and textures, the pervasive eroticism of mime and movement smacked of Broadway or the films—which then, as now, certainly employed more imaginative approaches to sound and sense than the Metropolitan Opera. Edward Johnson was courteously forgiving; Edward Ziegler was confirmed in his lack of confidence in the American Ballet. Hoping against hope, we still thought we might benefit by being attached to an establishment. Olin Downes, the omnipotent music critic of the *New York Times*, found it all "absurd," "impudent"; worse—"meddlesome." *Time* magazine and the rest followed his line. It was generally conceded we had thrown away our golden opportunity.

ORPHEUS AND EURYDICE:
Lew Christensen (Orpheus),
William Dollar (Amor)

DECEMBER, 1936: NEW YORK

Received Stravinsky's piano score and orchestration for JEU DE CARTES. Clean calligraphy, ready for the engraver. Warburg says it can't be called "The Game of Cards"; it must be "Poker Party." Balanchine tried it on his piano and found it rhythmically fascinating. Quotations from Rossini. This clinched for me the success of Stravinsky Festival next spring. Ballets to add: APOLLON and LE BAISER DE LA FÉE. To Tchelitchev's to beg him to do one or the other. He refused. After his experience with ORPHEUS, he won't work in American theater again. Wired Stravinsky thanks; asked him to conduct performances. To the Met; in MEISTERSINGER's "Johannestag" scene, boys found Sachse, the director, onstage urging them to change the choreography, so they let him have it, with truncheons. Ugly scene with Ziegler.

When Stravinsky had received Warburg's invitation to accept a commission, he was already at work on a new score, which he then turned to our use. We did not know its subject for months after a contract was signed. Stravinsky credited one Malaieff, a friend of his painter-son Theodore, with developing the *prétexte*, which emerged as three deals in a game of poker. Irene Sharaff set the work in a witty frame: an enormous green baize card table against a corner of which stood, in sharply forced perspective, a huge gilt three-branched candlestick. The pack of cards consisted of twenty-six dancers, drawn from the four suits, plus a joker. Balanchine explained:

Stravinsky and I attempted to show that the highest cards— the kings, queens, and jacks—in reality have nothing on the other side. They are big people, but they can easily be beaten by small cards. Seemingly powerful figures, they are actually mere silhouettes.*

The danced action followed rules according to Hoyle. In each deal, as Stravinsky said, the situation is complicated "by the endless guile of the perfidious joker who believes himself invincible because of his ability to become any desired card." Abrupt entries of the joker, to whom ordinary causality does not apply, destroy any presumed sequence in the dealt hands. At the end of every deal, giant *papier-mâché* fingers of an otherwise invisible croupier swept away the rejected cards. A short prelude to each deal (march, polonaise, waltz) was followed by group dances, *pas d'action*, and solos. Deal, bet, and pass were translated into the idiom of classic dancing; cards shuffled themselves at the start of each part. Balanchine was prodigal of invention, to such a degree that Stravinsky, always thrifty, insisted he should repeat one especially ingenious device, because the audience wouldn't have time to appreciate it on its first appearance.

Before his arrival, we asked Irene Sharaff (later to become Elizabeth Taylor's favorite costumer) to design scenery and fifty dresses. We suggested that she study the Tarot and other medieval packs for heraldic fantasy and symbolic sense. When Stravinsky saw her clever sketches, he complained that they placed his music in too particular a historical period, evoking a decorative but specific atmosphere that was the opposite of what he had intended. He wanted the impersonal, workaday taste of the usual card pack, forms and details to be immediately legible. There would be many poker players among the public; they should be able to read the drama in his three deals at once.

* Balanchine's New Complete Stories of the Great Ballets (Francis Mason, Ed.), Doubleday & Co., Garden City, N.Y., 1968, pp. 74–5.

Before I had much contact with theatrical working conditions, I was puzzled about an element commonly called "inspiration," a mysterious creative quantity without which nothing good gets done. I became accustomed to Balanchine's readiness in improvisatory composition; he analyzed the capacities of available individuals or elements and made dances from given materials just as a tailor cuts and sews clothes. Afterward these may be worn by others or adapted to other bodies, but "inspiration" more often than not turned out to be accommodation to necessity, making do with what one found at hand. Stravinsky was as impersonal as a surgeon, carpenter, or plumber. Imposed factors were not only acceptable but could be warped into constructs which made the factors more firm and clear. We had only a limited time allotted for rehearsals. Clocks ruled everything, starting with the duration of sections of a score. Stravinsky would sit for six hours at a stretch in our studio, then haul the rehearsal pianist off to his hotel for more work. He was a precision instrument, a corporeal metronome, but neither captious nor inelastic. When he saw that Balanchine needed additional music to permit a desired development, he would promptly decide whether to repeat measures or add new notes. If the latter, the necessary piano part would appear next morning, accompanied by its immaculate orchestration ready for the copyist.

Balanchine was accustomed to make his own piano reductions from whatever new orchestral score he was given. Marius Petipa's dancers had followed the piano alone; they would hear the orchestra only at a final stage rehearsal. Balanchine composed with full sonorities and dynamics already in his ear, and while dancers were frequently surprised to hear what eventually accompanied them from the pit, unsuspected sounds and silences were anticipated. As for choreography, Stravinsky expressed neither surprise nor preference. He had confidence in the partnership; what had now become his method was concentration without waste motion. He exhibited only muscular energy, patience, constant encouraging cheerfulness, no hysteria, and courteous attention. Realizing that when he came to conduct the performance he might have a tendency to accelerate tempi and thus dislocate the dancing, he had our accompanist play faster than his score's indicated counts, tempering them to his own discrepancies. He treated Balanchine like a junior assistant, although on an absolutely equal footing as an expert, since there was a presupposed agreement that the spectacle would be governed by music rather than by any overall concept of stylized movement.

THE CARD PARTY: Publicity photograph. *Seated at table, clockwise from left,* William Dollar, Edward Warburg, Igor Stravinsky, George Balanchine

JANUARY, 1937: NEW YORK

Tchelitchev has pushed Alice Halicka for the decor of LE BAISER DE LA FÉE. Coinciding with a snowstorm, Madame Halicka arrived in furs. Rather than sketches, her plans are collages, pasted up from paper lace, tinsel, silk, wood veneer, sequins. The effect of Swiss souvenir cuckoo clocks, boules-de-neige, glass balls filled with flakes which, when turned, make a miniature blizzard. The last scene defeats her; the Matterhorn glacier, upon which the hero disappears. Tchelitchev found a solution: a huge net, stretched across the stage, under which cold green light would be thrown in jagged points. The last scene would be a dance on a net.

Alice Halicka was the wife of the painter Marcoussis. She had charming gifts as a decorator and with sophisticated mock vulgarity made naïve pictures from a mosaic of materials, an elevated *Kitsch—la romance capitonnée* —stuffed and quilted. Her proposals for the Alps were composed of tufted satin sprinkled with glitter; her scale was a postcard view of a fretwork chalet, blown up to a travel poster. A danger was that her style might seem a parody rather than a proper frame, so that homage to Tchaikovsky's genius, which was the point of the piece, would appear to be mocked or diminished. The finale, which Halicka found difficult to design since it was in reality an interminable climb up an imaginary mountain, contains some of Stravinsky's most luxurious orchestration, but is so extended that it leaves no scope for building dances toward a dramatic climax. The ballet seemed finished long before it ended. Like the scenery, the score was a mosaic of quotations and variations on themes from early, then-unfamiliar Tchaikovsky scores, including a beautiful manipulation of the famous song "None But the Lonely Heart." This was a favorite of Warburg's urbane and generous father, who was polite enough to assume it had been included for his special pleasure.

But the ballet, in spite of a magical *pas de deux* between fiancé and fairy, did not really work. Alpine village and Tchaikovsky quotations offered a visual and musical landscape which seemed not only *déjà vu*, but *déjà entendu*; at best pastiche, although tasteful and dignified. The work entered the repertory of the Ballets Russes de Monte Carlo during the Second World War; Alexandra Danilova had considerable success in the part of the Bride, as did both Mia Slavenska and Maria Tallchief as the Fairy. Balanchine's group formations for the snowstorm were reborn in a variant when he came to choreograph THE NUTCRACKER for the New York City Ballet seventeen years later. The fortune-telling duet looked back to the "hand-of-fate" episode in his COTILLON of 1932. Balanchine continually reworked his own veins of invention; many motifs reappear in other guises in the sequence of his invention. This explains why he is so loath to revive works which have not had an immediate or complete effect. But one of the miniature masterpieces of the *second* Stravinsky Festival of June, 1972, was an extended divertissement derived from LE BAISER DE LA FÉE.

MARCH, 1937: NEW YORK

Dress rehearsal of Stravinsky ballets. Warburg's decision to use the Philharmonic rather than the Met opera orchestra certainly paid off. Stravinsky particularly liked scenery for APOLLON: "Ça fait riche; très Poussinesque." Lew Christensen was everything one could wish. Balanchine threw away his wig. His hair is long enough to be curled tight. Tchelitchev cut away half his gilt leather armor. Improved his makeup; little to do with a head like that but let it shine. At the end of rehearsal, Stravinsky thanked Lew.

I had first seen APOLLON at Covent Garden during Diaghilev's last season, in 1929. Through repeated experience of it, I gained an understanding of Balanchine's essential attitude about choreography. This differed not only from pre-Diaghilev dance design, but also from Diaghilev's own preference. The nineteenth-century philosophy of stage dancing was dominated by opera-house atmosphere, and before 1850, by opera itself. Diaghilev released it into an autonomous form. It is significant that in the chief national houses over the last half century, important diplomatic occasions have been celebrated in Paris, London, and Moscow by ballet rather than opera galas. Through APOLLON I came to understand that the classic dance, an expressive idiom in its own right, was not necessarily subsidiary to spectacle, employing equal ingredients of painted decoration, expressive pantomime, and brilliant dancing, but rather an independent language of visual plastic interest based on music unadorned. The preoccupation was with three-dimensional movement measured by opulent rhythm and sonority. And through APOLLON I realized that choreography clothed the dancer far more than costume, that the essence of important dancing lay in combinations and sequences of linked steps quite apart from intrusions by a star performer's accidental overlay of personality.

Originally, Balanchine had been ordered by Diaghilev to invent a work which would frame Serge Lifar, his last first-dancer. Lifar had the air of a postadolescent, self-indulgent boy of grace and energy, but he was by no means a fully equipped classic technician. Balanchine arranged steps for him which accommodated and capitalized on his limitations, accentuated his brusqueness, set off his strength to such a degree that in his triumph, pattern and structure were eclipsed by personality and idiosyncrasy. Hence an eccentricity in many parts of the female variations, which were organized and designed to be consistent with the unique masculine role, at first appeared as particularly disturbing. Diaghilev, deprived of his Russian source of young dancers in his later years, suffered from a weak corps de ballet. In APOLLON Balanchine used three ballerinas, not only as soloists but as a super corps de ballet, by means which were astonishingly innovative.

With the exception of a very few ballets still surviving, much of the late Diaghilev repertory from 1917 on substituted amusement for amazement. Ideas, poetic or shocking, with pantomime more or less primary, served as lyric drama. New sounds, the *musiquette* of the Parisian twenties, with its perverse polemical bias, mainly against heavy German symphonizing, was the ensign of *Les Six*, who repudiated the romantic background (Wagnerism in particular) by cultivating deliberate triviality. This Diaghilev encouraged as novelty, since he manipulated the casual snobberies of Paris like a puppet master. He had been responsible for novelty since his debut; his was a formula for planned obsolescence. APOLLON, in its apparent modesty of scale (four dancers; strings alone), its melodic insistence and rhythmic compulsion, its strict formal skeleton and heroic overtone, was not grandiose although it framed grandeur. It administered a serious negative electric shock, and what is rare in so deliberate a work, effected a consequential

reversal in taste. It was at first offensive to a smart public schooled to expect more and more clever, provocative silliness. Diaghilev knew that what Stravinsky and Balanchine had done was to reaffirm the importance of classicism itself with a neoclassic turnabout that had already been proclaimed by Picasso's renunciation of Cubism and his attraction to Pompeian wall painting. Classic wholeness and order were prime factors. Their constant potential for offering plasticity and temporal analysis depended on measuring lofty melody strong and suggestive enough to compel new and alert rhythmic motivation and resonance.

Balanchine used a number of devices that, at their debut, seemed ridiculous. Today this extension of a vocabulary has been so long and so deeply absorbed that there is no fraction which does not appear logical, gracious, and flowing. In 1929 much appeared quirky, "ugly"; in "bad taste." What it had done was to require new looking and listening. Shocking gesture and movement there had been before, notably in the seminal invention of the Nijinskys—brother and sister. But these had been more easily forgiven, since they were apparently derived from folklore and only decorated the rhetoric of the academic idiom. In truth, the Nijinskys invented from scratch. Vaslav, in no way a humorless or uncultivated innocent, solemnly assured one British critic eager for a briefing on his "inspiration" for LE SACRE DU PRINTEMPS that every step had been devised from original Muscovite documents of the fourth century B.C.! Balanchine could claim no such license for extending a classic language which was almost as well-known as counterpoint and harmony. He merely asserted new movement, and the more eminent White Russian critics howled as if he had committed rape. But Gordon Craig, who had hated LE SACRE for its sweatiness and oppressive subhuman (or superhuman) energy, left the Paris premiere of APOLLON before the final work on the evening's program, wishing to preserve in his mind its splendor undimmed by further impressions. This ballet proposing a renovated neoclassicism has in forty years become classic.

In its grave sequence Balanchine carved four cameos in three dimensions. Calliope portrayed the metric and caesura of spoken verse; Polyhymnia described mimicry

Diana Adams, Jacques d'Amboise, Melissa Hayden

APOLLO

and spectacular gesture; Terpsichore, the activity, declaration, and inversion of academic dancing itself. These are all subservient to Apollo, animator and driver; they are his handmaidens, creatures, harem, and household. He is the dance master whose authority develops from boy to man to god. Freed from swaddling bands, he feels and flexes muscle, matures into manhood, chooses his foredestined partner; finally assumes his godhead. The muses do not develop; they move in a temporal element which has no history, fixed in their idealized pre-ordained powers. Having expressed their Platonic nature, they are and remain eternal archetypes and values. Apollo, commencing as an awkward athlete, gradually emerges as if from a blunt four-square block, just as the early Greek stone *kouroi* over three centuries grew into the released humane prototype of Periclean and post-classical naturalism. By no accident, Balanchine used quotations both from Hellenistic sculpture (Apollo Belvedere, the Self-Scraping Victor of Lysippus) and from beginnings of the Baroque (Michelangelo's *God Touching Adam into Life*). The ballet is not, as it may be read from the piano score, only a series of divertissements. In the orchestra it assumes an urgent dramatic logic, ritual rather than narrative. There is no contest, no *agon*, except between the first dancer, his own body, and his self. Tension springs from anarchic muscular energy transformed into physical and moral grace or order. After the electrifying coda, in which his muses are harnessed (a troika) to the god's chariot, Stravinsky masterfully italicizes the serene majesty in motion gilded by Apollo's sunset apotheosis.

With Lifar, Balanchine had been given a boy who might conceivably become a young man. In America, with Lew Christensen, he found a young man who could be credited as a potential divinity. Praxitelean head and body, imperceptibly musculated but firmly and largely proportioned, blond hair and bland air recalled Greek marbles and a calm inhabitant of Nicolas Poussin's pastorals. Diaghilev had taken the decor from a "Sunday painter" in the line of the Douanier Rousseau. But André Bauchant's naïve canvases were irritating in their clumsy innocence. The aim was to cauterize a worn-out vision of Greece as a century-old archaeological reconstruction. But the shock potential in Bauchant's coarsely feeble paint was wiped out by Madame Chanel's "classic" haute couture costumes, which were contemporary tennis dresses, cinctured by striped men's cravats from Charvet. Long classic tutus were replaced. Chanel's small but apt explosion of chic fixed Balanchine's muses in a space far more immediate and surprising than Bauchant's vapid hills and blossoms.

When it was our turn to plan scenery and costumes, we knew the visual frame must not be assertive but, on an opera-house scale, tactfully splendid and solid. Our models were Poussin's backgrounds from his *Echo and Narcissus* and *The Arcadian Shepherds*. Colors of changeable taffeta drapery came from his *Inspiration of the Poet* in the Louvre. Christensen wore a light, supple, gilt armor of soft kid, with a short crimson silk mantle. His own hair, tightly curled and varnished, was powdered with gold dust. Stewart Chaney, an adroit and responsible designer, contrived a big Poussinesque cave, over which spread trunk and branches of a huge sacred laurel. Realized completely in three dimensions, lit to accentuate a late-afternoon glow, it filled the large stage as a sumptuous background. When Stravinsky approved, we were delighted; indeed it was expensive, but unlike Bauchant's decor, it never mocked the music. Stewart Chaney's (and Poussin's) harmonies of sunrise and sunset, glimmering accents of pewter, bronze, and gold, highlighted a sumptuous adornment to choreography (which, when APOLLON would be revived twenty years later, seemed to need none; by then it was known as APOLLO, or APOLLO, LEADER OF THE MUSES).

While ORPHEUS was a milestone in every sense, it had no issue. Spectacle, dominated by a painter's imagination, no matter how appropriate or inventive its dancing, would always remain for us, with few exceptions, beyond need or possibility. Tchelitchev retired, something important disappeared. He established a level of fantasy and achievement by which we would judge all future collaborations; few ever approached his. On the other hand, in our first Stravinsky Festival we found we could count on him for suggestion and support. It also meant that Balanchine's principal adjunct, apart from dancers themselves, would be music, and among the living musicians available, Stravinsky. He was and would be, for us, the most accessible and constant. Balanchine looked back on APOLLON from a perspective of thirty years
as the turning point in my life. In its discipline and restraint, in its sustained oneness of tone and feeling, the score was a revelation. It seemed to tell me that I could, for the first time, dare not use all my ideas; that I, too, could eliminate. I began to see how I could clarify, by limiting, by reducing what seemed to be myriad possibilities to the one possibility that is inevitable.*

APRIL, 1938: NEW YORK

Scandal at the Metropolitan. Two of the dancers were late for performance; not the first time. Mr. Johnson displeased with divertissements for LA JUIVE. Balanchine demoralized. He has offers from Larry Hart and Richard Rodgers for a Broadway musical; from Sam Goldwyn for Hollywood. Dimitriew prophesying doom; Warburg fed up. School, O.K. Touring out of the question. A real crisis. Ziegler refused to let me explain.

The genuine *succès d'estime* of the Stravinsky Festival merely delayed the inevitable rupture with the Metropolitan. In the late spring Balanchine withdrew his company. This barely forestalled our dismissal; it was hard to say who fired whom. We took comfort in considering that we preserved a moral advantage. Three years on 39th Street was a fair education in the devious politics and mechanics of establishment theater. We had foolishly imagined that if and when we penetrated such prestigious portals, all our energies and talents would be liberated to operate unhindered in the service of unalloyed creativity. It did not take long to discover that ancient formulae governing international opera-house practice had forged chains which were not to be broken soon. Edward Johnson had hired the American Ballet on the promise of its youth and Warburg's backing, but he was not prepared to support us in ambitious aims for the renovation of dancing in opera, or to permit us a free hand in the development of a ballet repertory within his house. He had neither wish nor ability to impose his instinctive optimism on a staff which had long held tenure, nor has anyone in his position attempted it since. I had known something of the history of opera management and of the current situation in Italy and France, and I knew how thirty years before, Diaghilev had been defeated by the imperial bureaucracy in Petersburg. But I

* *Balanchine's New Complete Stories of the Great Ballets,* p. 22.

THE CARD PARTY (CARD GAME): Todd Bolender, Janet Reed

was dazzled by our chance of working at the Met, and rationalized plans by which we could eventually gain our way by persistence, service, or boring from within.

Dancing at the Met was by no means easy for our dancers, who were barely permitted to practice on stage. For example, Lew Christensen was to appear as the partner of Rosa Ponselle in the "Lillas Pastia" scene of CARMEN. She refused to rehearse; she was saving her voice. She sent her own dancing teacher to arrange her stage business with Lew; she would learn it all, somehow, "later." When they met for the first time onstage and commenced their routine, she seized a goblet of wine (grapefruit juice), quaffed a gulp, and tossed the rest in his face. Then she pulled down his head and smacked him full on the mouth. For six seconds they were locked. It seemed sincere. In the intermission, he said: "I thought she was trying to make me in front of God and everybody." Ballet and opera rarely mix; interludes may be intended to rest the voice but they seldom tickle the eye.

Early in 1936 it had come to me that, all else failing, I had best attempt to form some sort of company by myself. I was personally attached to Lew Christensen and to his fiancée Gisella Caccialanza, an excellent soubrette and strong dancer, the godchild of Enrico Cecchetti, the famous teacher of La Scala. There were some dozen other dancers, including Alicia Alonso, Todd Bolender, William Dollar, Eugene Loring, Michael Kidd, and Erick Hawkins, to whom I felt obligated. I now had no role in managing the school, which had increasingly been turned over to Eugenie Ouroussow. I lacked a vocation. I felt that my recent crash-course in theatrical self-enlightenment under the aegis of the Met must count for something. I decided to organize a small troupe on my own and call it Ballet Caravan. It would be self-sufficient, using a dozen of our best dancers, who would also serve as stage managers and stagehands. We could travel by bus and truck with our own lighting equipment, portable switchboard, drapes, and bits of scenery. In this I had the good wishes of Eddie Warburg. Balanchine was off to Hollywood; Dimitriew regarded the venture with amused if tolerant disdain.

I was not helpless, for providence intervened as it had before and would again, this time in the trim figure of Frances Hawkins, an enterprising, adventurous, and imaginative concert manager, who was then booking Martha Graham and Harald Kreutzberg. The daughter of a distinguished labor lawyer in Denver, she had absconded from Bryn Mawr to perform for several seasons in vaudeville in an acrobatic adagio act. There was little about vaudeville she didn't know; American vaudeville was at once her preparatory school and postgraduate course in theatrical administration. She knew more about touring conditions across the entire continent than I would ever learn; she had excellent taste, and loved dancing. With little to go on — no newspaper reviews to sell us at the start, small capital, and a wildly overoptimistic program — she found some forty engagements for our first season. In the next two years, with no subsidy, she took us twice across the country from New England to Oregon and back.

Ballet Caravan was conceived as a miniature. I had no ambition to make it more than a pilot experiment, something I could manage by myself with the help of Frances Hawkins. Primarily it attempted to produce a new repertory by native choreographers, musicians, and designers working with national themes. Prospective audiences would come from colleges across the country, and we would play in civic auditoriums as we could find them. Musical accompaniment was planned for two pianos; if the music we selected or commissioned was of some intrinsic interest, later orchestrations might be made. Everything was planned for possible enlargement; nothing depended on it. My general aesthetic was based on two bricks: five years of college "art and culture" history, and ten years of attendance at Saturday evening concerts of the Boston Symphony Orchestra under Monteux and Koussevitzky, both of whom had been closely identified with Diaghilev. On this basis I hoped to summon out of the air an "American" style from something in our atmosphere — literary, musical, theatrical. Films, vaudeville, musical comedy, the popular arts in painting and sculpture — all could serve. Dependence on folklore, a cultural chauvinism, is always the first resort of pioneers in a new province. I was undaunted by the precedent of Franco-Italian ballet masters who went to Petersburg in the nineteenth century to produce Franco-Russian bastardies. In the *New York Times* John Martin had labeled Balanchine's efforts over the last three years *"Le Ballet Americain."* I was eager to drop the French pronunciation.

Through Frances Hawkins's connection with Martha Graham, and Martha's alliance with Bennington College, we were given an opportunity to open in that fortress of modern dance. Owing to the broad sympathy and generosity of Martha Hill, who in many ways was responsible for the early fame of Graham, Doris Humphrey, and José Limon, Ballet Caravan first appeared in an auditorium usually given over to the dauntless experiments of progressive dancing, supposedly in violent opposition to the academic classic ballet. Our performances at Bennington were no more than open dress rehearsals, but the audiences allowed us the benefit of many doubts, and in an important sense, Modern Dance may be said to have launched Ballet Caravan.

We prepared a repertory of five miniballets in six weeks. For dancers we had the strongest available from school and company, including a handful of ambitious, imaginative boys and girls who saw themselves as future ballet masters or choreographers. It was in fact a small academy; five of these would enjoy big reputations in years to come. Lew Christensen, after his army service, would be charged with San Francisco's ballet company and school; Erick Hawkins became a vocative theorist of the advance guard; Michael Kidd gained considerable reputation on Broadway and in films; Eugene Loring, after a career in ballet and legitimate theater, settled in Hollywood, where he worked in films and kept a school; Alicia Alonso became the Margot Fonteyn of Castro's Cuba.

We usually appeared in movie houses, whose nervous managers gambled that we would do no worse on off-matinees than bad films. Our tours were a parade of many comedies and a few tragedies. In Burlington, Vermont, we arrived to find competition from an American Legion convention, a county fair, and a square-dance contest. We played to fewer than a dozen people — but Frances Hawkins insisted we play, and the show went on. Bus and truck are the least relaxing forms of travel and transport. To drive three or four hours, unpack, set up, take class, perform, and eat later, if one is not too exhausted, hardly puts a performer's body in perfect condition. But Frances Hawkins, the Christensen brothers, the two girls whom they were about to marry, and many of the others were accustomed to touring in vaudeville. They were already professionals; the younger dancers learned to endure such schedules.

I had no instinct for directing a company and was notably lacking in that quality which the army calls "leadership quotient." I fancied that an "American" company, such as ours purported to be, should be run "democratically," with everyone doing as well as saying exactly what he felt about everything. Here, at least, I would be free of Dimitriew's ukases. I would not treat my dancers as serfs but as friends, and I was surprised and depressed to find this policy as impractical as it was irresponsible. The dancers soon came to me in a body: either one man must plan and manage, face and solve problems — in short, direct, or they could not perform. Their job was dancing, not administration. Frances Hawkins was busy organizing future tours, as well as her other artists' careers, but she reinforced the company's attitude. Gradually I turned into some sort of director.

Whatever the birth pangs of our Caravan's first season, a second seemed justified. Now, at least, there were some agreeable press notices which Frances Hawkins could edit into a brochure. Balanchine took many of our best members to California for the benefit of THE GOLDWYN FOLLIES, but somehow we managed to divide schedules and resources. Virgil Thomson says in his autobiography:

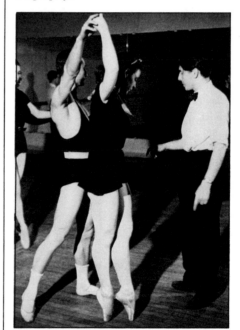

Balanchine rehearsing

My other work of 1937, almost wholly for me a year of theater, consisted of a ballet and a Shakespeare play. The dance piece, commissioned by Lincoln Kirstein for his Ballet Caravan, was a slice-of-life called FILLING STATION. . . . That midsummer I had found in Lew Christensen a dancer and director I knew I could deal with, and in the subject offered us by Kirstein a theme I thought I could at least take hold of.*

FILLING STATION was the result of an extended analytical process. As Virgil wrote, I'd dreamed up a number of libretti long before there was any company to consider them. When Ballet Caravan came into being, I had a mass of suggestions taken from "American" sources, some popular, others literary—from folktales and balladry to tales by Hawthorne, Melville, and Mark Twain. Before I had a company my notions were grandiose, more operatic or cinematic than choreographic. The existence of the Caravan was a precise determinant: fifteen dancers, a program of three units of twenty to thirty minutes each, little scenery, and two pianos.

Two other constants were Eugene Loring and Lew Christensen. A small, compact, exciting theatrical personality with little training as a classic dancer, Loring had energy and appeal. He wished to become a choreographer. Christensen needed suitable roles in a heroic genre within developed American balletic style—roles equivalent to Prince Charming or Prince Siegfried, knight-errant, crusader, romantic wanderer. These were not easy to translate into native terms. Hawthorne provided grotesque suggestions; Poe, morbid ones; Melville was too grand for our scale. Mark Twain's *Mysterious Stranger* seemed to have possibilities, but its medieval, romantic locale was reminiscent of GISELLE—a locus which at the moment was anathema. A site in which Jimmy Cagney might be at home seemed to hold the key; he would be comfortable in a filling station.

But the ballet could not be realistic; its style must derive from vaudeville, where Christensen had gained his polish. Visually, comic strips were appropriate. John Alden Carpenter had composed his KRAZY KAT for Adolph Bolm in 1922, but Krazy Kat danced through a landscape resembling Alice's Wonderland. I wanted an everyday, ordinary setting rendered magical. I made Cocteau's philosophy mine: theatrical, indeed all, lyric magic does not derive from the exotic, fantastic, or strange, but from a "rehabilitation of the commonplace." Paul Cadmus, a painter recently working for Roosevelt's Works Progress Administration, had caused a considerable scandal with his panel *Shore Leave*, which showed sailors ashore behaving in a manner which the Navy Department discountenanced. I was attracted by the exactness and vitality in his Hogarthian scenes of metropolitan and suburban life. He'd worked in an advertising agency and had an ironic eye on industrial civilization. He designed the interior of a filling station in terms of a rectilinear blueprint that might be handed to a builder. It had a big window, a gas pump outside, a neon sign in reverse, the door to a rest room. Except for Mac, the mechanic-attendant, who wore a handsome white uniform of translucent nylon piped in red with a red-and-white cap and tie, the other characters were in the style of comic strips or animated films.

* *Virgil Thomson*, Alfred A. Knopf, New York, 1966, pp. 274–5.

Mac centered the action; he served those in need of gas or a telephone, monkey wrench, or road map. A series of incidents occurred, not unlike those in Robert Sherwood's PETRIFIED FOREST. There were a tourist family, a pair of acrobatic-vaudeville Mutt-and-Jeff truck drivers, another pair of vaguely F. Scott Fitzgerald lovers, a gangster, and a holdup. At first there was a "tragic" ending; but Balanchine suggested that The Girl, who had intercepted the gangster's bullet and was borne off held aloft, would revive in midair and wave to the audience just before she reached the wings. Virgil, as he said in his autobiography:

wrote a score made up of waltzes, tangos, a fugue, a Big Apple [the popular dance-fad of the time], a holdup, a chase, and a funeral, all aimed to evoke roadside America as pop art. . . . Christensen, as a filling-station attendant in white translucent coverall, filled the stage with his in-the-air cartwheels and held us breathless with his twelve-turn pirouettes.*

Besides FILLING STATION we devised YANKEE CLIPPER, with music by Paul Bowles (who later abandoned musical composition for confessional prose) and choreography by Eugene Loring, and SHOW PIECE, with music by Robert McBride to choreography by Erick Hawkins. The first presumed to take a clipper ship's cabin boy around the ports of the world on a dance voyage from Salem, Massachusetts, to Tahiti and back. SHOW PIECE was a demonstration of the flashiest dancing we could muster. Performances in New York with a good orchestra, under auspices of the W.P.A. Federal Music Project, put some sort of seal of approval on our repertory, which in its small scale had a modest appeal through its consistency and taste.

While *Uncle Tom's Cabin* as transmuted by e. e. cummings had come to little except its publication (although David Diamond was later prompted to write a score for it), other ideas took firmer root. David Garnett, whom as a boy I had known in London, and whose *Lady into Fox* became a ballet for the early British repertory, had written an absorbing reconstruction of the life of Princess Pocahontas. Having finished it, he decided to come to Virginia and check the site, which we did together. In 1933 one of many subjects I'd proposed to Virgil was the Pocahontas story, which Florine Stettheimer, decorator of his opera FOUR SAINTS IN THREE ACTS, had also independently proposed. As he said: "For decor it was splendid, but it lacked drama." Virgil also refused an offer to collaborate with James Joyce on a ballet based on children's games (out of *Finnegans Wake*) for the Paris Opéra, and he'd found nothing to be done with cummings's *Tom*.

In spite of such implied warnings, I was still taken with the notion of Pocahontas, largely because the figure of the adventurer, John Smith, whose life she saved but whose hand she spurned, seemed to be an excellent foil for Lew Christensen as John Rolfe, the young subaltern who took his Indian savior back to England as a bride. Elliott Carter, whom at Harvard I had known more as classical scholar and mathematician than composer, agreed to write the music. I stipulated that the marriage-finale, in which Powhatan's daughter appeared in an Elizabethan wedding dress, should sound like an "American Indian" version of APOLLON MUSAGÈTE. Elliott fulfilled this strangulating condition with genuine beauty.

* *Virgil Thomson*, p. 275.

In *Flawed Words and Stubborn Sounds*, Carter's revealing conversations with Allen Edwards (1971), the composer speaks of our ballet:

POCAHONTAS . . . was my second work to be played publicly. . . . The character of the work came from the section of Hart Crane's *The Bridge* in which Pocahontas appears as a sort of "mother-earth" of America. There was an attempt to present this story as seen through the eyes of the English who came as colonialists, and their being saved from destruction at the hands of Nature. At that time the American past was being whitewashed, I suppose in a desperate attempt to make the "melting-pot" idea work. I myself had misgivings about the "colonialist" aspect of the subject, particularly as I have some Indian blood of my own, but hoped to make it a parable of cooperation.*

Just as dealings with e. e. cummings had been unhappy over *Tom*, I had something to regret in my occasional contacts with Hart Crane. When I had been an editor of *Hound & Horn*, overly influenced by the rigors and strictures of R. P. Blackmur and Yvor Winters, whose verse and criticism I took very seriously, we had rejected the subway, or "Tunnel," section of *The Bridge*, at the same time printing reams of verse of incomparably less quality. After he was drowned, we made feeble amends by publishing Crane's comprehensive letter to Otto H. Kahn, his generous patron, outlining plans for his magniloquent epic structure.

I watched Crane at Manhattan parties when I came down from college. His behavior after dark astonished, alarmed, and excited me, because had I the courage I might have enjoyed myself much as he did. Crane's friend, the photographer Walker Evans, who took pictures for our earliest souvenir program, told me more of Crane. Crane's epigraph for Part II of *The Bridge* bears the title "Powhatan's Daughter," and quotes the earliest English records of the Virginia Indians: "—Pocahuntas, a well-featured but wanton yong girle . . . of the age of eleven or twelve years, get the boyes forth with her into the market place, and make them wheele, falling on their hands, turning their heels upwards, whom she would followe, and wheele so herself, naked as she was, all the fort over." †

The costumes for the ballet were by Karl Free, an exceptionally gifted painter and draftsman, who suffered from self-doubt as drastic as Crane's, and who finished life in the same style. He drew heavily on the wonderful drawings by John White, who landed with the first Virginia settlers, and rendered naked Indians in terms of the English Renaissance. Even more in my mind as visual precedent was Degas' magnificent painting in London's National Gallery of young Spartan girls daring adolescent boys to wrestle. These Greeks are in fact archetypical, perennial, snub-nosed, flat-breasted, lean-hipped ballet students at the start of some progressive and permissive "modern" dance. Divested of any decorative or temporal reference, this might happen equally in forest clearing or ballet studio. Hart Crane saw his small ballerina-acrobat:

* Allen Edwards, *Flawed Words and Stubborn Sounds: A Conversation with Elliott Carter*, W. W. Norton & Co., New York, p. 57.

† *The Complete Poems and Selected Letters and Prose of Hart Crane* (Brom Weber, Ed.), Liveright, New York, 1966, p. 53.

SHOW PIECE: Fred Danieli,
Eugene Loring, Lew Christensen

There was a bed of leaves, and broken play;
There was a veil upon you, Pocahontas, bride—
O Princess whose brown lap was virgin May;
And bridal flanks and eyes hid yawny pride. . . .

A birch kneels. All her whistling fingers fly.
The oak grove circles in a crash of leaves;
The long moan of a dance is in the sky.
Dance, Maquokeeta: Pocahontas grieves . . . *

I knew how important Jean Cocteau had been for Diaghilev as poet and publicist for his early Parisian seasons, and I always hoped to find someone who could dream up concepts which dancers might incarnate. James Agee and I had been at Phillips Exeter; he sketched for Ballet Caravan several scenarios, one of which bore the working title "Bombs in the Ice-Box." Like so many of his marvelous conceits, this dissipated itself in endless conversation. As for two other considerable technicians and collaborators, Wystan Auden and Chester Kallman, they admired Balanchine, who directed the first performance in New York of their libretto for Stravinsky's RAKE'S PROGRESS at the Met. However, in spite of much talk, we would never have the luck of gaining a balletic PAID ON BOTH SIDES, DANCE OF DEATH, or BASSARIDS for our own repertory. Auden disliked the Bernstein-Robbins AGE OF ANXIETY; he reiterated that his services were purely verbal, but his passion for opera and Kallman's feeling for theatrical structure and high-camp continually teased our hard-dying greed for such capital collaborators.

We considered Melville's *Confidence Man;* Henry James's *Turn of the Screw,* from which Benjamin Britten extracted viable opera; *Brer Rabbit; Ethan Frome;* Scott Fitzgerald's "The Diamond as Big as the Ritz"; Thomas Beer's *Road to Heaven;* Carl Van Vechten's *Tattooed Countess.* We were by no means alone in a struggle to impose a native meaning on a recalcitrant alien dance tradition. Ruth Page in Chicago, Catherine Littlefield in Philadelphia, and before all or any of us, Ted Shawn with his cowboy and Aztec numbers, experimented with folkloristic material from barn dance, barroom, roundup, and various native mythologies. Possibly the most successful was no ballet at all but Martha Graham's AMERICAN DOCUMENT, a broad, masterful arrangement of solos and processions interspersed with spoken documentary quotations, encompassing many of the elements that led to the opening of our continent and the tragic drama of its aborigines.

In face and figure Eugene Loring, the protagonist and inventor of YANKEE CLIPPER, reminded me of Jimmy Cagney; both were alike in their stubby strength, concentration, and physicality. There was available the legend of William H. Bonney, bad boy from Brooklyn who was taken west in the sixties to become Billy the Kid and was betrayed and killed in 1881. Through Virgil Thomson I met Aaron Copland and asked him to write a score, which I feared he might consider could be overburdened with folkloristic themes impeding his own imagination. I had already become self-conscious about insistence on imposed Americanisms. However, I took the precaution of leaving on his piano an album of cowboy songs to which he might refer. This he did; a few, "Git along, Little Dogie," "Old Chisholm Trail," "Bury Me Not on the Lone

* *The Complete Poems . . . of Hart Crane,*
pp. 70, 73.

Prairie," inserted themselves into the most convincing and sturdy ballet to come out of Ballet Caravan. Paul Cadmus had shared a studio with Jared French, whose wall paintings for the state reformatory at Coxsackie, New York, were some of the strongest murals done under the W.P.A. I gave him Theodore Roosevelt's memoirs of the Far West, where as a youth he had been sent for his health. This fascinating book had been brilliantly illustrated by Frederic Remington; from his pictures French drew a series of dashing but simple costumes, as well as a backdrop of tall cacti, which immeasurably enriched the ballet.

BILLY THE KID opened in the Chicago Opera House in October, 1938, and had an immediate and lasting success. Billy's Mexican sweetheart was danced by Marie Jeanne. Perfectly cast and costumed, she was an exquisite personification. Ann Barzel, Chicago's faithful ballet historian and critic, wrote in that December's *Dance* magazine: "BILLY THE KID . . . marks a milestone in American ballet. . . . Loring's choreography is marked by inventiveness and imagination, and yet his work is never obscure. Loring's inventiveness is shown in the movements devised, whether it be to illustrate riding a horse or pushing West. His details are excellent."

There was the problem of the repeated sound for gunshots, which Copland solved with efficient simplicity. Loring also: the shots precipitated his triple air turns. The good-guy sheriff, Pat Garrett, was naturally Lew Christensen, who resembled young John Wayne disguised as the Apollo of Tombstone. Loring had a real scar on one cheek, which added to the sensitive brutality of his boy-brigand's mask. We invented a chameleon-like character under the name of Alias, who was everywhere and nowhere, an impalpable personification of danger, treachery, menace—admirably danced by Todd Bolender, who would also become a choreographer and ballet master. BILLY THE KID worked well; when I went into the army, it was assigned to the Ballet Theater, through my friendship with Oliver Smith, its cofounder. Before that he had served as an assistant to Tchelitchev. But soon the costumes and scenery changed; Loring no longer danced it, and it took its place as a historical fixture in a standard repertory.

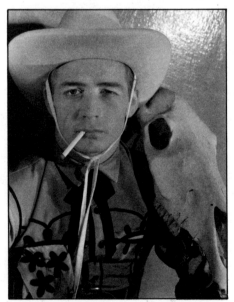

BILLY THE KID: Eugene Loring

FEBRUARY, 1939: MILWAUKEE

Eugene Loring's hometown. We wanted to do his two ballets, YANKEE CLIPPER and BILLY THE KID; the sponsors refused BILLY; it was no fit subject for ballet. What most provincial American sponsoring committees want is pocket-size Russian ballet. If it's American, it can't be ballet. However, our success was such that we were asked to do BILLY should we come again next year.

MARCH, 1939: VISALIA, CALIFORNIA

Sunday matinee. Owing to the presence of the local clergy, and their fear of competition, we were not allowed to dance FILLING STATION or BILLY THE KID.

MARCH, 1939: DALLAS

Local critic irritated by my "100% Americanism." Tried to show him that our program was not one of blind chauvinism, but a personal attitude, contrasting with a pervasive Russian ballet domination . . . I had wanted to present BILLY THE KID here, but because of recent big state celebrations, the sponsors felt they'd had enough Wild West. However, the next night, for the state women's college at Denton, Dallas newspapers sent over critics, and many people from the previous night's audience came too.

MARCH, 1939: SAN ANGELO, TEXAS

Local ranchers particularly pleased by BILLY THE KID. I feared that they might consider it pretentious of Easterners to show imitations of bronco-busting and gunplay, but they were pleased that we thought the Wild West a suitable subject for classic dances.

APRIL, 1939: TORONTO, CANADA

Official reception with the lieutenant governor-general, etc. Canadians would have preferred white tarlatans and Russian music. Everyone polite and cold as the weather.

While we learned much about the United States and Canada in our far-flung tours, and more about the organization and maintenance of a theatrical company, I began to realize we'd come to the limits of our particular operation. Long before, my father had told me that two kinds of energy determine the quality and character of operations: the energy to establish, and the interest to maintain. For me, maintenance was far more difficult than initiation. The routine of keeping performance at a high level is as necessary as the original invention of new work, but it is far more of a grind. Few of us wanted to cross the continent again, even under the increasingly favorable conditions which Frances Hawkins's stubborn ingenuity and courage had gained.

Back in New York, we had the irrelevant luck to appear with a first-rate orchestra on one of those peculiar programs which have nothing to do with anything except the momentary and inconsequential passion of individuals to indulge themselves in haphazard hobbies. A middle-American millionaire had conceived a passion for the melodies of Stephen Foster. He commissioned an opera to frame two dozen tunes, and since this alone did not seem quite enough for a genuine "festival," our Ballet

the New York City Ballet

52

THE FOUR TEMPERAMENTS

SYMPHONY IN C

BALLET IMPERIAL

ORPHEUS

THE PRODIGAL SON

PRODIGAL

SON

ILLUMINATIONS

CAKEWALK

ALLEGRO BRILLANTE

DIVERTIMENTO NO.15

SCOTCH SYMPHONY

Caravan was briefly attached. We also had skittish conversations about being absorbed by the Ballet Theater, which Lucia Chase was now directing away from the original Russian orientation of Mikhail Mordkin, her teacher. Our aimless flirtation with the Ballet Theater continued until I went into the army. Eugene Loring, taking BILLY THE KID with him, did go to Miss Chase and Oliver Smith and produced other works which, uncharitably, I could not commend.

However, as happened after the debacle of our American Ballet in Scranton, Pennsylvania, another providential patron now arrived in the unlikely guise of the Ford Motor Company. In the months of suspended animation anticipating World War II, owing to the weird and willful optimism of some obtuse businessmen, New York City organized a feckless World's Fair. People have often mistakenly believed that dancing on the edge of a volcano puts off the eruption. In our case I was approached by Walter Dorwin Teague, an industrial designer employed by Edsel Ford, to devise a spectacle which, through the ballet vocabulary, would sell their new 1940–41 models. Teague had provided a handsome circular pavilion in gold mirror-and-mosaic. Inside was a well-equipped theater with comfortable seats for five hundred people, a turntable stage, excellent dressing rooms, and a built-in canteen.

The pretext for our dancing was the fate of the horse in the path of the automobile. It added nothing to the history of The Dance, but it was an agreeable exercise and had important consequences. We never knew whether or not it sold a dozen automobiles, but for six months it provided food and rent for forty dancers in two teams that performed an eighteen-minute ballet entitled A THOUSAND TIMES NEIGH! every hour on the hour, twelve times a day. Logistics were complex, but they were solved efficiently. Every dancer had one free day a week; there was a "swing shift" to take up the slack of accidents and replacements. Dobbin, the horse, was made up of two boys, head and tail. He executed a soft-hoof bit of tapping.

MAY, 1941: FLUSHING MEADOW, NEW YORK

Lunch in a private dining room of the Ford Pavilion, given by Edsel Ford for Nelson Rockefeller on the scale of a diplomatic occasion. Mr. Teague had designed everything, furniture to gold plates, cutlery, and glassware. Nelson, cheerful as usual, bantered Mr. Ford about spending hard money on ballet. I tried to get a word in about the possibility of a national American company under their joint protection. Naturally it was hopeless.

A THOUSAND TIMES NEIGH!: World's Fair

I had known Nelson Rockefeller since 1931. My preceptors in the fine arts at Harvard had been Jere Abbott and Alfred H. Barr, Jr., who were soon appointed codirectors to plan New York's Museum of Modern Art. In college, with John Walker, who later became director of the National Gallery in Washington, and Eddie Warburg, we had organized the Harvard Society of Contemporary Art, which has been called a prototype for MOMA. With another classmate, the architect Philip Johnson, we had also been loosely attached to planning a program for mural decoration when Rockefeller Center was being built in the early thirties. A stormy exhibition of invited mural painters at the museum followed, as well as the destruction of Diego Rivera's fresco over the entrance lobby of 30 Rockefeller Plaza. In both altercations I was an observer. Recruited by Ben Shahn, then working as technical and political assistant to Diego, I served as a model for a "typical American Jew" (nose, mostly). For the exhibition at the museum I asked Ben to paint a mural fragment, which he based on Sacco and Vanzetti. (My father had employed Sacco's son as his chauffeur.) I was also attracted to several young union organizers working in the South and found myself embroiled in polemical battles which had little to do with art but a lot with life.

During this confusing if instructive time, in which I shifted from one false position to another, on the one hand scuffling with Raymond Hood, the architect, who feared Rivera's mural might bankrupt the rental agents for Radio City, on the other placating Ben Shahn and various fiery self-appointed protest committees, there was one person to whom I could go for sanity and assurance. This was Mrs. John D. Rockefeller, Jr. In a room next to a chamber in which, at that time, were hung the Unicorn Tapestries, now a glory of the Cloisters, Mrs. Rockefeller would give me tea and toast as she listened to my account of the day's skirmishes. She was a personal friend of Rivera's; she understood Ben Shahn very well; that we all stayed less than enemies was due in large part to her refusal to be frightened.

Occasionally I was asked to stay a night at Pocantico. I once met Nelson's grandfather on the golf course; he seemed as ancient as Amenhotep, but actively demonstrated the virtues of his windbreaker made of layers of paper which, he said, kept the wind out better than any leather vest. Nelson and I admired Gaston Lachaise, the sculptor, for whom Eddie Warburg and I posed and whom Nelson patronized. At Dartmouth, Nelson had thought to become an architect and was knowledgeable and interested in the plastic arts. He helped us in many striking ways from our start, and not with money alone.

In 1941 Nelson was appointed by President Roosevelt to head a new agency, the United States Office for Coordination of Commercial and Cultural Relations between the American Republics. (His short title was Coordinator of Inter-American Affairs.) This office was ostensibly under control of the State Department, but Nelson was hardly contained within an establishment which, so far, had done little to prevent that apathy which his young agency was created to combat. In any case, I acted in innocence of the hazardous and complex tensions at work in exalted political spheres. The dance is a universal language, transcending every local dialect of Spanish or Portuguese. In Washington in a climate of

unreal informality, unofficial optimism, and casual friendliness, a loose and quite unbusinesslike contract was contrived for a ballet company which would tour every Latin-American republic save Paraguay and Bolivia. An imprecise document assured us that the Coordinator's Office would pay minimum expenses for this company for half a year; further deficits would (more or less) be underwritten; we would defray necessary production costs, including a number of new commissions.

Later there were tiresome repercussions about money, but Nelson was always our responsible defender. When he was attacked in Congress for spending cash "on ballets rather than bullets," he pointed out that in the midst of the Civil War, Lincoln had ordered the expensive casting of new bronze entrance doors for the national Capitol, to show that he was sure of victory and that the Republic prized and deserved certain immaterial values.

Balanchine and remnants of our American Ballet had finished their stint for Sam Goldwyn in Hollywood. He returned to New York charged with Nelson's commission. In Washington I was given a check which seemed so large that I was as scared as if I had stolen it. The actual amount was rather less than what we now spend in a single season of the New York City Ballet at the State Theater. Anyway, I was so frightened that I became suspicious of my least decision. Dimitriew and Warburg were no longer aides or opponents; I was more or less alone, to make mistakes and face a future that I must guide as I could.

The expedition to South America was not undertaken lightly. With a grant from the Library of Congress, we were able to take along two musicologists who collected folk-song materials from each country. Through friends at Fordham University I was given letters to several Jesuits who I thought might show me parishes and parishioners—which they did to an extent that our official embassies never would. I learned a sort of Spanish in six weeks. We signed thirty-six dancers, a sizable group for the time and circumstances. Our repertory combined elements from the American Ballet and Ballet Caravan, with notable additions. Antony Tudor invented TIME TABLE to Aaron Copland's *Music for the Theater* of 1925. The ballet was a nostalgic reference to the First World War on the eve of a Second. In it Lew Christensen shone as a marine bidding good-bye to his girl on a suburban railway platform, reminiscent of the atmosphere of Edward Hopper's lonely paintings. PASTORELA was a folk ballet, with sung parts based on an indigenous Mexican nativity play transcribed and adapted by Paul Bowles. By this we hoped to show a veritable goodwill toward Latin-American material. But we discovered, on a tour which did not include Mexico, that Brazilian, Peruvian, and Colombian critics each considered his own culture autonomous, unique, and superior to all others. As far as they were concerned, Mexico was as remote as Siam, though less interesting. Alec Wilder put together a series of his delicate tunes for JUKE BOX, but the jazz element was not convincing when danced. The two strongest novelties, hardly to anyone's surprise, were both by Balanchine—CONCERTO BAROCCO and BALLET IMPERIAL, which persist in repertory after three decades.

the New York City Ballet

77

JUNE, 1941: RIO DE JANEIRO

Teatro Municipal, a marble monument more antiquated than the Met. Accommodations mostly for scenery made out of paper, locally permitted, but which our lighting equipment tends to ignite. In Ambassador Caffery's box he made no secret of his strong dislike, not of us personally but of the trouble we'd put him to by arriving; the ambiguity of our reception. It was no triumph. Later, Balanchine and some of the kids to a nightclub. For one bottle of champagne and ice cream they were given a bill for more than a hundred dollars.

Although we were accompanied by an official guardian or nanny dispatched by the State Department to prevent errors of tact and decorum, our connection with Rockefeller's agency was regarded by the ordinary Foreign Service diplomat as distinctly suspect. Ambassador Jefferson Caffery was a classic example of the professional career diplomat. He melted a bit at BALLET IMPERIAL, an affectionate pastiche of Petipa, but our so-called "modern" works convinced him that we had been sent to subvert both his embassy and the continent in time of war. Why had we nothing like SWAN LAKE? The Ballets Russes de Monte Carlo had toured South America the summer before, enjoying vast success with the standard repertory. There was no use trying to explain to Ambassador Caffery our philosophy of national coloration; ballet was an alien contraption; what of it that was useful for export should be limited to an accepted typology. São Paulo was a little more welcoming; we valiantly attempted to work with Brazilian composers and painters. Candido Portinari made a handsome backcloth for SERENADE, scattering stars in the constellation of the Southern Cross in the manner of Joan Miró. Balanchine invented a Radio City Music Hall version of supposedly native dances to music by Guarnieri. We were taken to some allegedly secret, exotic, underground, magical "samba schools." With all the goodwill in the world we were fish out of water, and chronologically out of luck. The newspapers were not entirely unkind; we could send to the Coordinator's office in Washington some evidence that they had not backed a losing horse. Montevideo was not much of an improvement, but the audiences were more sympathetic.

Mendoza park

JULY, 1941: BUENOS AIRES

Flew ahead to prepare the season. Arrived Thursday; company due Friday night. Delays; they arrived Saturday morning. At the dock all girls under eighteen were arrested and removed to a local jail; work permits don't apply. We were importing dancers for purposes of prostitution. Some sort of German-inspired plot? A weekend; unable to find a federal judge, the only person capable of springing the girls. Balanchine insisted on being arrested also. To the Ministry of Justice, but nothing to be done until Monday. Dreary theater, usually used for films. No advance at the box office. Baggage held up at Port Authority, owing to our legal status; loss of three days.

Our girls were eventually sprung, little the worse for wear. Performances at first were largely unattended; however, after the presentation of Tchelitchev's ERRANTE and Stravinsky's APOLLO toward the end of a ten-day season, there was an awakening of interest. Victoria Ocampo and her friend Maria Rosa Oliver gallantly stirred up a brush fire of enthusiasm. Miss Ocampo, dauntless mistress of the progressive literary magazine *Sur*, had survived generations of opposition, censorship, and prison to bring to Latin America the best that was being written there and over the rest of the world. They took me to visit Jorge Luis Borges in an ancient apartment lined with books. But Borges, who knew everything about everyone including us and our repertory, was nearly blind. I was taken to the Teatro Colón and wished we'd the luck to be dancing there rather than in a hideous movie house.

After other big towns, we proceeded by train to Mendoza in the high Andes. There, a terrific blizzard immobilized us for a fortnight, forcing us to miss our scheduled subscription opening in Santiago de Chile. The Andes were impassable; our scenery had to be routed, guarded by two dancers, up and through Bolivia. We appealed to our embassy in Lima, Peru, to send transport planes to rescue us from disaster. In the meantime, to maintain morale and gather in whatever fringe benefits might ensue from our persistence, we gave daily performances at the tiny but pretty municipal theater attached to the Mendoza gambling casino.

One morning on my way to class and rehearsal, I crossed a park in front of the theater, where a gentleman courteously approached and demanded why he should not kill himself. In his hand was a revolver; he spoke urgently but quietly; his seriousness was such that I could hardly doubt his insistence. He had lost the last of his money gambling the night before and was heavily in debt. I had nothing to propose except to suggest in my best Spanish: "When you're dead, it's for a long time." I began to realize that I had acquired a mythical reputation as a mad North American millionaire who amused himself keeping a ballet company performing night after night, in the high Andes, to a handful of spectators. Finally, since the man remained imperturbably courteous but obdurate, I told him that I must get on to my rehearsal. Tattered palms shivered in the ragged municipal park; a broken fountain dribbled; starved dogs skulked. His own hungry elegance matched the faded gilt of casino and theater. It was a scene from some fable by Jorge Luis Borges. In the auditorium when I was watching dancers at practice, I fancied I heard a shot; it may have been an automobile's exhaust or another sharp report. However, this indeterminate incident summarized our South American experience in its indecisiveness, frustration, and blunted impact.

The company, using oxygen masks, was finally flown across, or rather between, the Andes. It reached Santiago nearly two weeks late and from there proceeded north by coastal cattle-boat to Lima, Guayaquil, and Colombia. When we had budgeted the tour, a wholly imaginary sum had been allocated for income. After Buenos Aires, even before Mendoza, it became clear we would never approach half of it. In panic I left the company and flew to Washington to renegotiate with the Coordinator's office. I was an unremarkable negotiator; a general opinion prevailed that the remainder of the tour should be canceled. This meant eliminating Peru, Ecuador, Colombia, and Venezuela. I dealt with Wallace Harrison, the architect, who had been pressed by the national emergency into serving as Nelson's deputy. He wanted to know if the tour so far had been a "success."

Certainly this is the most frightening word in a theatrical lexicon. Success on what basis? We could claim little by way of improving the image of a North American government in a southern continent that had so far been ignored except for commercial exploitation. As for personal success, there was our ballet company, which had indeed performed in Brazil, Uruguay, Argentina, and Chile. In the light of historical precedent, might I not claim that the first tour of a sizable troupe performing at some level of efficiency throughout new territory was a kind of "success"? In the light of newspaper clippings collected and influential persons, many in the political opposition, interested or attracted, what could be estimated as the increment? Was success a cipher, amounting to less money lost than had been witlessly anticipated? We had been dispatched to stimulate goodwill, not to save cash. We could be considered a success insomuch as we had been chosen to be sent, and by many considerations had been no absolute failure. This seemed to be the single alternative to "success"—the smash hit, big prize, Top Ten, the Oscar. Was there nothing between 100 percent and zero? However, Wally Harrison, among others, had something more like a war to win; while he was a friend and a sensitive man, he confessed that it looked like curtains. Until, as usual, our guardian angel appeared in the grotesque guise of an accident high over Colombia.

Sharing our program of cultural penetration had been a famous tenor and film star. When his plane crashed, a whole string of personal appearances had to be canceled. If, hard on this catastrophe, our ballet's performances were also wiped out, what would be the prestige of our vaunted export culture through the highlands and lowlands of El Gran Colómbia? The Coordinator's office bowed to *force majeure*. The tour was continued; meanwhile our engagements throughout Venezuela were actually achieving "success," which made things easier when it came to sorting out the ghastly financial discrepancies. Nelson and Wallace Harrison made everything as equitable as they could.

CONCERTO BAROCCO: William Dollar, Marie Jeanne, Mary Jane Shea

THE FOUR TEMPERAMENTS

Nicholas Magallanes, Maria Tallchief,
Beatrice Tompkins, Todd Bolender

In fact, on the basis of contacts the ballet had made, I returned to South America within the year, supplied with funds to buy progressive Latin-American paintings for the Museum of Modern Art.

Back in New York, looking over newspapers from the South American journey, I was surprised to find how erudite, warm, and favorable much of the journalistic criticism had been. It was almost too scholarly, on too respectful a level. Perhaps it tended to keep popular audiences away by the very level of its seriousness. Ballet was made to seem as sacred as symphonic music, but not as much fun. Also, we had had little or no advance publicity; our embassies had considered us a sinister nuisance. Worse, we had no famous stars—and worst, our ballets were not remotely Russian.

MAY, 1945: BAYREUTH, GERMANY

I was last here in 1923 for the first Wagner Festival since the 1914 War. Mother and I were refused at the best hotel in spite of advance reservations. They said we would be happier in a kosher rooming house. At the end of MEISTERSINGER a rapturous audience, joined by the chorus onstage, broke into "Deutschland, Deutschland über Alles." Today, the stage was covered with tarpaulins on the shattered roof; Special Services will use it for films and name bands.

In the Army my energies were transferred from theater interiors to drama in the open air. The European theater, at least what I managed to see of it as courier or interpreter, was full of brilliant impersonations, among the most notable being George Patton himself. Headquarters had comic-opera overtones; as far as high-camp went, he was certainly among the more conscious and expert prima donnas of his era. Fringes of his command were extraordinarily permissive. In Normandy, momentarily confined to the Cotentin Peninsula before Patton broke loose at Saint-Lô, we spent happy wasteful hours building a movie theater, or at least transforming a cattle barn into an auditorium. From somewhere came dozens of fat rolls of tar paper which had the texture of dull black velvet. We tacked them up in the barn and inscribed them with linear murals, white-on-black in the Cocteau manner. This bit of interior decoration was achieved in off-hours; before it could be finished, on one electrifying day in late July, four thousand planes blasted a path for Patton, and our unit tore after him to Paris.

TIME TABLE: Gisella Caccialanza, Lew Christensen,
Beatrice Tompkins, Mary Jane Shea

MAY, 1945: TRIER, GERMANY

Bumped into Lew Christensen. He's in Graves Registration. Bad-for-morale to leave pieces of people around the place; his unit collects them, tags them, and cleans up the landscape. We were both so preoccupied with what looks like the end of war that we had little to say. We touched on plans for what could be done in the ballet; he doubts if he will dance again. No point in reminiscence; the last ten years seem ploughed under.

Lew was awarded a battlefield commission and ended up administering a small German town for another year. I found myself in the Austrian Alps, helping uncover Göring's spectacular cache of stolen art objects, but extricated myself from the Army by early October. I had enjoyed most of it, imitating Ulysses the polytrope, the sly fellow who passed, usually safely and anonymously, from one unlikely occasion to another. I found an interstitial existence not only desirable but possible, particularly for one who had a little French and German, no rank, and an authoritative if elaborately courteous and official manner. In fact, I was giving an impersonation of some type of shady character, possibly from a branch of Intelligence, to which I had no claim whatsoever. This sort of behavior is easy enough in anarchic, chaotic, or extreme situations; hence the Army gave me a taste for exercises of simulacra of free will. I gained an illusion that I might do much as I wished so long as I knew what it was and analyzed the factors. A former weakness for the tentative, accidental, or improvisatory was sloughed off, and with it, much insecurity and doubt. In the service I behaved much *as if* what I wanted to do could be done. And peacetime brought its immediate if momentary euphoria which increased this illusion.

I returned to find our school, under Eugenie Ouroussow, stronger than ever. Aims remained basically the same; we needed to form another company, a new audience; and sooner or later we needed a sponsor for a theater of our own. Through the spring and summer of 1946, Balanchine and I planned strategy. An analytical, conscious operation, it was overly ambitious, including a dozen projects which we never started and as many others which would abort. Perhaps the program sprang more from caprice than caution, but the famine of war years had made us hungry and now we were greedy. Our proposals were often reckless or, I suppose, "pretentious." That is, we would pretend to an impact which would be unprecedented in scope and quality. One thing we never considered was "success." There would be no compromise with good taste or establishment standards; to attach ourselves to these spelled death, as our experience with the Metropolitan Opera had proved. Balanchine and I knew that what had been done in the past had no place in a present or future. We needed fresh attitudes, new audiences, and our own theater; we set about obtaining these according to a rational schedule. We projected a private subscription organization called Ballet Society, Inc., and proposed a six-point program which was sent out in a brochure inviting membership. Some eight hundred people responded. They got quite a lot for the money, and so did we.

From the initial brochure inviting membership in Ballet Society, Inc., October, 1946:

PRESENTATION of new theater-pieces, including ballet, ballet-opera, and chamber-opera, either commissioned by Ballet Society or unfamiliar to the American public, as well as individual concert-dancers.

CO-OPERATION with other educational and cultural institutions, to enable the production of performances, exhibitions and publications, difficult or impossible to accomplish alone.

PUBLICATION of books, prints and articles that award to the dance a consistent and serious attention long enjoyed by painting, sculpture, architecture and music.

PRODUCTION and circulation of documentary dance-films recording contemporary activity in ballet companies, individual dancers, and national dances, as well as experimental films using dance as a main element.

PUBLICATION of record albums of music in the performances of Ballet Society, with photographic documentation and full program notes.

AWARDS of fellowships enabling talented young dancers and choreographers to work by themselves or with groups of dancers to develop technically and professionally.

It was something of a triumph that in the 1946–47 season, our eight hundred subscribers received everything we promised them, with the exception of record albums. Also included were a yearbook as an illustrated summation of our activities; a subscription to the magazine *Dance Index;* hardback monographs on Nijinsky, Pavlova, and Isadora Duncan; a bulletin; and invitations to demonstrations, rehearsals, and film showings. No tickets were sold for individual performances, which circumvented the necessity for a box office and clerical detail, and we eliminated the press list. If newspapers cared to cover our performances they could subscribe, like anyone else. We calculated that, instead of antagonizing critics (who by and large would be unfriendly anyway), this might pique their curiosity, while they would scarcely ignore productions of such intrinsic interest. We guessed right. We gave away tickets to poorer friends and enthusiasts, among them students, artists, and poets; these were the best propagandists we could pay. Typography and presentation for the initial announcements were elegant; our opening campaign had panache and a calculated arrogance which was attractive. There were no large individual backers; however, we dimly felt that somewhere, somehow, somebody would be waiting in the wings in the guise of a guardian angel, and that there must be some future use for what we presently proposed.

SEPTEMBER, 1946: NEW YORK

Tchelitchev's studio, with first programs for Ballet Society. Final refusal to do anything himself, except offer criticism. I'd already made commitments—for example, to a designer for L'ENFANT ET LES SORTILÈGES. He snapped that she was a nice enough woman, a good cook, but a total amateur; another example of my irradicable amateurism. He again brought up ideas for THE CAVE OF SLEEP, his MEDEA, and EPISODES. We haven't enough money even to start on the costumes he would want. He said: "Very well; take Kurt Seligmann; he is an intelligent man." "Intelligent?" "Yes, you have too much enthusiasm, not enough brains."

Working with the composer, Balanchine had produced Maurice Ravel's ballet-opera L'ENFANT ET LES SORTILÈGES (here translated as THE SPELLBOUND CHILD) twenty years before in Monte Carlo for Diaghilev. It had not been given in the United States. The charming libretto by Colette was ostensibly a children's extravaganza; actually it was an extremely sophisticated adult's-eye view of childhood, its terrors and wonders. Aline Bernstein had encouraged me in a variety of ways. She allowed me into her workroom to watch the procedures of a professional scenic designer. The fact that she could not draw very well in no way impeded the execution of her tasteful and imaginative costumes and stage sets. In fact, the naïveté of her watercolors recommended her talent for the infantile elements in Ravel's ballet-opera, in which an armchair is animated and china teapots sing with amorous cats and dance with a choir of frogs and insects. A twelve-year-old boy soprano sang The Child onstage and moved with the dancers. The solo singers and chorus sat with the orchestra.

A main problem was the theater itself. Lacking any possibility of hiring a Broadway house for a single performance, we rented the auditorium of the Central High School of Needle Trades. It had nothing resembling proper equipment, lights, hanging space, or dressing rooms, and it was available only when school schedules permitted. The auditorium was huge, drafty, unappetizing; the proportions of the stage, which was hardly more than two yards above the floor, were broad and very low. However, it had a certain amplitude; here at least nobody bothered us, and Balanchine as usual forced something unusual out of harsh conditions.

In the late thirties he had managed to save some money working with Dick Rodgers and Larry Hart on Broadway and Sam Goldwyn in Hollywood. He had spent it to commission from Paul Hindemith, then in exile teaching composition at Yale, a ballet for string orchestra in the form of a theme and four extended variations. We had first proposed to use the piece for our Latin-American tour. Tchelitchev designed a series of sixty impossibly extravagant costumes on the *prétexte* of four systems supporting human anatomy—the bony structure and the lymphatic, nervous, and muscular systems. Inspired by Vesalius (with an assist from Gray's *Anatomy* edited for first-year medical students), he boasted to Balanchine that when these were executed and worn they would wipe out all choreography and obliterate music; that the audience would be *bouche bée* at such splendor. The splendid designs for his THE CAVE OF SLEEP joined others now deposited in the Museum of Modern Art.

The Hindemith score remained unused until Balanchine resurrected it for Ballet Society. Tchelitchev suggested Kurt Seligmann, an erudite painter with a big library of alchemy and magic lore, for decorations. Using a blend of personal symbolism and arcane ikonology, encouraged by Tchelitchev's own insistence on visual aspects, Seligmann swathed our dancers in cerements, bandages, tubes, wraps, and tourniquets, so that dancing became more a dress parade than a display of human bodies in motion. (They were soon rejected for practice dress, as has been the case with CONCERTO BAROCCO, APOLLO, and other works of overwhelming choreographic rather than atmospheric interest.) To complicate matters, stage proportions were such that Balanchine was forced to align his patterns largely as bas-relief, in linear sequence across a low, broad platform which had no central focus and which was so narrow that it could barely accommodate dancing in any depth. His finale was a volcanic fountain or atomic eruption of bodies; later he also replaced this with the ending still used today. THE FOUR TEMPERAMENTS (the new title for the unproduced THE CAVE OF SLEEP) was an abstract kinetic gloss on the canonical medieval concepts of corporal and physio-psychological types—melancholic, sanguine, phlegmatic, and choleric. Todd Bolender, whose supple body and tubular limbs were remarkably serpentine, made a powerful impression as a fluidly sluggish acrobatic mendicant.

Whatever its hazards and discrepancies, Ballet Society's debut was a positive success. The Hindemith, *sans* costumes, entered a permanent repertory to be danced in the next twenty-five years by a dozen companies from Canada to Covent Garden. Now, with a new beginning under our belt, we hunted for a theater which would allow us more possibility. Our audience grew; we seemed to be well on our way—somewhere.

During three ensuing programs we offered a dozen new ballets of varying interest, as well as Gian-Carlo Menotti's opera THE MEDIUM and his brilliant comic curtain raiser THE TELEPHONE, which we had commissioned. These were immediately transferred to Broadway for a commercial run. Apart from strict ballet, we introduced some lovely Javanese court and popular dances performed against an opulent transcription for Western orchestra which Colin McPhee had made in Java from a Balinese gamelan. Merce Cunningham and Isamu Noguchi collaborated on THE SEASONS, which had visual perkiness or quirkiness, but John Cage's score (for full orchestra rather than his then notorious prepared piano) sounded no more provocative than Christian Sinding's "Rustles of Spring."

Ever since Bennington College's generosity to us, I had done my best to appreciate the so-called Modern Dance, and we would later be able to work briefly with Martha Graham and Paul Taylor. Their individual qualities of personal intensity and integrity were exhilarating. But I never lost the sense that their idiosyncratic styles derived from accident or incomplete training, that the antagonism of such dancers toward ballet (as they then understood it) stemmed from the historical condition of dance education in the United States when they were learning to perform. Their intense individualism hardly lent itself either to their inclusion in repertory or to their attachment as performers to a traditional company. In attempting to work with them we were prompted by their value as novelty for a ballet-oriented audience, rather than by any charitable broad-mindedness or genuine preference. A single unique personality, however magnetic it may be, when canonized for its own sake, restricts itself within its own accidental limits and tends to repeat itself. As far as repertory goes, works designed to frame an individual protesting theorist dissolve in the hands of other dancers, or wither when the protest loses its immediate polemical bite.

In its first season Ballet Society produced one small but exquisite work that sticks in the memory as something completely realized. This was Stravinsky's miniature opera RENARD, produced first by Diaghilev in 1929 as Serge Lifar's debut in choreography. Now, Tchelitchev advanced Esteban Francés, a young Catalan post-Surrealist, as decorator. A superb draftsman, having been trained as an architect, he designed costumes for Cock, Cat, Sheep, and Fox that were marvelously executed by Madame Barbara Karinska. The elegant and very witty translation of the Russian rhymes by Harvey Officer, who knew his Gilbert and Sullivan, were easy to sing and understand. On its small scale it was as perfect a production as might be imagined.

From the YEAR BOOK OF BALLET SOCIETY, INC., 1946–1947:

The productions offered by Ballet Society in its first year combined unfamiliar works by eminent composers with new works by musicians, choreographers, painters and dancers who are embarking on their careers.

The performances of these works were a fusion of professional standards and amateur taste (the word amateur understood in its original meaning of careful selection, a cultivated taste, but an absence of timeworn formulae of production intended to guarantee safe commercial success).

Not in the last fifteen years have so many first performances been offered by a single sponsoring unit in this country. The programs, however, were presented not for their newness alone, but because performing them offered a threefold experience in education. Collaborating musicians, choreographers and painters learned how to work with each other in unsuspected ways; dancers could develop themselves through the performance of the results; while the audience accustomed itself to unfamiliar aspects of the youthful spectacle.

During the war years, Frances Hawkins had worked in New York for the Museum of Modern Art in key positions of management and public relations. Ballet Society had now reached a point when it needed a full-time business manager who might also implement policy and organize production. Improvisation at its most nervous and fitful had been our main strategy since we started. Frances Hawkins brought us not only energy and imagination, but also her wise logic distilled from long experience in the theater. Her first move was to insist that all future performances be held in the same house. Our use of dispersed auditoriums all over town was confusing and accentuated an aura of impermanence and unprofessionalism. Changes from one dissimilar backstage space to another made the construction of scenery awkward and wasteful. Stage floor-space, dressing rooms, and storage had been inadequate. From years of touring vaudeville in every conceivable climate and condition, she had sympathy for the performers' minimal requirements. She searched the city endlessly; abruptly our guardian angel manifested itself, this time in the drab but far from uncomfortable quarters of the City Center of Music and Drama, Inc.

RENARD: Lew Christensen (The Rooster), John Taras (The Ram), Fred Danieli (The Cat), Todd Bolender (The Fox)

Built at the command of a now bankrupt fraternal order, Mecca Temple on West 55th Street has the pasteboard exterior of a one-dimensional mosque. At that time it was surmounted by a huge gilded tin star and crescent, which the wind toppled to hang by a thread before it was finally removed. Over its proscenium of geometric Islamic tile was inscribed a welcoming *Salaam Aleikum.* The auditorium seated some thirty-five hundred; numerous large lodge rooms made good rehearsal floors. The building had been added to city properties for nonpayment of taxes. Newbold Morris, president of the City Council in Mayor Fiorello La Guardia's benevolent administration, and Mrs. Lytle Hull, who had organized an emergency relief committee for musicians in our worst of depressions, conceived a plan whereby the city would gain, at no cost, premises for a people's theater. The necessary transformation of the house commenced with Leopold Stokowski's broadcast concerts. New seats, a raked floor, and lights were installed. While little could be done to enhance the cavernous interior's moresco-baroque decor, it offered an inexpensive and inviting space. Frances Hawkins hired it for Ballet Society's second season at five hundred dollars a night. Little suspecting it, we had found our first real home in thirteen years.

In charge of City Center's finances, and its virtual if anonymous managing director, was Morton Baum, a citizen of incomparable value. He had graduated in 1928 from Harvard Law School to practice in New York with his brother Lester, a former New York State senator. Morton was special tax counsel to the city and devised the first city sales tax. He was assistant U.S. district attorney under Governor Dewey's racket bustings and was elected alderman in the initial La Guardia administration. A man of consummate warmth, toughness, political sagacity, and sterling integrity, he was also an able pianist and, in the true sense, a musical amateur. At the start of Ballet Society's connection with City Center we never met; he appeared to be a business executive and ordinary lawyer with whom our dealings were casual and official. As relations developed, we came to realize our fantastic luck in latching onto a landlord and legal champion who became a close friend.

At the outset Baum had no knowledge or even particular interest in ballet. He was familiar with musical literature, operatic and symphonic. He encouraged the fledgling New York City Opera Company to balance the standard Cav & Pag ham-'n-eggs with works unfamiliar to its audience. He sight-read easily at the piano and was knowledgeable in the romantic repertory for voice and chamber music. Most important, he understood that hysteria is concomitant with the arts of performance, that without it — since after all, it is mainly a sign of high spirits or excess energy — nothing of much intensity can be achieved on stage. He knew that "efficiency" lies in the impact of performance rather than in tidy accounting systems. In addition to other prime qualities, he was a genius in the peculiar craft of deficit financing, of raising unsuspected funds in emergencies — which, considering our needs and natures, were permanent. He knew without waste motion how to make do with little or, more often, nothing. Later he would be accused of tyrannical secretiveness. He held cards firmly close to his chest; no one except Baum and Ralph Falcone, his endlessly

THE TRIUMPH OF BACCHUS AND ARIADNE:
Tanaquil LeClercq, Nicholas Magallanes, George Balanchine

faithful accountant and accomplice, ever knew in any detail how much cash was touchable, how much was promised or could be counted upon, or how much was owed. Falcone had his own sense of justice; although he worked long hours in the theater, he never endangered his sense of equity in handling finances for ballet and opera: he kept himself clear of any taint of unfairness to either starveling simply by never attending one single performance of either.

Baum (and Falcone) somehow maintained both the opera company, which had been in existence for three years, and now the ballet so that they were not only alive but continuously growing. Most important, Baum, unlike most harassed executives, was accessible; he would always appear at the other end of a telephone, never employing the convenient connivance of a secretary except when he was on the street or in conference. And his long intimacy with intricacies of state and municipal government did the City Center no harm. While official support was, for long, token or vestigial, even this gave City Center some appearance of being the meritorious public-service institution which indeed it became in fact. Apart from dancers and ballet masters, the pair most responsible for guiding the New York City Ballet through its early, most difficult years to eventual independence were Frances Hawkins and Morton Baum.

Before encountering Baum, we had been lulled into an illusion that Ballet Society, Inc., might somehow proceed successfully on its own as a progressive, autonomous organization. Our production program was full, subscriptions had grown, our present scale was so extravagant (at least in proposals) that there was general curiosity as to what in the world would be done with our gross accumulation of orchestral parts, scenery, and costumes after the very few performances we announced and produced. We always answered that the city was full of big, clean warehouses; however, this

PUNCH AND THE CHILD:
Beatrice Tompkins, Herbert Bliss

hardly clarified the vagueness of plans which were to lead somehow, someday, toward a viable permanent repertory. We were so concretely preoccupied with arranging four more evenings of novelties that we had little time to consider an abstract future; that could be left to Baum and Hawkins.

Balanchine projected a three-act ballet based on *Beauty and the Beast.* Ballet Society had presented the American premiere of Jean Cocteau's lovely film made from Madame de Beaumont's fairy tale. Music for the ballet would be by Alexei Haieff, whose DIVERTIMENTO was one of the genuine triumphs of our first season; decor would be by Esteban Francés. This might have been a fascinating work, but Ballet Society had run out of money, Haieff of energy, Esteban of patience. He returned to Spain where, far away from dancers, he could paint in peace.

DECEMBER, 1947: NEW YORK

To Noguchi's studio with Igor and Vera Stravinsky. Isamu had beautiful scale models of ORPHEUS' decor, which they both loved. Nothing Greek about it or the costumes; Arp- or Miró-like shapes for bones-and-flames. Pluto no devil with horns, but more a King of Death like the Hindu Kali. Handsome lyre for Orpheus, carved in balsa wood. Costumes — embroidered wool, timeless, suggestive of ritual tattoos. Stravinsky thanked him for forgetting about Greece. The music is not "Greek," nor the dancing "like Duncan."

Twenty years before, our Harvard Society for Contemporary Art had given Isamu Noguchi, then a very young Japanese-American sculptor, his first one-man show. It was mainly bronze or brass portrait heads, among which were stylish likenesses of George Gershwin, Buckminster Fuller, and other celebrities; later he became distinguished for his beautiful pottery fired in Japan, as well as exquisite paper lamps and masterfully cut and polished stone figures. He developed a special gift for theater, particularly with Martha Graham and John Gielgud; his carving, modeling, and placement of three-dimensional shapes enhanced the plasticity of the space in which dancers and actors moved. Clear colors were thinly washed over metallic surfaces; these attracted light admirably. He had also a sharp sense for the surprisingly or shockingly appropriate. For the moment when Orpheus, in Hell, finally feels Eurydice's hands placed on his own so that, although blindfolded, he is able to start his long ascent to earth, Noguchi designed a slim pennant-shaped streamer of cerulean blue which sliced the infernal darkness on a musical cue. A glimpse of heavenly sky promised hope for the lovers to regain a living world.

the New York City Ballet

85

We commissioned ORPHEUS from Stravinsky in the fall of 1946. This collaboration between him and Balanchine was one of the closest since Petipa dictated to Tchaikovsky the precise duration of each section of THE SLEEPING BEAUTY. For example, Balanchine estimated how long he thought the big duet between Orpheus and Eurydice should take: "about" two and a half minutes. "Don't tell me 'about,'" insisted Stravinsky, with the exactness of cook or carpenter. "It's either two minutes and twenty, thirty, or forty seconds; no more, no less." The action in ORPHEUS and its musical springboard are exceptionally concentrated if deceptively bland. There is only a single sequence of violent and fully orchestrated sonority: the final onslaught against Orpheus by the Bacchantes. Rhythmically this passage was disconcertingly complex; Stravinsky was constantly present, analyzing and authorizing the intricate tempi, while Balanchine composed it for dancing and directed stage rehearsals. The most generous and rewarding of partners, Stravinsky always placed himself at the service of ballet master and dancers. He felt that it was his responsibility to change what he'd proposed if it was neither useful nor legible. All his effects, from the most calm and subtle to the fullest, fastest, or most melodramatic, were structured for urgent plasticity in physical movement, visually as well as aurally.

His early renown, fixed by the overwhelming impression of FIREBIRD, PETROUCHKA, and LE SACRE, made three later generations of audiences hope for a continual reprise of these same pieces. Utilizing folkloristic material, they employed massive orchestral forces, strange sounds, and rude noises for a first thrilling shock. But PULCINELLA, OEDIPUS REX, APOLLON, and DANSES CONCERTANTES were melodic and, though rhythmically disturbing, "simple" or "small" in format. Audiences accustoming themselves to the signature of one sort of prestige commodity were loath to reexamine or reevaluate his continual shifts of manner and material. Stravinsky programmed his constant self-repudiation, moving always toward new frontiers and disdaining previous formulations, particularly those which had already proved "successful." ORPHEUS was APOLLON's heir, not alone in the ancient myth, but in the essence of his music-drama. Although it added brass and woodwinds to APOLLON's band of viols, it was not calculated as a noisy smash hit which a prepared public could acclaim at first hearing. Indeed, ORPHEUS, for all its beauties, has never

achieved the orchestral repertory, and neither have Stravinsky's symphonies or most of his scores after 1930.

Balanchine conceived ORPHEUS as a ritual ceremonial, in its plangency and pathos. It is rare in the theater for artists of like intensity and talent to work together in harmonious tension. The partnership creating ORPHEUS was a triangulated collaboration in which music, sculpture, and dancing were lightly and tenderly balanced; the result could not but have been recognized as compelling, even in the dominant calm and quiet of its mood.

When Tchelitchev designed ERRANTE for Edward James's Ballets 1933, he invented for its finale a surpassing *coup de théâtre*. The archetype Wanderer, having passed through fire, flood, revolution, love, hate—all life's changes and chances—was engulfed in an enormous mass of thin white China silk released from the flies. This translucent, light-reflective spun gossamer mass overwhelmed the hero who was enmeshed in its folds and thrashing against destiny. Meanwhile his alter ego, shadow-twin, or daimon, visible as a silhouette against the blinding backdrop, mounted a loose rope ladder, higher and higher, to skies from which the silken cloud had fallen.

To separate the three scenes of ORPHEUS Balanchine ordered a similar translucent curtain of China silk, but one which would, when necessary, veil the entire stage picture. It would never fall released to the floor; instead its billows, blown by backstage drafts and the motion of dancers, would reveal dozens of bodiless arms dragging Eurydice through its voluminous folds back to Hell. The silk for this curtain cost over a thousand dollars. Having it sewed and delivered to the theater cost even more, and such was our situation that we had no cash to pay for it two days before a dress rehearsal. Frances Hawkins had already raided her own savings; we had spent what there was and could borrow no more. We seldom discussed money with Balanchine (this was a courteous fiction, since he could not help knowing exactly what went on, but it helped morale). Noguchi was a model of patient despair, having been refused further credit from one scenery shop because previous bills were unpaid. Between rehearsals there were emergency conferences in corners of the School of American Ballet. We were approaching that desperate moment when we must suggest to Balanchine that he cut his beautiful *pas de deux*, alter his action, and submit to crass blackouts for the linking music between scenes. We did not notice

that Balanchine had disappeared from rehearsal. Suddenly he reappeared with five hundred dollars in cash in each hand and tossed the money to Frances Hawkins. We begged to know where he'd found it; he would say nothing except that he hadn't robbed a bank.

The dress rehearsal of ORPHEUS proceeded far too smoothly for the peace of mind of any superstitious watcher. But with Stravinsky, any irrational or apotropaic fear of disaster was sentimentality; he knew what he was doing and results were not luck but logic. And our guardian angel, marking time, now fluttered in the wings, about to proffer peculiar promises.

MARCH, 1948: NEW YORK

To Nelson Rockefeller's office, 30 Rockefeller Plaza, to meet George de Cuevas, who married a granddaughter of J.D.R., Sr. An engaging birdlike creature, he embraced Balanchine and offered us the Cosmopolitan Theater in Columbus Circle. It was built for Marion Davies by Hearst and renovated by de Cuevas for his own ballet company three years ago; it's been empty since. Too good to be true. We are to participate equally, except in rental, which he promised free.

Too good to be true it was; the Marquis de Cuevas, like Aladdin's djinn, vanished in a cloud of delicious scent (lime or acacia); he was neither seen nor heard from again. This apparition was typical of a bevy of false starts, disheartening stops—suggestions and projects which in early stages glowed like rosy dawn but faded by dusk, or before any firm contracts could be drawn. Hope springs eternal; no stone was left unturned in our chase after stability in the frame of a permanent house. Every empty film or legitimate theater, on Broadway or off, seemed to hand us an invitation; but even the Cosmopolitan, which de Cuevas had refurbished with luxurious taste, seated only a little over one thousand persons. Frances Hawkins outlined a plan for using it a possible thirty-six weeks, during which we might share the house with a variety of like-minded attractions. Such plans always had to be reconciled with popular prices—a policy to which we were committed, and which seemed never to cover the costs. So we contented ourselves with our haphazard rentals of City Center, trying to forget its shortcomings, congratulating ourselves that we could at least spend two days rehearsing on a proper stage, that we had a little time to adjust lights and organize our irregular forces.

Isamu Noguchi

ORPHEUS: Noguchi model

the New York City Ballet

Francisco Moncion, Nicholas Magallanes

86

Maria Tallchief

ORPHEUS

MAY, 1948: NEW YORK

With Frances Hawkins to Morton Baum's office. Baum congratulated us on ORPHEUS. Asked what we intended to do with scenery and costumes we have accumulated. I was short and irritable, nervous about the money we owed. He took no offense; asked if we would form a ballet company for the City Center, like the NYC Opera. But "I am only one person; there is, after all, a board of directors." We had heard this before, and often, at the Metropolitan Opera.

Mr. Baum did well to temper our hopes for speed and ease in the formation of a company. He had his own problems, financial and otherwise. On his board, in addition to various complications, was Gerald Warburg, Eddie's older brother, a gifted cellist, who for years had regarded me as the chief villain in the American Ballet's catastrophic tour after Scranton, Pennsylvania. Gerald warned Baum hotly against any enthusiasms of ours, which could but lead down the garden path to disaster. In addition he avowed that ballet was an impure form, anti-American, elitist; in fact, not even "healthy." There should be no place for ballet in a decent people's theater. However, Newbold Morris, the nominal chairman of the City Center, could be persuaded otherwise. Sooner than we might have hoped, a comfortable agreement had been drawn and signed. Baum's financial wizardry never exceeded the limits of the possible; after all, he was both tax expert and agile counsel. He was also an acute political analyst and knew how small palliatives might affect broad policy. A loose arrangement was effected to put us under the protective custody of a semiofficial institution, which in turn gave us a chance for further development.

We would continue to cover our deficit, but day-to-day services provided by the City Center's staff would reduce this figure. We would also serve the New York City Opera and thereby furnish additional employment for underworked dancers. Our season was concurrent with the opera's; we performed on Monday and Tuesday (the poorest nights in the week), the opera on Thursday through Sunday. Beggars aren't choosers. We saved on costs of stagehands, orchestra, front-of-the-house personnel, advertising. We were in possession of a considerable and varied repertory which had barely begun to be exploited. We had found a home, or something approximating one. When we prepared future seasons of new ballets, despite rainy weather, Morton Baum held over our heads the sturdy umbrella of the City Center of Music and Drama. In 1933 in London, I had promised Balanchine that by the time I was forty, he would have a company and a theater of his own. So far he hardly had either; the war cost us only a year's delay, but our future was open.

Emily Coleman in NEWSWEEK magazine, October 25, 1948:

It has always been Lincoln Kirstein's purpose in life to "do things nobody else would do"; that, he explains, "is the only reason I exist." . . . Now he finds himself on the same hot seat occupied by so many others. The New York City Ballet must support itself or leave the boards. This season, appealing to a broader public [than Ballet Society], at popular prices, is Kirstein's final stand. "This," he says, "is the last formula I can think of."

Our "season," restricted to weak Mondays and Tuesdays, pulled only fifty percent of capacity. It cost around fifty thousand dollars (which in current money would be roughly three times that). Immediately before we opened, the Ballets Russes de Monte Carlo enjoyed a successful engagement at the Metropolitan, draining the curiosity and purses of many ballet lovers who were accustomed to standard repertory and well-known stars. Our situation was certainly sticky. However, Balanchine was not particularly unhappy; to him profit or loss rarely meant much. He would contrive to busy himself; if one theater seemed shut to him, there was, or always had been, another that was open. Maintenance and continuity would be someone else's job; his was to weld a company and furnish it with new works. If our repertory was in itself a failure, if we did not now possess negotiable properties, if our artistic planning had not justified itself (none of which we believed), then and only then might there be cause for suicide. Morton Baum agreed, and offered us a separation from a subsidiary position with the opera. We would become autonomous; he would grant us our own week-long "season" the next January. This meant that from now on City Center, rather than Ballet Society, assumed our deficits. We—that is, the New York City Ballet as a company with no legal entity—would be charged only for new productions. Novelties

CAPRICORN CONCERTO:
Maria Tallchief

DIVERTIMENTO:
Francisco Moncion, Maria Tallchief

Swan Lake

THE CONCERT

AFTERNOON OF A FAUN

were (and are) what we lived by and for, but *how* we lived would now be up to the City Center.

Through new friends we also began to raise a certain amount of money from outside our own circle. Alice Pleydell-Bouverie loved dancing and dancers; she, her sister-in-law (then Mrs. Vincent Astor), and J. Alden Talbot and his Ballet Associates (a previous benefactor of both Ballets Russes and Ballet Theater) helped to organize gala evenings. They were usually held at the Waldorf Astoria, which not only gave us some politically important social cachet but also brought in cash. Before this, we had had no position among the hereditary Manhattanites who supported the Met and Philharmonic and might have become interested in a native ballet company. Ballets Russes opening nights attracted flashy audiences, which yielded effective unpaid publicity in the press. Such glamour stimulates public excitement which overflows into the box office on subsequent nights.

We would never acquire much social status; we would never enjoy a well-heeled board of directors, or any legally independent status. The City Center stood *in loco parentis*, and we welcomed both the paternal advice and paternalistic patronage of Morton Baum. He did not wish to spend or waste time on cosmetic socializing, and he spared us the ennui of board interference. We learned that the price of "entertaining" prospective patrons was higher than providing free entertainment for essentially unserious enthusiasm, based on no real interest except the idle warmth of casual personal contact. We aspired to a popular policy; but this was not easy, since we were promulgating an aristocratic form of entertainment. But the idea of combining populist service and aristocratic quality appealed to Newbold Morris and Mrs. Lytle Hull, who after all were so secure in their long public services that they could discount the infrastructure of New York snobbery.

As for Baum, he would always be from the wrong side of the tracks. He suffered over his recent rejection by the Metropolitan Opera, where he had been briefly on the board at the behest of the municipal tax administration. But he had asked too many questions for comfort; covert or clear anti-Semitism was seldom absent from the red-and-gold purlieus of 39th Street and Broadway. Baum would turn this snobbery to his advantage; an affluent section of New York's industrial families was siphoned into the City Center, where he made them feel at home. A people's theater could also be classified as an amusing charity or even an "entertainment" rather than an exclusive social club. Baum magnetized a new audience of second-generation New Yorkers with a long tradition of musical appreciation in Middle Europe — an audience which was scarcely made comfortable by the heirs of Dutch patroons and the Hamiltonian succession of Murray Hill's rich, well-born, and able.

However, from this very aristocracy sprang Alice Bouverie, who threw a considerable weight of fair opinion and prestige our way. In England during the war she had worked in a munitions factory. She had also been close to the tribulations of a nascent British ballet, which was then enduring most of the hazards that we would, with such rare help as hers, eventually surmount. Her admiration and affection for Frederick Ashton was to

have crucial implications for us; her interest in our company was never loudly enunciated; she was shy, born, as she said, under the sign of Cancer; her benefactions, though many and large, were granted sideways, crabwise, apologetically. If she couldn't do more at the moment, she'd try later. Her interest, and that of Mrs. James Fosburgh, J. Alden Talbot, and, later, Joseph B. Martinson, gave us an air of somewhat raffish respectability and a bit of extratheatrical glamour, whether or not it reflected any long-range promise of security. Such ancillary or ephemeral factors had undeniable importance; even a sketch of our story would be inaccurate if it did not acknowledge these people's lively and providential help.

Stability we had not and would not have for another twenty years. In England, with the inestimable advantage of Lord Keynes's patronage, Lilian Baylis, Marie Rambert, and Ninette de Valois were beginning to enjoy the results of their Herculean labors ever since Diaghilev's disappearance. Maynard Keynes's profound attachment to all the arts, and through his wife Lydia Lopokova to ballet in particular, would transform the Sadler's Wells Company by patent into a Royal Ballet. That title was magic; the surreal but numinous magnetism attached, however tenuously, to crowned personages in a constitutional monarchy was an enormous popular advantage to the Royals, both in Britain and abroad. How we longed to touch some of that magic, knowing even then (as Wystan Auden said of himself thirty years later) that we were not Americans but rather New Yorkers, and that our ballet must represent one city in its immediacy rather than remotely personifying a nation.

After a reasonably successful season early in 1949, we faced nine months of layoff. Here again was a threat to our company. As usual, however, there were merciful injections which revived our faltering feet. From Sol Hurok, Morton Baum shrewdly acquired Marc Chagall's scenery and costumes for Stravinsky's FIREBIRD, in which Maria Tallchief made an electrifying appearance, emerging as the nearest approximation to a prima ballerina that we had yet enjoyed. And Jerome Robbins, who had studied under Fokine and danced with Ballet Theater, cast his lot with us for several seasons and created THE GUESTS for Tallchief with an acerbic jazzy score by Marc Blitzstein. He also took Leonard Bernstein's symphonic reading of Auden's AGE OF ANXIETY and, using ingenious photomontage by Oliver Smith, made a popular piece, although the poet prized it not at all. Robbins's genius for improvised comedy, his canny instinct for the artificed use of the apparently accidental, were also evident in his PIED PIPER (1951) set to Aaron

Copland's Concerto for Clarinet and String Orchestra (1948).

A third, less noticed but potent addition to our forces was Madame Barbara Karinska, who arrived from Hollywood with an Oscar awarded for her costuming of Ingrid Bergman's JOAN OF ARC. The supreme mistress of theatrical wardrobe in our epoch, she now gave us perky tutus for Balanchine's BOURRÉE FANTASQUE, his second recension (after COTILLON in 1932) of Chabrier's piano pieces. It ended with the finale of *Le Roi Malgré Lui* but, alas, without its rousing chorus. For years to come Balanchine kept proposing in vain the production of this opera. The score would be offered, a producer or opera manager would express delight, then nothing would come of it, either here or abroad, although Balanchine continued to design dances after Chabrier and never lost hopes for the whole opera.

Todd Bolender, Lew Christensen, William Dollar, John Taras, and Antony Tudor now began to revive or invent ballets for us. Balanchine welcomed other choreographers, but the fact that, except for Robbins's, their works seldom stayed long in repertory naturally gave us the tag of a "Balanchine" company. It could not have been otherwise, granting his qualities. However, none of the "younger" choreographers who have been asked to work with us have ever publicly faulted him for lack of warmth in offering them whatever facilities of rehearsal or production he could furnish.

Our School of American Ballet was growing from strength to strength. From the start Balanchine had organized a structure of strong instructors from whom he himself had learned. Dancers, however admirable as performers, are rarely gifted as teachers. Usually they are either models of deportment, style, and capacity who can be followed or imitated as a criterion, or analyzers who break down or demonstrate components of efficiency in their motor elements. It is seldom that the two capacities of model and analyst are found in a single master. Pierre Vladimirov was as pure an exemplification of *danseur noble* trained in the early twentieth-century Petersburg school as was then alive. Anatole Oboukhoff graduated from the Imperial School to follow Vladimirov as first dancer at the Maryinsky. It was Vladimirov who had been the Prince Charming of Diaghilev's production of THE SLEEPING BEAUTY in 1921. Oboukhoff was a strong, even harsh teacher who frequently behaved as if he were training big cats, horses, or poodles rather than adolescent bipeds. He barked

Balanchine

Children from the School of American Ballet, Edward Villella center

ILLUMINATIONS

Tanaquil LeClercq (top); Nicholas Magallanes (bottom)

commands and corrections like a drill sergeant; his own gestures seemed violent to the point of physical aggression; yet he was the gentlest of men as well as the strictest and clearest of analysts. Muriel Stuart, an English girl recruited and trained by Anna Pavlova, was an excellent classicist who also had a sympathy for Martha Graham's expressivity and free forms outside the academic orthodoxy of ballet. Consequently her teaching added a dimension of movement which prepared the way for Balanchine's outlandish innovations and his violations of classic order when her students came to face these in professional rehearsals. Felia Doubrovska, Vladimirov's wife, and Alexandra Danilova, the last ballerinas of the later Diaghilev seasons, had continued to perform into the thirties and forties as popular favorites. Doubrovska's regal authority and elegance, Danilova's sparkle, humor, and attack, gave innumerable girls and many boys the cool, selfless efficiency that Balanchine would use to forge a new style which, though based in Petersburg, found sharp definition and athletic accent in Manhattan.

In ever-increasing numbers our school produced recruits tailored to Balanchine's taste and requirements. Besides students from the school, there were older and more experienced dancers trained by Fokine, Mordkin, Bolm, and other Russian teachers in Paris, as well as Russian dancers scattered over the American provinces following Diaghilev's tours. These came first to join Ballet Society, then the New York City Ballet. Performers of youth and merit, Melissa Hayden, Francisco Moncion, Todd Bolender, Nicholas Magallanes, and Patricia Wilde, turned into company stalwarts. Audiences at City Center adopted them as members of a family whom they delighted in watching develop from season to season. Very young girls and boys entered our school; within four or five years they joined their seniors on the Center's stage. In one early generation emerged Jacques d'Amboise, Edward Villella, and a brilliant, capable, and strangely personal ballerina of wit, Tanaquil LeClercq, who was the epitome of Balanchine's lyrically athletic American criterion.

DECEMBER, 1949: RHINEBECK, NEW YORK

To Alice Bouverie's with Freddy Ashton and Cecil Beaton. Bitter cold above the Hudson; roaring fire and enormous English high tea. An album with Rimbaud's drawings, nineteenth-century carte de visite photographs of acrobats. Cecil thinks there should be no color in ILLUMINATIONS: all dancers in clown-white. At the end, a huge enlargement of Rimbaud's blotted sketch of street, steeple, and sunburst. After dinner we returned to ILLUMINATIONS, but the staff had everything tidy, stowed away, so Fred gave marvelous impersonations of Pavlova, Sarah Bernhardt, and Ida Rubinstein, with whom he had danced: "a giraffe on pointes."

On leave in Paris during the last year of the war, I had heard Benjamin Britten's setting of some of Rimbaud's *Les Illuminations*, ten pieces for high voice and string orchestra (1939), beautifully played and sung by a contingent of British artists-in-uniform. Britten and the tenor Peter Pears had lived in Amityville, Long Island, in 1941 before the United States entered the war. At that time we were preparing for our Latin-American tour and asked Ben to orchestrate two suites of Rossini's piano pieces called *Matinées musicales* and *Soirées musicales*, to be used as a divertissement to conclude an evening. For DIVERTIMENTO—a name we were to use again—we again used André Derain's delectable dresses designed for LES SONGES, which was originally produced by Edward James in 1933 and later mounted for our American Ballet. I first met Britten through Wystan Auden; they were collaborating on a folk-opera commissioned through Columbia University's department of music. I admired both words and music, but Britten withdrew his score unpublished, and Auden reprinted only the lovely dialogue of Cat and Dog—"The single creature leads a partial life." *Paul Bunyan*, revised, could have been an attractive repertory piece, but it vanished, one more work ploughed under in two dauntlessly prolific careers. ILLUMINATIONS, on the other hand, would hold the stage from its debut through frequent revivals.

I had known Cecil Beaton since 1927, when he befriended me in London. Ashton I had met through Chick Austin in 1934, after Ashton had come to Hartford for his miniature ballets for black dancers in Virgil Thomson's FOUR SAINTS IN THREE ACTS. He is a scrupulous, imaginative, highly professional choreographer, an old friend of Pavel Tchelitchev's. Pavel provided him with the perfect dancer to impersonate Arthur Rimbaud: a young Mexican of grace and presence, Nicholas Magallanes. Tchelitchev used him as a model for paintings and sent him to our school, where he found his real vocation. He danced Rimbaud in the ballet biography compacted from the time the poet quit Charleville, through the eruption of the Paris Commune and the stormy friendship with Verlaine, to his abdication from poetry before he'd hardly come of age. Ashton realized half a dozen tableaux fusing harshness, violence, and lyricism which had a genuine ferocious impact. Beaton imagined the performers as a troupe of clowns in a one-ring circus somewhere off the Boulevards—mostly white, pale green, mauve, with metallic accents. His was *le style chiffonnier*, a poor man's chic, framing a meager, post-adolescent, half-lit pathos in a tradition which reaches from the brothers Le Nain, through pink-and-rose Picasso, to LES FORAINS, waifs, mendicants, and wanderers of Christian Bérard's ballet for Roland Petit in 1945. Ashton, with his considerable skills inherited from the long tradition of English narrative gesture and pantomime, gave us a European ballet. It was unlike any of our more or less "native" American works and an addition we needed for variety at this particular time. Also, we had our eyes on London for some future connection, a possible contact through hands-across-the-sea programs.

Balanchine

MOTHER GOOSE SUITE: Janet Reed and Todd Bolender

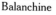

the New York City Ballet

THE DUEL

Melissa Hayden

The premiere of ILLUMINATIONS provided us with the pretext for a gala. The British ambassador was present; national anthems were played; John Martin of the *Times* gave Ashton a brilliant notice; Alice Bouverie was delighted with what she had, first and last, brought into being. We were now very conscious of the name we carried and pressed a quasi-official alliance with our city on every opportune or opportunistic occasion.

Later that season we improvised JONES BEACH, on which Jerome Robbins and Balanchine collaborated. At its debut were Robert Moses, the redoubtable commissioner of parks who had caused the vast Long Island pleasure ground to be built, and representatives of the Dutch government, since the score was composed by Jurriaan Andriessen, a very young Hollander here on a Rockefeller fellowship. His music had not been written for us; he had showed Balanchine a lively diploma symphony, sunny and cheerful as a day on sand and shore. Its first movement we called "Sunday"; the adagio was "Rescue from Drowning," entrancingly danced by Tanaquil LeClercq and Nicholas Magallanes; its allegro was "War with Mosquitoes" (largely by Robbins); the finale, for no particular reason, "Hot Dogs." This was typical of a dozen works which were invented backward. We had spent most of our available money on ILLUMINATIONS. As costumes for JONES BEACH, we wanted something more festive than the practice dresses which Balanchine increasingly favored. Bathing suits offered approximations of nudity and were available in every shape and color. We approached a well-known manufacturer with a magnanimous offer for the firm to donate undress for a classic ballet; its response was as generous as the ensuing publicity. Apart from rehearsal time, JONES BEACH in all its topical chic cost hardly a penny.

During our early seasons at City Center, we were in the enviable position of having Leon Barzin as musical director. For Balanchine, the orchestra has capital importance; our scores needed attention, discipline, and dispatch in rehearsal beyond the interest or capacity of the ordinary contract type of Broadway bandsmen. For years Barzin had led the National Orchestral Association, which enabled student instrumentalists and con-

London, 1950. Balanchine, Robbins,
BBC interviewer, Tallchief

ductors to obtain training and exposure under professional circumstances in series of seasonal concerts at Carnegie Hall. Barzin himself was an experienced viola player. In him Balanchine found an eager colleague with whom he could speak as a partner—a conductor who embraced contemporary music enthusiastically while having a wide familiarity with the entire scope of orchestral literature. Our lighting expert and technical administrator was Jean Rosenthal, who had done wonders for Orson Welles and John Houseman since the days of W.P.A. and the Mercury Theater. She worked magic with patched or rented electrical equipment and rickety portable boards—veterans of the Ballet Caravan tours, which she had originally serviced.

Because of the increasing accumulation and persistence of our appearances, our introduction of piquant novelties, and the incidental social functions of two galas and their attendant publicity, we managed to finish this season with our smallest deficit so far. Our achievement was also due to help from Mrs. Bouverie, Mrs. Astor, and J. Alden Talbot. Morton Baum could face his board of directors with some vindication for his rashness in having taken us on. We had not yet bankrupted City Center; on the contrary, we'd managed to attract a different, often younger audience, open up a new sphere of public service, and create a fresh excitement.

MARCH, 1950: LONDON

Frances Hawkins and I wait endlessly for David Webster, absent for the weekend. Negotiations at a complete impasse. Our conditions unacceptable; he doesn't want us at Covent Garden. Onstage, rehearsal for Balanchine's revival of BALLET IMPERIAL. Margot Fonteyn and Michael Somes danced beautifully. Frances decides to fly home tomorrow; I'll wait for IMPERIAL. Cyril Beaumont's ballet bookshop, Charing Cross Road, with Lydia Lopokova; found postcards of her in THE GOOD-HUMORED LADIES. Heavy tea with Dickie Buckle, editor of Ballet. He says that Webster is always like this at first.

The first night of Balanchine's BALLET IMPERIAL, invented originally to give us a "grand" Petipa-type work for the Latin-American tour, was, in London nine years later, all it should have been. Beryl Grey, Michael, and Margot were strong and stylish; there were seventeen curtain calls. Finally Ninette de Valois, creator and director of the Royal Ballet, came onstage with George, who was handed a big wreath from the dancers. Frances Hawkins had her ticket to New York in her pocket; she'd be leaving at dawn. She bade goodbye to David Webster, General Administrator of Covent Garden, at the party Balanchine gave in the crush-bar of the Royal Opera House. Webster, all smiles, stopped her farewells; she must not leave London until he had signed our contract. We would appear at Covent Garden for five weeks, commencing the middle of next July, then tour the provinces for three weeks more. His terms were generous; he would even pay half transportation to and from New York: our ultimate condition, which clinched the deal. It seemed too good to be true. When Frances took her leave, Webster said: "My dear, believe it or not, I'm happy to have the New York City Ballet; however, I can assure you London will make or break you." We appeared under the sponsorship of the Arts Council of Great Britain. Our visit was considered a semiofficial exchange for the Sadler's Wells 1949 season at the Metropolitan, where the British dancers had received the greatest ovation in their brief history. To an important degree, an alien audience establishes the artistic, economic, and political importance of a luxury export. Acceptance by a foreign public affixes a convincing seal of prestige for home approval.

We were scarcely "official," however, except by the grace of City Center; and we were far from being royal. Our particular American qualities, no matter how they might be prized in New York, gave no special assurance of being warmly embraced by London. So far we barely qualified as a national treasure. I was apprehensive; England meant much. My real education had commenced there; my criteria of sensibility and intelligence were based on British models, living or dead. Nothing less than absolute victory would bring me much satisfaction. One appearance at Covent Garden was a culmination, beyond which there could be nothing: on this I staked everything. It was ridiculous overexaggeration; I would pay for my lack of historical perspective. But I had not been in London since 1933; for me it was still Diaghilev's town; we would be dancing on the stage of vividly remembered triumphs. My sense of competition was factitious; I was not rational; as Frances Hawkins wisely diagnosed: "He's not crazy, he's hysterical."

George Platt Lynes

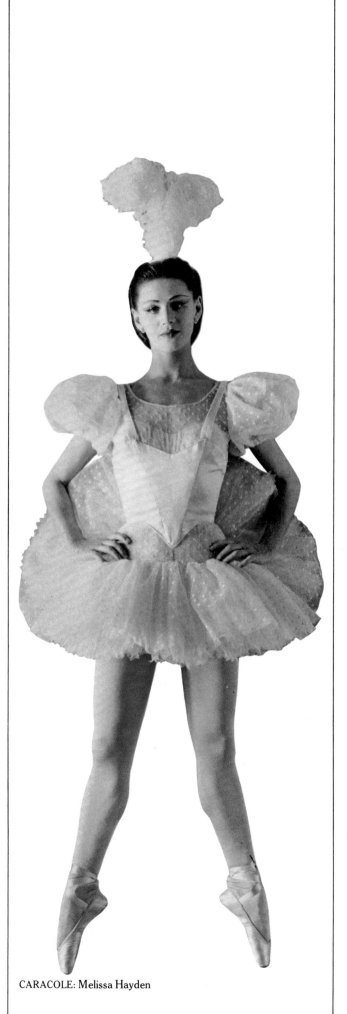
CARACOLE: Melissa Hayden

JULY, 1950: COVENT GARDEN

Debut of ILLUMINATIONS. The Queen is not coming. "Mixed" reception. Fred led us underground to a passage which would take us up into the Duke of Bedford's private box. A steel door locked us in the cellar. We yelled in unison; finally a night watchman heard and let us through. Marina, Duchess of Kent, glacial. She was not amused by Ashton's pantomime in which a king and queen have their crowns knocked off, while the mob delights in an orgy. Not the sort of thing Fred would have been allowed to do here. I tried to explain to Her Highness. Fred, delighted. He'll do another piece for us next year. Wired Alice Bouverie "love and thanks," but it was no jolly occasion.

Predictably, the anonymous reviewer of the *London Times* loathed ILLUMINATIONS as much as or more than he had hated FIREBIRD at our opening the week before. I responded to his shocked stance far too seriously and felt impelled to draft a letter, with the help of Morgan Forster, a friend from Bloomsbury summers. I was much consoled when complimented on it during a quiet weekend in Cambridge where, at the high table in Kings, one of Forster's colleagues said: "Jolly well done." It might be a footnote to the complete letters of the master of *A Passage to India*, for its tone and terseness were more his than mine:

Sir,
Your critic's unfavorable opinion of Mr. Frederick Ashton's ballet, LES ILLUMINATIONS, in your issue of July 21 was, so far as I could judge, not shared by the audience, for the reception was enthusiastic. Your critic is presumably aware of the mixed beauty and grossness of Rimbaud's life and work and it is regrettable that he could only recognize grossness on the stage. As for his condemnation of THE FIREBIRD I would ask leave to correct him on a point of fact. He states that "The whole ballet was danced without the slightest trace of the atmosphere of Stravinsky's music." He seems unaware that the choreography was revived with the composer's desire and approval and that he conducted the work in the February, 1950, season in New York.

London's reception of our company was doubtless not as drastically ignominious as I chose to imagine. The Opera House for our five weeks sold about seventy-five percent of capacity. Many reviews were sympathetic, some even favorable. What might I have expected? Something vague, impossible, absolute—like death or transfiguration? David Webster now turned into kindness itself; he suggested, and should not have, that we play a sixth week. We did, and should have. In reckless compulsion we even felt obliged to produce a new ballet, THE WITCH, by John Cranko, who was presented to us by Ashton as the best of "young" English choreographers; in return, Balanchine gave the Sadler's Wells junior company Haydn's TRUMPET CONCERTO. Neither was

remarkable except for the genuine exchange of goodwill prompting them. Our provincial tour was lamentable; ghosts whom I hoped had been laid for keeps in Scranton, Pennsylvania, reemerged howling.

There were compensations, or more precisely, memorable incidents. During an intermission after a performance of ORPHEUS to which I'd asked T. S. Eliot, we spoke of a possible sequel for which his words might conceivably be set by Stravinsky, as he had handled André Gide's *Perséphone*. But Eliot knew of the composer's notorious difficulties with French prosody and Gide's poetics, and was not enthusiastic. A sung prayer for dancers could be imagined, but would take consideration. Eliot, remote, courteous, attentive, thought dancing was sufficient unto itself, requiring nothing by way of words, at least from him. I reminded him of his excellent notices of dancing and music halls when he edited the *Criterion;* he replied that those were "evocation not invocation." There would indeed be a sequel to ORPHEUS, but AGON was some seven years in the future.

An enormous party in a huge mansion seemed to revive for a night Edwardian Mayfair in its heyday. It was given to celebrate the coming-of-age of a Marquess of Hartington, and our entire company was invited. I was introduced to Clarissa Churchill, later Lady Avon. She inquired—implying, I imagined, some trickery—how we

BOURRÉE FANTASQUE: Tanaquil LeClercq, Jerome Robbins

FANFARE FANFARE FANFARE FANFARE FANFARE FANFARE FANFARE FANFARE FANFARE FANFARE

Patricia Neary

had chanced to come by Chagall's scenery and costumes for FIREBIRD. I started to explain, in overelaborate detail, the convolutions surrounding Morton Baum's negotiations with Sol Hurok over the transference of property which had fallen to him. She cut it short: "What I really want to know is why your dancers can't keep in step." I was puzzled; "keeping in step" implied a Rockette type of paramilitary discipline, whereas most of our choreography was insistently contrapuntal, phrasing deliberate imbalance, syncopation, and calculated offbeats. It was characteristic of my mild paranoia that I imagined her hostile.

In New York we had anticipated a London deficit of twenty-five thousand dollars. Owing to our week's extension at Covent Garden and the provincial tour, we lost twice that; Morton Baum would have to cover it in ways one dared not ask. Arnold Haskell, an old friend from 1933 when he and I collaborated on Nijinsky's biography, gave us in print a generous summation. Richard Buckle, critic on the *Observer*, as well as editor of *Ballet*, rebuked his colleagues for a general "impercipience" toward our manifestations. But the most comforting farewell was small handmade bouquets of red and white carnations bought early at Covent Garden's flower market and delivered to every girl in the corps de ballet, with cards reading:

LILAC GARDEN (opposite):
Hugh Laing, Tanaquil LeClercq,
Antony Tudor, Nora Kaye

Herbert Bliss

In gratitude and with admiration for your wonderful dancing throughout the season from your friends in the Gallery and Amphitheater at Covent Garden. Please come back.

Despite ups and downs, before the company flew back to Manhattan, David Webster offered us a return engagement for the summer of 1952. At that particular moment, such was my manic depression that this was the last thing I wanted. There was no evidence that we would even be in existence by 1952.

The stage floor of the Royal Opera House had scarcely been repaired since its honorable wartime service, and our dancers suffered from cracks and splinters. Maria Tallchief sprained an ankle opening SERENADE; there were other injuries for which the patched surface was not blameless. But Richard Buckle, with his genius for the preposterous which elevates him to a dukedom of the absurd, awarded us a floral tribute of bomb-site weeds and this citation: *"To those Americans who fell at Covent Garden: July–August, 1950."*

From the NEW YORK TIMES (John Martin), November 22, 1950:

It was a joyous evening at the City Center last night, for the New York City Ballet company opened its three-week season at the top of its form in three of George Balanchine's best ballets. There is no doubt whatever that the successful outcome of the young company's daring invasion of London's Covent Garden Opera House last summer has done wonders for its morale, and it has returned to its home stage in the finest of spirits raring to go.

And what a company it is! Without any stars in the narrow sense of the term . . . it has a brilliant set of leading artists. . . . Here too is an ensemble of note; there was not one of them last night who did not dance as if she were herself a ballerina, yet with a feeling for the unity of the group and the framework of the composition. What more can one ask of any company it would be difficult to say.

John Martin's conversion to our cause, after his earlier misgivings about Balanchine and our chances for creating an "American" ballet, was just as important as our London season, since weekly news magazines which covered city and nation followed the lead of the *Times* then, as they do today. However, in 1950 there were half a dozen papers in New York which regularly sent reporters to dance events. With due respect to David Webster's prophecy, Covent Garden neither made us nor broke us. Our financial footing was no firmer over the long run.

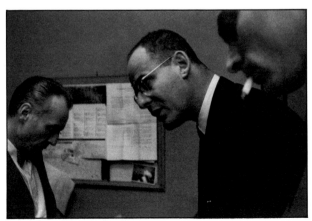

Balanchine, Kirstein, Bigelow

London did, however, add a status which we had not enjoyed before, especially with dancers who had not been schooled within our orbit. Janet Reed, a sprightly, swift soubrette, came from Lew Christensen in San Francisco. She was that American who, for me, most recalled Lydia Lopokova. Melissa Hayden with her formidable strength and attack was already a favorite. Maria Tallchief stayed as our standard-bearer. Now Diana Adams, with her cool linear plasticity, joined us; a little later came Nora Kaye, the most intense and melodramatically effective dancer-mime of her generation. Hugh Laing brought his dark suavity and firm elegance to Antony Tudor's ballets; Harold Lang captivated everyone with his jazzy snap and sharpness. André Eglevsky, premier *danseur noble* of his time, terminated an impressive career after several seasons with us and later taught a generation of boys in our school.

As we proceeded, reinforced by such experienced artists, the School of American Ballet continued to provide new soloists who formed continual support in depth. There were, of course, comings and goings, enforced by personal sentiment, fate, or history. Edward Villella, on the brink of a spectacular development, having studied in our school since he was nine, disappeared for more than five long and unprofitable years in the Merchant Marine Academy. Nora Kaye had been rapturously received on her initial appearance in February, 1951. For her Jerome Robbins created THE CAGE, which, as he admitted, was a ferocious updating of the second act of GISELLE. More accurately, it was a manifesto for Women's Lib, twenty years *avant la lettre*, in which Nora mimed and danced a predatory, unprayerful mantis. In this and in Tudor's repertory, she was incomparable.

City Center stage door

Herbert Bliss, Melissa Hayden

Tanaquil LeClercq, Nicholas Magallanes

JONES

BEACH

Jerome Robbins, Maria Tallchief

Our aesthetic did not suit her, however. She was a tremendous personality in her own idiosyncrasy and could have been nothing less; we were unable to frame so overpowering a presence in roles which she felt were satisfactory. But her success in THE CAGE, which was due as much to her dancing as to Robbins's design, encouraged Baum to risk our first "summer season" which, in spite of a superstition that "no one stays in New York in the summer," succeeded.

Sol Hurok now offered us a national tour, which we might take as a basic commercial accolade. He had been most helpful in arranging our contract with Covent Garden, and it had been through him that we obtained Chagall's decor for FIREBIRD. He planned to have local symphony orchestras accompany us wherever possible; there could be extended seasons in Chicago, San Francisco, and Los Angeles. But when Frances Hawkins and Baum projected actual costs and calculated the amounts that transportation and commissions might subtract from any gross we might earn, and when we considered that our repertory would be unfamiliar and probably unattractive to many new audiences, we decided not to risk it. I had hoped that our company would remain comfortably a tale of two cities, New York and London, which was scarcely realistic or farsighted. Balanchine, who (always wearing a Zuñi bracelet) had driven across the continent from New York to Los Angeles some dozen times via the Dakotas, the Rockies, and the Southwest, naturally wished our ballets to be seen beyond the Mississippi. Where had all my nationalist sentiment gone? What had happened to the doctrinaire programs backing BILLY THE KID, YANKEE CLIPPER, and FILLING STATION? My nationalism was alive and fairly well at the City Center. But now we knew for sure that we were not Americans in general, but specifically New Yorkers.

APRIL, 1951: CHICAGO

Huge parade celebrating Douglas MacArthur. Handfuls of people in the Opera House. Negative satisfaction of knowing I was right in not wanting to move out of New York. Beautiful studio party given by Ruth Page and Tom Fisher. Chicago is a big town in which nobody lives; hard to get home by the Illinois Central to suburbs after dark; only two theater nights, Friday and Saturday. Baum underestimated losses.

On my return to New York, Baum would give no definite date for our company's further appearance. The City Center was undergoing one of its permanent crises, which continue into our present. There were various anonymous characters upon whom he could call in direst need, but since need was always dire and sources few, he was slow to cry wolf too often. However, within a month we were back at work; Baum had uncovered a new patron in a manufacturer of kosher matzos. All this was long before any real support came from the state or federal government or charitable foundations.

Our Chicago experience was sobering, if only temporarily; we would play there again with better luck for several years on a more or less seasonal basis. The main point of touring, as far as I was concerned, was to employ dancers and so avoid the erosion of personnel and the costs of replacement. Dancers were paid about half the

FIREBIRD: Maria Tallchief

the New York City Ballet

SERENADE (previous page): Jillana, Nicholas Magallanes, Mimi Paul
AGON (upper left): Arthur Mitchell, Diana Adams
THE PRODIGAL SON (upper right): Edward Villella
PULCINELLA (bottom): Michael Arshansky

BUGAKU (upper left): Allegra Kent, Edward Villella
ALLEGRO BRILLANTE (upper right): Anthony Blum, Patricia McBride
SLAUGHTER ON TENTH AVENUE (bottom): Arthur Mitchell, Suzanne Farrell

JEWELS
RUBIES: Edward Villella, Patricia McBride
DIAMONDS: Suzanne Farrell,
Jacques d'Amboise
EMERALDS: Conrad Ludlow, Violette Verdy

rate of musicians and a third of what stagehands made. Their labor-union history was shorter, but they ate as much as their elders or betters. Soon we were appearing rather regularly in Washington, Philadelphia, San Francisco, and Los Angeles. These jaunts eked out our City Center engagements, but costs mounted increasingly (and continue to mount; over the last decade, for example, the company has been able to leave New York only for foreign tours and summer seasons in Saratoga, Washington, Cleveland, and Ravinia, near Chicago).

In the meantime, at home base in City Center Balanchine completed a series of repertory pieces larger in format than any we had handled before. Ravel's LA VALSE had been in part instigated by Diaghilev who, when he read the piano score, pronounced it undanceable. Ravel's original inspiration may have been Schubert's piano waltzes from 1823, which Diaghilev could have considered superior. Also, in 1912, Ravel's first version had been used dubiously for dances by Natacha Trouhanova, a dancer much disliked by Diaghilev. For our Ballet Caravan, William Dollar had made a ballet from Ravel's *Valses nobles et sentimentales*, the suite of piano pieces from which the big tone poem was later derived. LA VALSE had later been used for ballet without notable success; it was too brief and abrupt to sustain a dramatic extension which initially it seems to propose. Balanchine, however, adapted the early piano pieces, fully orchestrated, as a prelude to the developed grand waltz.

Diaghilev's original prejudice has some justification; LA VALSE is less a canonization of the waltz as a form than a definition of its cataclysmic disintegration. The big themes shatter, rhythms dissolve, a persistent beat grows tenuous, and as a succession of feverish motifs dissolve, the climax becomes chaos. If there is any substratum of narrative, it lies in the suggestion of dancing on the edge of a volcano. Karinska's skirts and bodices fused a Parisian Second Empire theme with a timeless but immediate present, fixing their permanent elegance so that even the waistlines have not been changed in twenty years. At the start, Balanchine developed oddly "Chinese" gestures in a provocative overture that focused on the soloists' long white gloves and introduced a pervasive mood of heartless ritualized flirtation and broken impersonal encounters. Tanaquil LeClercq, with her exceptional nervous energy, grace, fragility, and pathos, strongly supported by Nicholas Magallanes and Francisco Moncion, ensured its persistence in our repertory. Before this we could not have commanded an orchestra capable of mastering a score so large in scale, but Leon Barzin had strengthened his forces, and Morton Baum permitted us to pack a dozen more musicians into the Center's crowded pit.

We deliberated over the problem of revivals. Certain names of older ballets stick in the public mind, although they may never have been seen. Some of Balanchine's European successes ought to be produced here. A few had entered the repertory; APOLLO, which would be given new vitality by André Eglevsky and later by Jacques d'Amboise; Prokofiev's PRODIGAL SON, with Rouault's decor newly painted from original watercolors bought by Chick Austin for Hartford; Bizet's once-forgotten SYMPHONY IN C, which Balanchine had invented for the Paris

FIREBIRD: Francisco Moncion

FIREBIRD

Francisco Moncion,
Maria Tallchief

Opéra in 1947 as LE PALAIS DE CRISTAL. Lacking Christian Bérard for a revival of COTILLON, Balanchine revised an homage to Emmanuel Chabrier in BOURRÉE FANTASQUE. Bérard's decor for MOZARTIANA was lost; we had exhausted his costumes in our own recension for the American Ballet. Balanchine staged CARACOLE from Mozart's Divertimento No. 15 as a replacement for his SYMPHONIE CONCERTANTE, created for Ballet Society in 1947 and too soon forgotten.

We did not yet have a nineteenth-century work on our roster—no SLEEPING BEAUTY, no GISELLE, no SYLPHIDES. We were not a museum of past masterpieces, or a guardian of an "authenticity" which at best is no better than the dubious or radical restoration of once splendid but long eroded paintings. Balanchine's practice of altering his own works from season to season as he saw fit would continue to cause rancor among the journalistic confraternity. He would be governed by prevailing conditions as much as or more than by indecision. Often the determining factors were the presence of new dancers with novel capacities and his own altered insight into choreography he felt could be improved. But then, what of "authenticity" and an absolutely "correct" version? We were dedicated to a fresh repertory suited to new habits, our own audience, dancers we'd trained, and circumstances under which we now operated. We were no official agency; we had no imperial ballerinas to accommodate, or princely patrons to flatter. We could do much as we pleased, within limits imposed by our consistently uncertain economic situation. Often it was practical to be capricious, inconsistent, and irritating.

SEPTEMBER, 1951: NEW YORK

With Balanchine to Morton Baum's to thank him for fall and winter seasons. He was against Bartók's MIRACULOUS MANDARIN but consented because of aid from the Bartók Foundation. Orchestral pieces considered—Strauss's Don Juan or Tyl Eulenspiegel. Again brought up Brahms's LIEBESLIEDER WALZER. Voices too expensive. What about SWAN LAKE? Only the second act is interesting.

Baum was not moved by considering cash for itself; he was interested in repertory which would or would not attract customers. His emphasis was not stupid; he never interfered (directly), but he was persistent. Balanchine had admired the talent of Lev Ivanov even more than that of the far more famous Marius Petipa. Much less prolific, shaded by the Frenchman, Ivanov was equally professional but more musical, less synthetic and mechanical. Ivanov was responsible for the success of Act Two of SWAN LAKE in its 1895 revival, when Tchaikovsky's marvelous score vindicated itself (the initial failure in 1877 was due to a presumed "Wagnerianism" and to lusterless choreography). When we consented to face the idea of presenting SWAN LAKE, Balanchine made it clear that what he intended would be a personal abridgement which, while incorporating elements recalled from Ivanov, would be more his individual homage to Tchaikovsky than any "authentic" archaeological reconstruction. In the twenty years since Balanchine revived the second act, many changes, omissions, and replacements have been made. Sections in the score which Diaghilev and others had eliminated were re-

Tanaquil LeClercq, Francisco Moncion, Edward Bigelow

stored; music from other sections was inserted. The unison quartet of "little swans," an unfaltering applause-machine, was soon suppressed; the male solo variation was changed variously to suit a succession of first dancers.

SWAN LAKE in whatever version, produced by whatever company, bolsters weak programs. It is the favored role of favorite ballerinas, and a legible metaphor for classic ballet in the minds of people who care little for dancing. It is, in truth, reliable insurance. If we wished to consider a production of *Tyl Eulenspiegel*, then to cover its large risk we must make room for SWAN LAKE. At the moment it seemed a glaring retreat from our staunch principle of resisting revivals, adapting prior prestige to present opportunism. And some of the same people who, ten years before, objected to our insistence on novel or unfamiliar music now considered our use of SWAN LAKE an abdication. Yet Balanchine's production was hardly a revival, although he was inevitably accused of lack of reverence for the Ivanov-Petipa "original," wherever that dubious touchstone was thought to exist. Opinions on any strict choreographic adherence to half-forgotten ballets are comparable to divisions over details of an orthodox liturgy. A gloss considered heretical by one ballet master is taken as a standard of correctness by another. Balanchine considered himself a colleague of Tchaikovsky's rather than a protector of Ivanov or Petipa.

In his design for our production Cecil Beaton took as a precedent sixteenth-century draftsmanship as rendered by Urs Graf or Hans Baldung Grien. Their wiry calligraphy proposed handsome linear patterns of white ink used negatively on dark paper. We had a strong cast — Tallchief and Eglevsky in the big roles, Patricia Wilde and (later) Caroline George in subsidiary but scarcely less brilliant dancing. Balanchine's pattern for the finale was a notable example of intensity accumulated by blocks of cross movement. Our SWAN LAKE turned out to be precisely the sort of success Morton Baum desired. When paired with FIREBIRD, our "bird program" served manfully in many mutations. Beaton's stylish setting was too small when we moved to the State Theater. Rouben Ter-Arutunian, inspired by Albrecht Altdorfer, painted a moss-banked forest lake with enchanted-island cliffs;

again Balanchine altered Ivanov's design; but the music, as always and everywhere, was an indestructible scaffold for satisfactory dancing.

As for the tone poems of Richard Strauss, we went deeply into *Don Juan* and discussed the ballet endlessly with Eugene Berman, who had interesting pictorial ideas. But, as with *Tyl Eulenspiegel*, the brevity of the piece precluded much development and might have resulted only in a sequence of abrupt or truncated vignettes too compact visually for the scale of orchestration. TYL was produced as a repayment of sorts for our willingness in the matter of SWAN LAKE. It was one of several productions which should have had a long life. Large in format successful at its premiere, novel in treatment, triumphant in visual realization, with a witty performance by Jerome Robbins in all Tyl's tricky impersonations, it was the most elaborate work we had so far presented at the Center. Esteban Francés's scenery was a clever borrowing from the anxious and fantastic world of Hieronymus Bosch. It received unanimous approval from many who felt that we usually skimped on decoration. The music, however luxurious in sonority, gave Balanchine small scope to exploit characterization or incident. There were no possible musical repeats which might have expanded the opportunities for action. To gain a few more minutes he introduced a prologue accompanied only by ominous drum rolls. Two children were revealed opposing each other, playing on a gigantic chessboard. The boy king, Philip II, deployed a toy armada of model ships; the young Tyl blocked him with a blunt loaf of peasant bread. The Spaniard knocked the bread off the board; fisticuffs followed, and then the first chords of the tone poem were heard. Now Tyl, grown into a folk hero, taunts the tyrant invaders by his tricks and rouses his people against the might of Castile and Aragon. *Life* magazine gave us a double-page spread in color; everything promised a long and rewarding run in repertory. But fire swept our warehouse; costumes, beautiful little galleons, masks, all were lost. Jerome Robbins left the company. But most of all, Balanchine felt frustrated by the scale of the score, so there was neither impetus nor energy to attempt its salvage.

APRIL, 1952: NEW YORK

Final talk with Sol Hurok over 1953–54 tour. He wishes to reduce number of dancers, take only small ballets, use a half-size orchestra, and include one-night stands. Few dancers eager to go, leaving empty apartments; no salary increase. Eleven rehearsal weeks, thirteen playing weeks, and it's not enough. Trouble over possible European tour; Jacob Potofsky, president Amalgamated Clothing Workers and a director of City Center, resigns from the board because we are invited to Franco's Spain.

Our situation was again awkward. A chance of cashing in nationally on whatever success we had built in Manhattan interested Mr. Hurok, but conditions governing financial feasibility pleased neither Balanchine nor our principal dancers. On the other hand, we were now offered a five-month tour of Europe, commencing in Barcelona. Mr. Potofsky had been a good friend of my father's; we were aware of the justice of his protest as well as the injustices that prompted it. The negative political implications of our appearing in Spain were to be echoed continually over the next twenty years — particularly when we went to Japan in 1958, the Soviet Union in 1962 and 1972, and Greece in 1968. Many vocative persons with indignant memories held that we should have no traffic with former foes or present tyrannies.

From the early thirties I had had ample experience of confrontations between art and politics. In 1932 I arranged a show inviting contemporary artists to paint mural panels which might lead to jobs decorating Rockefeller Center, then under construction. Ben Shahn sent an effective panel, which he could hardly have expected to be chosen, for a series detailing the agony of Sacco and Vanzetti. It showed A. Lawrence Lowell, president of Harvard, gloating over their coffins, and caused exactly the offense that was intended. I was also involved in a rather violent attempt to prevent the destruction of Sergei Eisenstein's Mexican film footage. In 1939 for Ballet Caravan, Eugene Loring had choreographed CITY PORTRAIT with music by Henry Brant, a proletarian, proto-agitprop ballet with a rust-red guardrail around a manhole as its main scenery, and outraged dancing (if not very outrageous for mass movements) by a furious mob of fifteen. Marc Blitzstein and Jerome Robbins had Leftist attachments, and their ballet THE GUESTS (1949) was an ambiguously compassionate demonstration of what a black friend called "the cluded and excluded."

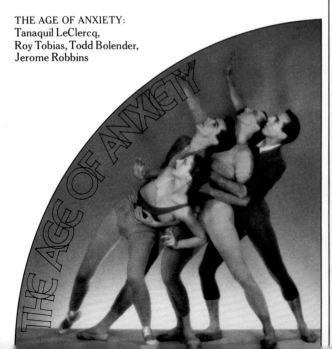

THE AGE OF ANXIETY:
Tanaquil LeClercq,
Roy Tobias, Todd Bolender,
Jerome Robbins

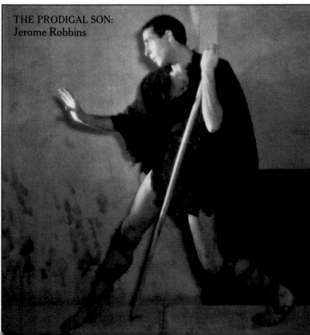

THE PRODIGAL SON:
Jerome Robbins

THE PRODIGAL SON

Maria Tallchief, Jerome Robbins

Years spent in the Army, however, had depoliticized me. Irresponsibly or not, I came to consider politics as a whole and politicians as they affected our company mainly as jugglers of intermittent or endemic apathy. Severe experiences with State Department agencies all over the world taught me that direct involvement with abrasive issues and most attempts to satisfy opposing public opinion would only impede my real business, which was our survival on my terms. The energy or talent needed even tangentially for devotion to valid causes was incommensurate with what energy I had to keep our company working. That we were vaguely considered representative of our city was honor and convenience. That we were to represent the nation's culture overseas in a country where our chief concern was naval bases to control the Mediterranean meant no more than necessary weeks of work. Since we could not presume to affect foreign policy either by going or by refusing to go, I would not let objections, however justified, stand in our way.

MAY, 1952: BARCELONA
Maurice Rapin, FIGARO, Paris, May 8:

SYMPHONY IN C concludes the performance and introduces the homage. The last strains of music end; a rain of rose petals and laurel leaves starts to fall from balconies and boxes in the upper tier while stage attendants begin to bring in baskets of multicolored flowers to the dancers, grouped around their *maître de ballet*. The whole stage becomes a garden. Now, the supreme and rare tribute that Barcelona shows to admired artists: a flight of doves flies from every direction over the entire auditorium. . . . Eight minutes by my watch, the audience applauded the dancers who by now had almost stiffened "to attention"; Balanchine was visibly moved. It was a great night in Barcelona.

Three weeks before this, such glory could not have been anticipated. We had been irrevocably scheduled to open on Tuesday of Easter Week. Just as "everyone" leaves London for Bank Holiday, or New York over the Fourth of July and Labor Day, so "no one" stays in Barcelona during Easter Week. Annual subscribers to the Liceo Theater's programs determine success. However—and doubtless from political considerations—word filtered down that the provincial governor, diplomatic and consular corps, and local city officials would attend our premiere. Then "everyone" else who was anyone felt obliged to be present. Our repertory was appreciated, the dancers even more so, which was lucky since it gave confidence before our imminent attack on Paris.

There we had been invited to appear at the Palais Garnier for a festival entitled Masterpieces of the Twentieth Century sponsored by the Congress of Cultural Freedom, whose secretary-general was Nicolas Nabokov. As a youth he had been discovered by Diaghilev, and in 1928 he wrote the music for ODE (Massine-Tchelitchev). During and since the war, he had served in several of our cultural embassies. In Paris there were numerous impressive participants, including the Boston Symphony Orchestra. But Serge Lifar, who had been ballet master at the Opéra since 1932 (at Balanchine's own suggestion), was offended because his company, a national standard-bearer, had not been invited. Reasons for this glaring omission were personal, political, devious, reflecting no honor on anyone. None of it was our fault; we had known nothing of the circumstances,

which were internecine and local. However, owing to the ancient connection of Balanchine, Nabokov, and Lifar, we were vulnerable to attack. In the Parisian fashion there were angry exchanges of letters in the press, which blithely contributed to black-market prices for our premiere. The situation of ballet at the Grand Opéra over the last two centuries has been, at best, uneasy. There have been good times when capable administrations found private individuals who personally covered deficits, but at other times the Opéra has been subject to disastrous political pressure when some official bureaucracy assumed control.

Only recently Paris had welcomed other American and English companies, as well as Roland Petit's young

SWAN LAKE:
Maria Tallchief

and tasteful Ballets des Champs-Élysées. The traditional, indeed legendary supremacy of French lyric theater—which was a semipermanent actuality in *opéra comique* and in ballet at least from the thirties through the forties of the last century—has long been compromised. Hence there were patriotic critics who, like others in years to come, would be lamenting our lack of soul, or *âme frigidaire*. As Balanchine later retorted to similar Russian complaints: "When you say we have 'no soul,' it merely means our 'soul' is unlike yours." For decades before the First World War, there was universal admiration for *l'âme slave*, which Anna Pavlova personified to an often inordinate degree. Dancers whose most adored role is Giselle incarnate "soul"; it is the blood of Swan Queens.

In any case, we could not have wished for more success than we had at our opening performances both at the Opéra and subsequently at the Champs-Élysées Theater. Stravinsky conducted his ORPHEUS in the presence of the president of the republic. Jerome Robbins's

PIED PIPER, a happy improvisation on Aaron Copland's Clarinet Concerto, was performed on the same program. To a Parisian audience, the gravity of ORPHEUS seemed modest or monotonous. LE SACRE DU PRINTEMPS of forty years before was still the type of Stravinsky which spelled a smash; nothing less loud could be expected to elicit so warm a welcome. Robbins's CAGE benefited from considerable coverage in the picture press; any number of erotic and quasi-pornographic journals regaled its metaphorical ferocity.

A fortnight at the Florentine Maggio Musicale followed, packing the Teatro Communale's forty-two hundred seats at each performance. There was even loose talk of Florence acting as a permanent host to our company, just as Monte Carlo had served Diaghilev after the First World War. A similar offer had come from Milan after Balanchine had mounted BALLET IMPERIAL at La Scala the preceding March. North Italian dancing masters of the sixteenth and seventeenth centuries were responsible for a codification of steps which remain the basis for our discipline. Yet ballet as an institution declined there, and recently has been represented chiefly by sporadic or token activity. However generous Florence or Milan may have been, it was impossible to take their enthusiasm very seriously. Italian audiences are oriented toward voice rather than dancing, and their system of municipal subsidies makes any consecutive program questionable. However, the gossip about these proposals did no harm at home. At least it showed that we were appreciated, and that we might hope for similar but firmer appreciation from our own municipal or federal government.

JUNE, 1952: THE HAGUE

Frans Schokkink (sic), Burgomaster, The Hague, insists we remove THE CAGE from all programs; two local critics who saw it in Florence decided it was "pornographic" and "shameless." The burgomaster has appealed to our ambassador, who says this is beyond his diplomatic competence. If CAGE goes, Robbins will withdraw all his work; Nora Kaye will refuse to appear in other ballets. Our embassy wants thirty tickets; none to be had.

Possible censorship made THE CAGE more popular than ever; our engagement was sold out; we were invited to return the following year. The historic progression of permissiveness in theater over the next two decades is exemplified by its development in Holland, where the national ballet companies in the late sixties flaunted frontal nudity as thrilling aesthetic innovation. Balanchine for years had opted for an approximation of the body unimpeded, unencumbered by redundant adornment. However, Lord Clark's distinction between nakedness and nudity is a governing consideration. Balanchine continued to clothe dancers in music, movement, and gesture; frontal frankness has its ephemeral piquancy, but sustains only marginal choreographic interest. Often it represents desperation on the part of dance

SWAN LAKE: André Eglevsky

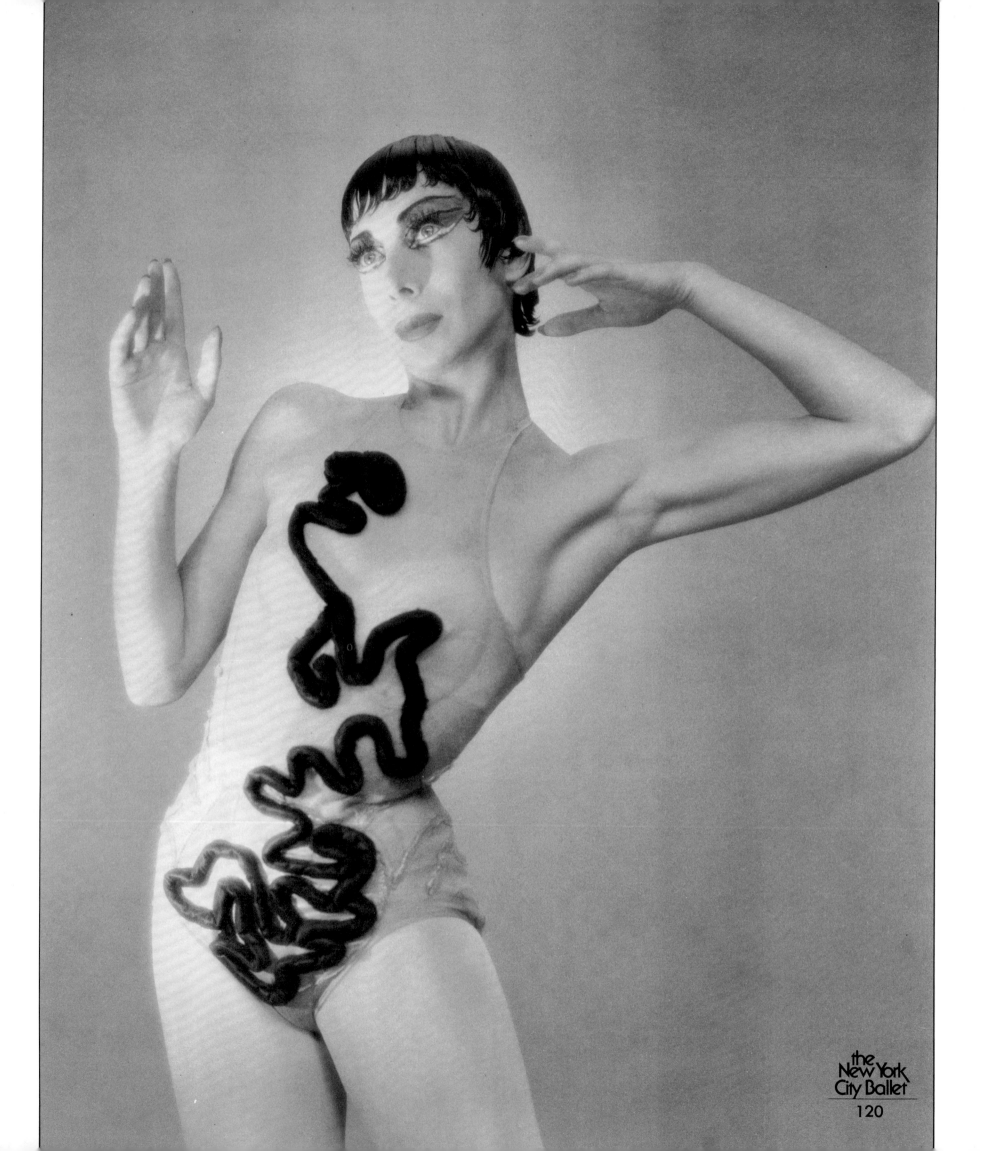

designers, who judge that a wholly exposed body is more fetching than exposure of their notions of movement. Obligatory shock is as tiresome as the resistance or apathy of conservative subscribers. Ballet, since it involves bodies in close contact, possesses erotic dimensions that have long been presupposed, but after the revolution of Isadora and Nijinsky, bankruptcy of imagination in many "young" choreographers (any male under forty-five) proposes genital display as a substitute for plastic invention.

Our second European tour ended with six weeks at Covent Garden, followed by another at the Edinburgh Festival. Our continental travels had been efficiently promoted by Leon Leonidoff, an experienced impresario who became a foster-father to Balanchine and our dancers. He would devotedly handle our European wanderings over the next two decades. This London engagement was less rousing than our first. THE CAGE was received with unflappable calm, perhaps influenced by the parochial nervousness of the Dutch. Nora Kaye had a genuine success. Even SWAN LAKE, despite its predictable lack of "authenticity," caused little discomfort. The critic A. V. Coton wrote: "In fact it has been much like a season by any other foreign company; more people approve than disapprove simply because it is strange and novel and unlike what they are used to."

If we had been French, our product would have been more appetizing and familiar; the English cherish the suave, cosmetic sagacity of French chic. Whatever their insularity, however fond or firm the bonds of our common language and our hands-across-the-sea, London is closer to Paris than to New York. Even after two centuries and four wars, Americans must bear the burden of having behaved like rebellious or ungrateful offspring whose naïve energy may be forgiven, but whose arrogance is not forgotten. Normal envy, residual resentment derive partly from a difference in the manner by which Americans measure time, and a national discrepancy in notions of speed, pace, grace, and motion. We share the same speech, but spelling, accent, tone of voice, and slang differ.

Before he left Russia, Balanchine knew that the twentieth century needed its own tempi, which were jazzy and syncopated, and that asymmetrical rhythm was deep in the motor dynamism of advanced industrial societies. The nineteenth century dies hard; its stronghold is still a constitutional monarchy, socialized indeed, but as firmly stratified as ever. The New York City dancers epitomize in their quirky legginess, linear accentuation, and athleticism a consciously thrown away, improvisational style which can be read as populist, vulgar, heartless, overacrobatic, unmannerly, or insolent. It is also a style of living which may be interpreted as having small respect for its forebears—its elders and, naturally, betters.

Offering the excuse of my mother's recent death, I did not accompany our company on this tour. I might have served in a social capacity, but I absented myself for a more useful conservation of forces. I detest the ritual of first nights, press conferences, confrontations with friendly or unfriendly journalists. I realized that this was all part of the impresario game, but I wasn't an impresario. I was, and would remain, a buffer for Balanchine outside the theater. In Europe he needed none.

THE CAGE: Nora Kaye

OCTOBER, 1952: NEW YORK CITY

No money for scenery for Hindemith's METAMORPHOSES. We need something exotic: Chinese? Balinese? Bought three hundred wire coat hangers on Seventh Avenue. Hung a ladder of them; on it, Jean Rosenthal threw gold light; a spidery pagoda. Problem of insect wings that don't flop.

Hindemith's *Symphonic Metamorphoses on Themes by Carl Maria von Weber* (1943) uses and shifts quotations from Weber's Piano Music for Four Hands, whose theme for the second movement was supplied by an "authentic" Chinese melody quoted from Rousseau's *Musical Dictionary*. This Weber had first used in incidental music for Schiller's TURANDOT (1809). Our ballet had nothing whatever to do with Franz Kafka's horrific parable, although there was indeed a huge and monstrous buglike creature (Todd Bolender) who ambled over the stage in glittering armor. Dancers were bejeweled grasshoppers or mineral dragonflies; there was a skitter and flutter of delicate vibrating membranes accompanying entomological quadrilles. In the three parts of the ballet, costumes changed themselves imperceptibly upon the dancers' bodies, so that what was seen first became entirely transformed. There was little suggestion of growth from egg to extinction, but only of continual mutation in a strange aura which was less oriental or exotic than insectile.

Ingenious and elegant carapaces and wings, which Karinska constructed of wire overlaid with metallic stuffs, were a unique happy solution to a perennial difficulty. Costume wings that carry much conviction are a severe trial to fabricate.

Tchelitchev had been expert in his use of feathers: "Tutus must look like chicken feathers," with no spot plucked bare between legs or at the seat. In his ERRANTE he crossed twin wings over the breasts rather than fixing them to the backs of his "angels," a solution found in the cherubim and seraphim of his favorite Byzantine mosaics in the Karieh D'jami, Istanbul. In his ORPHEUS AND EURYDICE, Amor wore a pair of wings scrupulously constructed of genuine goose feathers in graduated lengths. These sprang from the dancer's bare body with convincing naturalism and were based on a structure of feathering borrowed from Caravaggio's *Angel Dictating the Gospel to Saint Matthew*. When we were costuming SWAN LAKE, Cecil Beaton made wings in many sizes and models. The difficulty lies in attaching wings to a bodice so that they seem to spring logically from shoulder blades instead of being crudely stuck on. Later Balanchine and Madame Karinska found a solution which, while eliminating separate wings, seemed more satisfactory. When Rouben Ter-Arutunian redesigned SWAN LAKE to fit the larger stage of the State Theater, tutus were cut high and short in front, sweeping back in a bustle-like gathering of feathery tarlatan. The whole of this filmy bulk of tulle suggested folded downswept wings, yet the mass moved integrally with the body's shift. While Balanchine pays little attention to most run-of-the-mill costume designers, preferring those who are excellent draftsmen and easel painters in their own right, he is extremely conscious of costume's importance, particularly when it supports choreography itself, as in METAMORPHOSES.

METAMORPHOSES:
Tanaquil LeClercq

CON AMORE:
Karin von Aroldingen

LA GLOIRE:
Francisco Moncion

OCTOBER, 1953: NEW YORK

Inspected scale model for Christmas tree in second scene of NUTCRACKER. City Center's stage is not trapped; the tree must rise from the floor surface. Balanchine insists on a three-dimensional tree rather than painted canvas. Jean Rosenthal's model is built of umbrella-like spokes, lying flat; when pulled up, it springs out in high relief. Estimates run from five to ten thousand dollars. Scared to tell Baum. We order it with no firm figure in contract.

Our 1953–54 season introduced THE NUTCRACKER, our first "full-length" work, the most elaborate we had so far attempted. While the music's familiarity, due to Walt Disney's FANTASIA, led most people to call our ballet "The Nutcracker Suite," we used the entire two-hour score, not the diminished pop-concert version. The budget was high, although physical conditions of the City Center's stage restricted much extravagance in transformation scenes. There was literally no offstage room—no space for marshaling regiments of children in platoons of mice and toy soldiers, no space for storing their artillery and bulky mouse-dresses. Logistics were mapped as for a miniature invasion. The smaller students recruited from our school were silently bivouacked in stairwells and corridors leading up to dressing rooms already crammed with adult dancers. A system of hand signals, relayed by stagehands to prompter parents, hurried everyone onstage, on cue as needed.

The Christmas tree was a triumph of engineering. While in actuality only a half-round, its shivering branches of stiff pine needles jogged thrillingly, loaded with ornaments, toys, and glittering festoons as its invisible spine was hauled up. This always drew storms of applause from small fry who, many for the first time, found themselves in a true theater which could vanquish the notion that magic exists on television alone. In early performances, electrical short circuits of small bulbs wired to the tree contributed alarming special effects; they sparked, sizzled, smoked, threatening to burst into flame. But the branches were fireproof, and eventually the "candles" were put under safer if less exciting control.

THE NUTCRACKER had been patiently analyzed for its style and historic ambience. Balanchine accentuated the bourgeois atmosphere of a comfortable but by no means aristocratic home. Some productions (notably that of Leningrad in 1962) set the opening party in a veritable palace. We placed it in an unassuming middle-class parlor, so that the fantastic sequences might be revealed as all the more surprising and strange. The diminutive Prince and Princess continued to be chosen from the most talented children in our school; many boys and girls who later danced as soloists commenced careers as small angels, mice, or toy soldiers.

When we transferred to the State Theater in 1964, we were forced to abandon Horace Armistead's attractive scenery. A greatly enlarged picture-book production within a three-dimensional gilt paper-lace frame (of molded plastic) was ingeniously designed by Rouben Ter-Arutunian. His huge front curtain, on which a benevolent angel protected Christmas Eve roofs, might have been painted by one of the German Nazarenes. Our gift tree was now nearly twice as tall; at the finale, Prince and Princess are drawn skyward in a sleigh upholstered in tufted satin by a team of jeweled reindeer. NUTCRACKER

immediately became a fixture of New York's holiday season, and soon we would be giving more than a month of matinee and evening performances, on convenient early schedules, with three separate relays of adult dancers and as many teams of children. For several years the ballet was a Christmas telecast over the Columbia network. Balanchine continually changed solo variations, group dances, pantomime, and incidental stage business. In early years, Tanaquil LeClercq, a diamonded bouquet as the Dewdrop Fairy, led the "Valse des Fleurs"; Madame Karinska's gilt-bronze, rose-pink skirts for the corps transformed the stage into a revolving bed of Fabergé's enameled roses.

While NUTCRACKER represented a major effort, the year 1954 was also distinguished by three other novelties. These were of primary musical interest and precipitated much arresting and durable choreography. While I was working on POCAHONTAS with Elliott Carter in 1936, he mentioned the existence of a mysterious and marvelous musician, a businessman living in Danbury, Connecticut, who was perhaps the most original of American composers and a leading innovator of his epoch. However, extravagant peculiarities in the scale and nature of his orchestration exceeded the resources of even the larger symphony societies. This hardly recommended him to our small company, which was then accompanied by two-piano teams or an occasional pick-up orchestra. But in the fifties Balanchine, voracious for new music, recalled the name of Charles Ives. Leon Barzin, our adventurous and widely informed musical director, found and combined a suite of his pieces under the title IVESIANA. Long before *The Unanswered Question* or *Central Park in the Dark* had become popular repertory pieces, Balanchine's dramatic use of Ives's music drew widespread attention to his rich and eccentric beauties.

When I researched facts about Ives in 1953, the 1939 edition of the *International Cyclopedia of Music and Musicians* (for which I'd written a section on dance music) stated flatly that his scores, "both vocal and instrumental, are based on a polytonality that makes them almost impossible to perform." This opinion was still widely held fourteen years later. Resistance to unorthodox orchestration by instrumentalists is no new phenomenon. In 1911 the Vienna orchestra balked at PETROUCHKA for its "wrong notes"; in the summer of 1972 the strings of the Boston Symphony virtually struck in protest over rehearsing and performing a stubbornly unorthodox score. By 1937 the American Ballet had presented three of Stravinsky's late, and to America, unfamiliar ballets. Our use of musical novelties in a theatrical frame often marked debuts of orchestral pieces which later would be accepted and appreciated for autonomous musical quality, unsupported by any dancing. In IVESIANA, *The Unanswered Question* made a strong immediate impression on audiences. A boy seeks the answer to some insoluble cosmic riddle from a sphinxlike girl who, supported by a tribe of anonymous hands and arms, is never permitted to touch earth. The metaphor of equivocal, otherworldly response to his ceaseless appeal was incarnated in the sinuous soarings and collapses of Allegra Kent, a very young dancer of supple eloquence whose bare body seemed boneless, a kid glove of skin firmed with coils of steel.

TYL ULENSPIEGEL:
Jerome Robbins

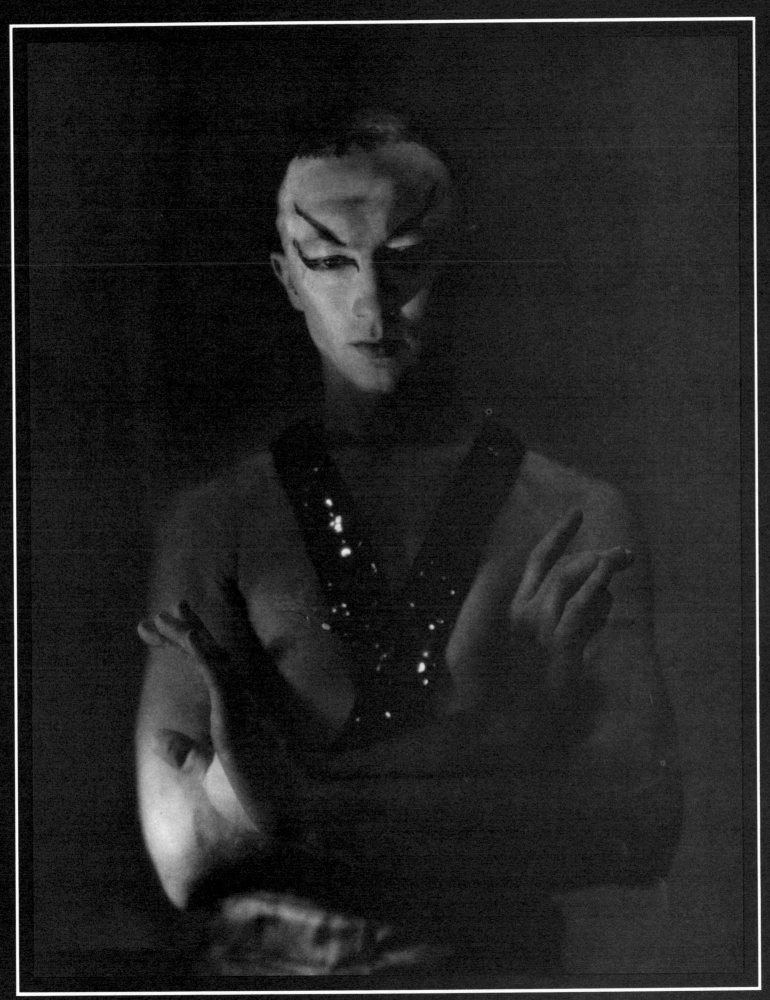

THE MIRACULOUS MANDARIN: Todd Bolender

WESTERN SYMPHONY

Tanaquil LeClercq

AGON

STARS & STRIPES

MEDEA

the Seven Deadly Sins

EPISODES

Liebeslieder Walzer

Liebeslieder Walzer

Jazz Concert
Electronics

BUGAKU

A MIDSUMMER NIGHT'S DREAM

MOVEMENTS
FOR PIANO &
ORCHESTRA

MEDITATION

Piège
de Lumière

Tarantella

Dim Lustre

Shadow'd Ground

147

Summerspace

At the same time, Balanchine used Arnold Schoenberg's Opus 34, his *Begleitmusik*(1930), for a cinematic scene in some nonexistent film. (Stravinsky had drawn Balanchine's attention to it.) He repeated the piece twice with the orchestra, presenting a provocative exercise in the possibilities of separate treatment of the same score. OPUS 34 was the first dodecaphonic composition that Balanchine found suitable for dancing. While comparatively simply orchestrated in a then radical twelve-tone system, its sonorities were unknown to ballet audiences. However, the fresh use of a twelve- rather than a seven-note scale impelled a family of gesture that was somehow related only to itself, in uncomfortable or abrasive sequences. These seemed visually as taut and relentless as was their aural basis.

By this time, any public reaction vaguely admitting shock at the music chosen by Balanchine had subsided to welcoming or enlightened curiosity. While the novel or unfamiliar aroused anticipation, their piquancy guaranteed no deep or prolonged attention, nor that suspension of habit which might have made looking and listening less conditioned or capricious. In the first of Balanchine's two arrangements based on Opus 34, he ignored the composer's narrative rubric: "Peril Threatening," "Fright," "Disaster." The music itself, divested of pretext, triggered elliptical or tangential curlicues of action which related only to its own hermetic, sonorous climate. When Balanchine had first tackled APOLLON in 1928, at the start of his kinetic research of which OPUS 34 was the most recent test, he deliberately inverted an ideal academic idiom against some of Stravinsky's most mellifluous measures. This deformed the open, *en dehors* positions perversely (or as it seemed to many, petulantly) into *en dedans*, the closed or shut accentuation. In OPUS 34, his assertions of disruption were in an entirely different vocabulary, holding by neither inversion nor deformation any relation whatever to any traditional language. Later, some would see it as a first sketch for AGON, the serial technique of which Stravinsky would claim, at its moment of composition: "A series is a facet, and serial composition a faceting, or crystallizing, way of presenting several sides of the same idea." Both the Webern EPISODES—also set to serial music—and AGON achieved a place in our permanent repertory, while OPUS 34 was ploughed under.

The 1954–55 season was the first for WESTERN SYMPHONY (initially with no scenery and in hand-me-down tutus), which Hershy Kay wittily and efficiently compounded to Balanchine's bracing prescription, making a formal classical symphony from cowboy themes. We had considered a new version of BILLY THE KID for the sake of Copland's touching score, but his RODEO for Agnes de Mille was being danced by the Ballets Russes. BILLY had been conceived more as dramatic pantomime than classic ballet; no one wished to supplant Loring's choreography, which was in the current repertory of Ballet Theater.

In 1955, Balanchine took another unfamiliar symphonic suite of Bizet's—his *Roma* (1860–1868)—and composed beautiful dancing. It was richly decorated by Eugene Berman in a Piranesian townscape of ruined arches, which at a climax were festooned with colorful lines of tasteful laundry hung in a frame of doors and windows remembered from Trastevere and the Tiber suburbs. Neither ROMA nor the unsuspected but lovely GOUNOD SYMPHONY of 1958 (a lively parade of metamorphic flower beds laid out by Lenôtre turned ballet master) enjoyed the instant popularity which seemed to justify retention in repertory. They lost out in the unending competition for rehearsal hours scheduled for more urgent or hopeful novelties. Balanchine is so masterfully inventive that if a new work is not immediately popular, he's inclined to forget it. Having exhausted his initial interest in the musical possibilities, he proceeds to something else which may prove luckier and hold public attention longer. Yet what we have abandoned, sometimes too summarily, might make rich fare for some extravagant if unlikely company.

Our reasons for discarding a ballet have frequently been as much accidental as commercial or aesthetic: the disappearance of dancers originally identified with the debut roles, its similarity to later work which seems at the moment more successful, warehouse fires, personal petulance, impatience. But ROMA, GOUNOD SYMPHONY, Alexei Haieff's DIVERTIMENTO of 1947, the Mozart CARACOLE of 1952, BAYOU of the same year (Virgil Thomson's charming *Acadian Songs and Dances* with delicious decorations by Dorothea Tanning) were losses regretted by those who prize delicacy of texture or quiet sweetness of expression. The criterion smash-hit "success" also extends to ballet repertory; while we have fought it harder and longer than most, whenever a company works for a popular audience, it is their taste, inertia, or attention rather than the preference of a director which will predominate.

APRIL, 1957: WESTON, CONNECTICUT

Balanchine preoccupied with roses; more satisfactory than choreography or cooking. Blossoms are perfection, blooming without excuse or complaint; they smell good, die quickly; hundreds of old, plenty of new kinds. Later he called me, having received piano score for Stravinsky's AGON; the music was more "appetizing" than roses or kitchens.

In college my freshman adviser had been S. Foster Damon, a supreme authority on William Blake and an early explicator of Melville when *Moby Dick* existed only in a limited edition and *Billy Budd* was an inaccurately deciphered manuscript in Widener Library. Foster's roommate was the scholar John Marshall, who after leaving Cambridge edited *Speculum*, a learned journal of medieval studies. It was Marshall who gave me Joyce's *Ulysses*, Ezra Pound's *First Cantos*, and Huxley's *Point Counter Point*, all of which meant more to me than Whitehead's lectures on metaphysics. Marshall was already a famous chef and later would write an admirable practical cookbook. He left scholarship, to become charged with the support of the arts and the humanities for the Rockefeller Foundation.

Serving as director of the City Center of Music and Drama, Inc., and holding brief authority over both opera and drama as well as ballet, I applied to the foundation for a grant-in-aid of considerable proportions to commission new works, among which were Aaron Copland's opera THE TENDER LAND and Stravinsky's AGON. John Marshall had a special affection for ballet; his youngest daughter hoped to be a dancer; her goddess was Maria Tallchief, whose photos she enshrined—but she shot up tall and leggy. (Later, failing, in her own eyes, to become either dancer or horse trainer, she found a lasting voca- tion in one of the severest of contemplative religious orders.) Through John Marshall and his superior, Burton Fahs, the Rockefeller Foundation initiated a patronage of the performing arts which, after this courageous and generous precedent, was later pursued by other important benefactors.

Ever since ORPHEUS, we had longed for a third work which might compose a full evening's sequence, commencing with APOLLO and ending with the tragedy of his poet-heir. But all proposals for a narrative sequel were killed by Stravinsky. By this time, through the insistence and persistence of Bob Craft, he had become increasingly occupied with the music and method of Arnold Schoenberg, Anton Webern, and Schoenberg's dodecaphonic system. As a point of departure for AGON, although the casual ballet-goer would hardly guess it, Stravinsky took two collections of French Renaissance dance melodies and adapted some twelve of them for a dozen dancers, in the twelve-tone scale which would also frame a "classic" *pas de deux* as climax.

Regarding repertory in general, and ours in particular, which is the richest extant in musical quality and variety, it has become habitual to presuppose a precious if precarious factor which has managed to get itself called "creative." This factor, not very accurately named, characterizes gifts and a relationship which Balanchine and Stravinsky shared in ways peculiar to both. Each held to an identical philosophy which precluded any consideration that what they were or did was—"creative." That is, neither invented *de novo* constructs whose root particles had not previously been in existence. For both men, "creativity" was and is a more methodical process than the opportune discovery of some flagrant chanced novelty. As far as talent, genius, or superior endowment extend, these are only viable to degrees of manipulation of extant elements, which however unsuspected or unfamiliar are always available, offering themselves to the observation and choice of self-elected sensibilities. They believed, as Albert Einstein apparently did, that "God doesn't throw dice"; that Order holds some, however fractional, advantage in cosmic play over Disorder. This imagined Order can be called God, in which case He is seen as Creator outside the dimension of time.

WESTERN
SYMPHONY

Time, as we clock it, is a fiction or device of our measuring. Before and After are loose concepts in relation to an Order which permanently *is;* God, then, is a de-timed source, the sole originator of "creative" energy, before and after whom is naught and all; whose ordering is the one possible irreversible Creative Act. Additions, contributions, selections from such ordering by individual historical brainy bipeds comment on such order but hardly "create" or "discover" anything absolutely "original." Creativity, on the human level, is simply what might be called an *uncovery* of commentary on innumerable facts of measure and order (parts of which may include disorder—chaos, hazard, cruelty, injustice, and death). Stravinsky was savage enough about certain notoriously "creative" contemporaries whom he felt were tasteful, or even erudite, anthologists whose reputations were chiefly based on aggressive idiosyncrasy. Fame formed an ephemeral aura around them which was the unique component that had any claim to having been in a true sense invented or created—however factitiously.

It's no secret that Balanchine is a creature of tradition, that he conserves past uncoveries as well as his own abandoned constructs, frames, contraptions, like a well-pruned forest from which timber may be hewn, planed, and joined to produce new furnishings. His polymorphic style, his "soulless" or impersonal manner, his belief in "angelism"—in elements, human or immaterial, that are on occasion sent—are reflected in methods which are, of necessity, economical. This attitude comes from a long and deep familiarity with a multiplicity of repetitive factors. The more these are manipulated, the more supple and dissimilar they appear, thereby gaining or retaining seeming diversity, surprise—indeed, even "originality" or "inventiveness."

Balanchine's arrant distrust of Personality, the negotiable bundle of negotiable formulae which the *prima ballerina assoluta* is wont to purvey, springs from rigorous notions of what a creator, on the terrestrial plane, may presume to be: in what manner, to what degree, performers may claim to be "creative." Stravinsky has often been accused of mannerism, that is, subservience to the styles of others—predecessors who in their turn adopted preferred habit already iterated. Stravinsky was a prime neoclassicist, subscribing to an academy which extends through the ages, having been taught by prior instructors and models—inventors, uncoverers, joiners. In the perspective (and modesty) of their judgment, these instructors recognized with dedication and gratitude their own descent from precedents which derive from a single stream, always fresh, and more potent than any purely personal rivulet diverted for a moment to green some small patch.

From the earliest times, music and dancing have depended upon mathematics and metaphysics. Recently, however, a borrowing of myth as pretext for theater has often been more a prestige-hunting literary caprice than testimony to superior order. Athletes, instrumentalists, dancers, acrobatic virtuosi who live by their bodies' central control, rather than by their minds' rationale, are rarely counted as "creative," or even as "intellectual." They "express," "interpret," "impersonate"—in fact, Realize. On the other hand, composers of music and dances, like Stravinsky and Balanchine, have supported a virtuosity in body, mind, or fingers by a structuring of ideas, but neither on an abstract level of "pure" mathematics nor in a vein of fashionable philosophizing. There are many systems of geometry more ingenious than Euclid's. To makers of a certain temperament it is important that as measures or counters, they hold historical ideas in a resonance of order and build on them. Finally, this saves time, which in theaters and concert halls must

be measured by contract hours or else by time-and-a-half charges for overtime. Knowledge of notions already enunciated anticipates errors; unviable paths have already been marked and need not be tried again. This knowledge is acquired less from fear of failure, or as insurance for success, than from recognition that many proposals have not worked and never will, that others time and again have worked and always will. Attempts to command the unworkable earn prestige for "experiment" and for what, over the last three decades, has been considered the instinctive courage of "originality." Incompetence, stubbornness, vanity, and the greedy acceptance of unthinking critical attention has not contributed much to the standard repertory, but has filled a sizable graveyard with moribund work, defunct organizations, and delinquent promises.

It is often asserted, with that naïveté which awards a facile acceptance to its own ambitions and careless authority, that Stravinsky really "put it all together" only once—in LE SACRE DU PRINTEMPS of 1913—and that, on a different scale but perhaps to a currently more relevant degree, Balanchine did the same only once, with AGON. This may be, but neither work exists in solitary self-satisfaction or containment. Elements which in one direction reach back to a pair of Renaissance dancing manuals, in another to Max Planck or Einstein, in another to Webern, Berg, or Schoenberg are braided in a collaboration which should be an admonition to creative, inventive, and original "young" choreographers who imagine that instinct, chance, personality, and loose autodidactic energy are fair substitutes for conscious measurement and concrete knowledge of more than a few faddish styles or systems.

AGON: Diana Adams, Arthur Mitchell

Stravinsky, whose Hollywood home was crammed with marvelous clocks and watches, said: "Portions of AGON contain three times as much music for the same clock-length as some other pieces of mine." AGON presents more concentrated structural dance material in twenty minutes than most nineteenth-century full-length ballets. These, apart from brief solos and extended *pas de deux*, are padded with filler pageantry in a repetitive roster of parade and pantomime, all in the insistent tempi of 4/4, 3/4, 2/4. AGON was the full harvest of Stravinsky's seventy-fifth year, half a century after APOLLON, which was a first capital proclamation of Balanchine's mature attitude and found authority. In 1968, Balanchine wrote:

Music like Stravinsky's cannot be illustrated; one must try to find a visual equivalent that is a complement rather than an illustration. And while the score of AGON was invented for dancing, it was not simple to devise dances of a comparable density, quality, metrical insistence, variety, formal mastery, or symmetrical asymmetry. Just as a cabinetmaker must select his woods for the particular job in hand—palisander, angelique, rosewood, briar, or pine—so a ballet carpenter must find dominant quality of gesture, a strain or palette of consistent movement, an active scale of flowing patterns which reveals to the eye what Stravinsky tells the sensitized ear. . . .

Stravinsky's strict beat is authority over time, and I have always felt that a choreographer should place unlimited confidence in this control. For me at any rate, Stravinsky's rhythmic invention gives the greatest stimulus. A choreographer cannot invent rhythms, he can only reflect them in movement. The body is his medium and, unaided, the body will improvise for a little while. But the organizing of rhythm on a large scale is a sustained process, a function of the musical mind. To speak of carpentry again, planning a rhythm is like planning a house; it needs a structural operation.*

Balanchine's New Complete Stories of the Great Ballets, p. 11.

MARCH, 1958: UNITED NATIONS, NEW YORK

Lunch with Dag Hammarskjöld, 38th floor of the U.N., to meet Birgit Cullberg, Swedish choreographer. Office walls hung with Matisse, Braque, Juan Gris on loan from Museum of Modern Art. He asked if Wystan Auden could not "write a ballet" for Miss Cullberg. He showed us the new Meditation Room with its table altar made of polished iron ore, one of the hardest substances known.

Anyone operating the arts as a public service holds constant and constantly frustrated dreams of encountering a Lorenzo de Medici, a Catherine the Great, or in our democratic republic, at least a Thomas Jefferson, a Theodore or Franklin Roosevelt. American Maecenases like J. P. Morgan, Sr., or John D. Rockefeller, Jr., left rich legacies of visual art, not alone in magnificent panels, canvases, and tapestries but in painted and printed books, written pages, and precious objects. Yet in New York, of all tycoons in his generation and the one after it, only Otto H. Kahn had much affection for lyric theater, and that mainly as an adjunct to the Metropolitan Opera House. The first Roosevelt admired our greatest sculptor and obtained from Augustus Saint-Gaudens our finest gold coinage. In a serious Depression Franklin Roosevelt (through Harry Hopkins) sponsored many excellent artists and even theater projects which (under Hallie Flanagan) included dancing, before a churlish Congress killed its great possibilities as "boondoggling." It is almost impossible to imagine discussing the specifics of theatrical sponsorship or performance with most heads of state, enmeshed as they may be in obligations more pressing than the cultivation of popular taste or pleasures of the mind. None of our elected leaders could compose for the violin as well as Frederick the Great, or execute an *entrechat* as well as Lully's star dancer, *Le Roi Soleil*. Only Jefferson, as an enlightened amateur and student of Palladio, brought a cultivated mind to his commonwealth as a matter of course.

Dag Hammarskjöld was something approaching a philosopher-king. His appreciation of poetry, painting, and skills in performance was neither pretense nor light adornment. He had a warm heart, cool hand, and cold eye; he was born to a manner of life which was luxuriously equipped with ideas and their concrete realization—well-framed, well-printed, well-played. He had little embarrassment or hesitation in talking to technicians; artists did not frighten him; they genuinely interested him, as did scientists, mountain climbers, soldiers, pilots, and politicians. He was happily aware of his position as secretary-general and employed his modest panoply of office at the United Nations toward the furthering of those arts whose exchange might serve international understanding. He forwarded the nomination of Saint-John Perse (the French diplomat Alexis Saint-Léger Léger) for the Nobel Prize, although there was resistance from de Gaulle's Quai d'Orsay at that time. He visited the City Center often, became a good friend of Wystan Auden's in both his official chambers and the seclusion of his home, and lent the considerable energy of his support to our efforts and those of many others.

He was not in any casual sense an easily humorous man. In a personal, even priestly commitment he felt afflicted by this world's evil and presumed himself capable, to some degree, of its alleviation. Indeed, he felt chosen for services and sacrifice. A "sense of humor" usually means quick reaction to the comic, ridiculous, or preposterous, but humors that he possessed were so attuned to endemic horror and tragedy on a global scale that, although he had a ready smile and much personal charm, he found little that was superficially amusing. Nor was he exactly "humorless," but pressure from the world's woes were more commanding, seen from his thirty-eighth-floor windows, than individual appetite.

the New York City Ballet

This perspective extended far past his own pleasure. He permitted himself appreciation of pictures and poems as symbolic delectation. He felt that those responsible for the weal of nations do well to acknowledge the healing aspects of art as the purest memorials of men's best hope.

Balanchine, in a fit of what was taken by some to be sheer perversity, now chose to exploit the treasure of our best brass-band master, John Philip Sousa. When asked why, why, why, he replied: "Because I like his *music*." This was not alone for Sousa's famous martial marches, but also for portions of an opera and other forgotten pieces. Hershy Kay, who had done yeoman service for WESTERN SYMPHONY, turned his talent to rearranging Sousa's brass choirs for symphonic orchestra with strings and woodwinds. Balanchine carefully indicated the instrumentation. The grand *pas de deux* would be scored not for violins, but for plaintive vinegary brass, with the tuba blatantly predominant. This he saw as a tribute to Dwight Eisenhower, in his senior year at West Point, engaged to Mamie Doud. The ballet was conceived as a musical joke, and STARS AND STRIPES was generally received as such, then and since.

Not by Dag Hammarskjöld. He was a stranger to Radio City Music Hall and the Rockettes in their perennial patriotic drills. He had no comprehension of Balanchine's parodistic irony, his ingenuity in transforming a vaudeville parade into balletic beauty; and in the finale when an enormous Old Glory unfurled itself as a gigantic backdrop, swept by a storm of wind machines, the secretary-general took offense. Such a display approached a call to arms, a shameless exhibition of chauvinist sentiment when Korea still spelled war, and this planet could do with a lot less flag-waving. There was nothing one could do to explain, as a gloss on the background of the ballet. The fact that the finale brought a loud and wryly enthusiastic demonstration, which in itself was a parody of patriotism, was no help. We had to suffer one of the worst pains this side of physical torture —enduring an inexplicably and hopelessly false position. We were not warmongers; we were even gentle censors of preposterous hyper-Americanism. But Hammarskjöld judged that the cause of peace among nations was not served by the blatant effrontery of our imperialist gesture.

Hammarskjöld was also a student of the classics and knew that antique myths of aggression, envy, and revenge were no more legendary than reports in the daily papers. He admired Balanchine's ORPHEUS and APOLLO; he was a patron of Birgit Cullberg, choreographer at the Royal Opera in Stockholm, and brought us together. She was shy, energetic, appealing. She proposed her already successful melodramatic ballet on Euripedes' version of the legend of Jason and Medea, to Bartók music, for Melissa Hayden, our strongest dramatic ballerina, with Jacques d'Amboise and Violette Verdy. This legend had prompted the most popular of Noverre's reformative *choréodrames* in many recensions through the eighteenth century all over Europe. Balanchine, as always, was pleased to entrust his company to someone, indeed anyone, other than himself, on the chance of broadening our basic repertory. Miss Cullberg's MEDEA played well enough. There were problems about dragging her two murdered children offstage without scraping their shins; a ruby light which meant murder spelled gelatin rather than blood. MEDEA remained in repertory for some seasons; it was mortally serious and provided energetic exercise for its loyal dancers. It was a European, or rather a Northern European, concept which was not hard for an American company and audience to adopt. Hammarskjöld infinitely preferred it to STARS AND STRIPES. Also, he had performed his function as a Swedish civil servant and world citizen. We had done ours as representatives of a quasi-municipal institution; neither were much the worse for it.

AGON: Stravinsky and Balanchine rehearsing Mitchell and Adams

Balanchine and Stravinsky

MEDEA: Birgit Cullberg rehearsing

APRIL, 1958: TOKYO

In the palace, performance of Gagaku by dancers and musicians of the imperial household. Splendid ceremonials, part religious, part military, of enormous gravity, elegance, and strangeness. A chamberlain took us through the huge greenhouses, with wonderful bonsai, centuries old, arranged in miniature landscapes. A daughter of the emperor at our performance. In the intermission, a private audience. Ice cream, like malachite flannel, but delicious. My left big toe stuck out through a hole in my sock. She regarded it with interest; neither of us smiled.

In those days, the flight to Japan took thirty-six hours. We broke the trip at Wake Island, sleeping fitfully in old Army barracks. Most of our Tokyo performances took place in an arena used more often for boxing than ballet. To hide the scene changes the curtain rose from the floor rather than fell; there was a topsy-turvy quality to the whole town. Tickets had been completely distributed on some mysterious schedule by which few were available for sale, while the auditorium was usually half empty. However, the experience and existence of Japan was so amazing, provocative, and compelling that we scarcely bothered to worry about audiences. That had become our embassy's problem, to manage as it might.

Having been raised in Boston, where from clipper-ship days there had been an exchange of tea and artifacts between West and East, I knew the oriental wing of the Museum of Fine Arts, but its wealth of Chinese and Japanese carving and pictures had always blurred vaguely in my eyes, schooled to look mostly at French or Italian painting. I told myself there was no use trying to absorb the Orient: "East is East." But at boarding school, aged thirteen, I'd made friends with a lean, diminutive Japanese who spoke good English although he'd not been away from home before. In a log cabin in the woods we cooked and ate two pounds of crisp bacon with no drastic result, while he told me true adventure stories about himself and his land. His name was Jujun

Balanchine rehearsing Tallchief

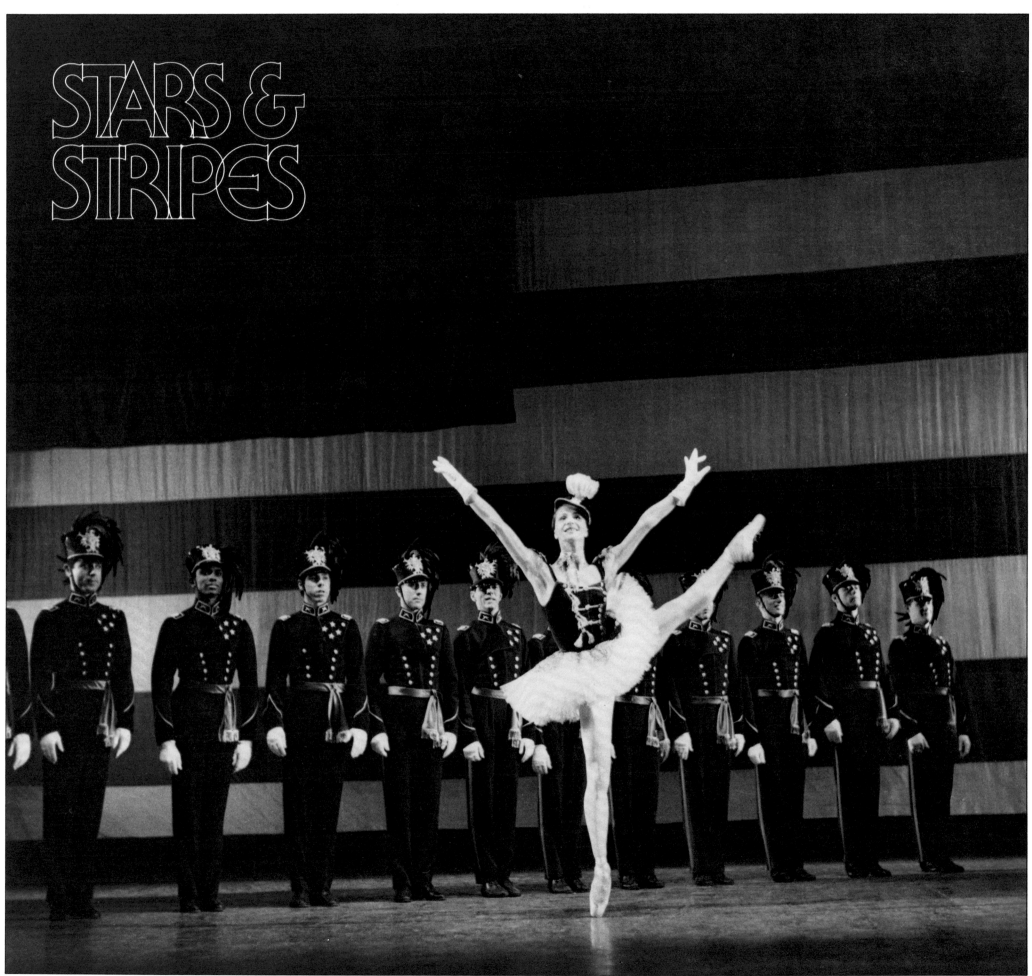

STARS & STRIPES

Melissa Hayden

Saigo; once he played with an imperial princeling around a palace pool, in which swam ancient coral-colored carp. The prince, a twig of his own age, wore a dress-kimono gloriously embroidered with the identical fish. Saigo wished to wear it more than anything in his life. He contrived to trip himself up over the brink; splash! With obligatory largesse, the prince hauled him out, dried him off, and wrapped him in the gorgeous fishy garment. The image of those carp, swimming in silk, stayed in my mind for forty years. Jujun himself disappeared one night, recalled to Japan by his father's death; doubtless to further adventures with carp and princes.

At a pleasant reception given by the American ambassador, conversation grew thin. I asked an obviously Westernized guest the kind of tourist's question that makes natives smile: "Do you happen to know a Mr. Saigo?" This gentleman replied: "Ah, so. He is that gray-haired man there." It was indeed Saigo. This was but one of a train of "coincidences," if such they were, which convinced me I'd come to Japan to fulfill some special purpose, that I'd always been coming, to find a style of life to be embraced with no further persuasion, as if I had always known it.

We were lucky in latching onto Donald Richie, then dance critic on the *Japan Times,* who'd lived in Tokyo since the first days of our military occupation and who was intimately in touch with an area which few foreigners ever penetrate. He held an open sesame to an extralegal, subterranean society which one could barely believe in, yet it existed in a downtown section which had alarming resemblances to the less protected parts of Brooklyn. In Shinjuku, the district in which our theater stood, a submerged life went on under the fierce hierarchy of gangs and fearsome, masterless men, much as it had since the seventeenth century. The Americans had reduced the local police to the status of traffic cops, but Richie knew the men who really ran the wards.

We were invited to watch, at six in the morning, the daily practice of unfledged sumo wrestlers, whose uncropped hair had not yet been tied up in the professional chignon. Big boys trooped in from the provinces to seek patronage, fame, and fortune in this proudly competitive and ritualized sport. Few aspirants ever reached those heights where, forcibly fed like Strassbourg geese, they were enthroned as imperturbable monsters of a majestic championage. Through Donald Richie and his friend, the adventurous publisher Meredith Weatherby, an early intimate of Yukio Mishima and patron of many Japanese writers and craftsmen, I met Masayuki Nagare. An ex-Kamikaze pilot, a sword maker, and now a master carver of the most intractable granite in his islands, Nagare would in a few years be executing important sculpture for the United States. Together we spent a memorable week in Kyoto, where he showed me the entire panoply of surviving martial sports, and not only kendo, judo, eikido, karate, archery, sacred football, and jiu-jitsu, but also water walking and the traditional women's fencing with staff, ball, and chain. Most marvelous of all was nin-jitsu, the skill of samurai espionage: sudden vanishment and bilocation, the art of being seen in two distinct places at once—a mystery to be mastered by all theater directors.

Members of our company became acquainted with dancers and musicians of the imperial household. In the spring of 1959, through Dag Hammarskjöld's diplomatic brand of occidental wizardry, for the first time in a thou-

sand years the oldest ballet company in the world left the palace precincts and their own islands. They performed their splendid sober ceremonial dances first under Hammarskjöld's aegis in the General Assembly hall of the United Nations, and later for a season on the same program with our own company at the City Center. In Washington, Mrs. Dwight Eisenhower received them on a memorable afternoon at Dumbarton Oaks, where they danced in the open air on a reproduction of their own red-and-gold stage against a background of magnolia japonica. For one of their dances they used branches of keyaki, the sacred laurel, one of the many exotic plants in the beautiful gardens endowed by Robert and Mildred Bliss for the nation.

In Osaka we opened a handsome new festival hall, sharing programs with the Soviet State Symphony. This was the finest new theater in which we had so far played. Later we would inaugurate auditoriums in Seattle, Montreal, and Saratoga, as well as our own home in Lincoln Center. There is a special excitement in facing the hazards of untried houses, including unexpected pitfalls which no architect is ever able to anticipate.

As for sightseeing in Japan, there were innumerable marvels, but for me the foremost would remain Noh drama performed in Kyoto's old wooden theater. "Perfection" is a word whose claim and meaning are so subjective that pronouncing it brings on a sense of superstitious awe lest this highest accolade shrink to nonsense. If perfection means anything, it is something approach-

ing the irreducible gleam and wholeness of pure gold, faceted diamonds, or the evening star. Noh is the only theater I'd dare call "perfect" in sight, sound, gesture, symbol, without offending those guardian spirits who estimate excellence in the performing arts. Removed to its proper dimension, far from occidental time and space, yet no more verbally incomprehensible than *bel canto* Italian opera, its essence glows like an even blaze of camphor logs—azure, sulphur, malachite—or the wings of a dragon moth fixed in translucent amber. But Noh defeats rhetoric, and is itself defeated when transferred fragmentarily to the West. It demands its immaculate pine walkway and floor, its own curved canopy and painted pines, its own airless airs. In the West, Noh seems like a beautiful pebble brought home from the shore which loses its sheen in your pocket on the way home.

Once, when I was working on TWELFTH NIGHT with Katharine Hepburn, she grew impatient at my voluble criteria of perfection in past performances. She held that the term indicates only a state of mind, a splinter from personal memory. For me it was Noh; for her it was the mating dance of Australian lyrebirds she'd come on somewhere in the bush. Sometimes in performances of ballet, energy is glimpsed in crystal fractions of precise movement, attached like invisible silk to music's structure. In the West I have never seen a sustained peak of ordered action simulating emotion that lasts for more than twenty minutes. In Noh, it is visible for hours at a sitting.

NIGHT SHADOW: Allegra Kent

PICNIC AT TINTAGEL: Jacques d'Amboise, Diana Adams

JANUARY, 1959: NEW YORK

With Martha Graham, discussing possibility of a collaborative work half by her, half by Balanchine, in which part of her company could dance in ours and vice versa. Spoke of key characters of feminine distinction so far unattempted, she having already drawn from ancient Greece, the Bible, Joan of Arc. I proposed Alice in Wonderland, which seems to me the essence of Martha's spirit; she thought I meant the Red Queen or Ugly Duchess. But she consented to consider Elizabeth or Mary, Queen of Scots.

I met Martha Graham through Frances Hawkins, her early manager, when they shared an apartment. I had been in college with Erick Hawkins who, among other roles, danced Powhatan, the Indian chief, in Elliott Carter's POCAHONTAS. He left us to join Graham's company and later married her. I had written an unpleasant piece about her, mainly on the basis of her self-designed solo as the Chosen Maiden in Massine's version of LE SACRE DU PRINTEMPS under Stokowski. (This was the first American-staged performance in an initial proprietary crusade for the classic dance.) However, at Bennington College, where she was artist-in-residence when our Caravan performed there, I had suffered a conversion upon seeing her perform as various personae of an Indian princess in her processional AMERICAN DOCUMENT. She taught me many things, including the importance of keeping a more humble, open eye on the Orient, its ideas and objects. This had long been one of her vital sources, gained partly through association with Ruth St. Denis. We met again when, under the auspices of Merle Armitage, our Caravan first played Los Angeles in 1938. I knew and admired Louis Horst, Martha's musical collaborator, who had a consuming interest in preclassic dance forms. In my ignorance I had thought that these were the property of ballet alone, but he appropriated them as a teaching system for choreographic structure and made them the ideological basis for his work with a generation of heterodox modernists. My contact with Graham was of some duration, despite temperamental differences which were apparent in the nature of our separate preoccupations.

Around 1952 Balanchine learned about the figure and fate of Anton von Webern. Bob Craft had recently brought Webern's sonorities to the attention of Stravinsky, with whom they became a seminal enthusiasm. Balanchine himself had not so far been attracted by atonal music. To him, as he said, Schoenberg stood as the Albert Einstein of twelve-tone systems, incomparable in his own genre but useless for dancing. Craft was then in the process of recording Webern's entire work, and Balanchine wrote later:

I listened to everything and liked it. The songs were the best of all, but they were written to be listened to [only, with their words]. The orchestral music, however, fills air like molecules: it is written for atmosphere. The first time I heard it, I knew it could be danced to.*

*Balanchine's New Complete Stories of the Great Ballets, p. 133.

Stravinsky was asked if, in the end, he did not think Webern's music "too narrow in scope." He answered in words which apply also to his own manipulation of temporal measure and dimensions:

[Too narrow in scope?] Not for Webern . . . I cannot understand the word in musical terms. Webern's time-scale is tiny, his quantity is minute, the variety of his forms is small, but whether these are measurements of scope I am unable to say. If, for example, scope is also a question of depth and not merely width and expanse, then Webern's can be very great. . . .*

As was his usual method with unfamiliar scores, Balanchine took the Webern piece he had chosen and transcribed much of the orchestration for a rehearsal piano, committing new sound and structure to memory for prompt use in plastic composition. The title—EPISODES—had stuck in our minds ever since Pavel Tchelitchev had, before World War II, proposed his spectacle to us and to Martha Graham. He imagined her as a feminine archetype, partner to his troika of Don Quixote, Don Juan, and Hamlet, corresponding to the ideals of Dulcinea the rational innocent, the various women who were Don Juan's victims, a guilty Gertrude, and a daft Ophelia. Like most of his fancies they never achieved the stage, but they stuck in our memories stronger than many sights actually seen. The notion of interchanging dancers shuttling between our two groups was only partially realized. From our side, Sallie Wilson portrayed Queen Elizabeth with authority, while Graham lent us Paul Taylor. For him Balanchine invented a variation of such fey eccentricity within the range of his highly articulated athletic presence that we soon had requests from other "modern" dancers for similar extensions of their possibility.

EPISODES I (Graham's section), was based on Webern's Opus 1 and Opus 6 (both from 1909), composed before he'd found Schoenberg's use of the twelve-tone row. The opening *Passacaglia*, followed by his Six Pieces for Orchestra, summarized and canonized the passion of Mary of Scotland's memories as she mounts the scaffold in Fotheringhay Castle. Francis Mason encapsulates the action:

The setting is austere, a black platform across the back of the stage with steps on both sides approaching it; in the center of the platform stands a black box and a halberd-like heraldic device. The music begins with an ominous plucking of strings. Mary, in black, stands below, tense. Her stiff dress seems both to armor and to imprison her. Suddenly high on the platform, she is free of it, stepping out as a young girl in white to meet her lover Bothwell. She comes down again and her black dress remains standing like an empty cage on the platform, accusing her worldliness. She rejects the crown-craving Bothwell, the love of her life, and is in torment.

Four girls now dress Mary in blood red and she begins her long contest with Queen Elizabeth of England. The music shifts to the *Six Pieces for Orchestra*. The black box on the platform becomes a throne. Elizabeth sits there in burnished gold. She descends. The two queens play a fateful game of tennis, a formal court tennis.

As Elizabeth wins, she is lifted high. Mary then sits for a moment on the throne. But now the throne is the scaffold. Mary

*Igor Stravinsky and Robert Craft, *Themes and Episodes*, Alfred A. Knopf, New York, 1966, p. 117.

EPISODES: Paul Taylor

Paul Taylor

Martha Graham

EPISODES

kneels before it, the tall halberd, now an ax, turns in the air and a bright red light illumines her cast-off queenly garb.*

Madame Karinska's spiderweb carapaces and freestanding farthingales worn by the rival queens were simultaneously costumes, props, and scenery. David Hays's austere planes and steps stacked with heraldic emblems were spiky, mineral, as leanly profiled as Webern's thorny sonorities. Too soon, when it became impractical for Martha Graham to appear in our repertory because our separate schedules seldom coincided, her entire section was abandoned. Paul Taylor departed also to pursue his independent course, and there was no one remotely capable of replacing him. His oddly mindless mask, sub- or super-human, the peculiar quality of his cheerful in- or a-humanity implementing a serpentine athleticism, exactly corresponded to Webern's fractured glass-snake noises. We called him the Geek; he had his own sweet and sour individuality; one might have wished he'd been trained early as a ballet dancer rather than beginning, as he did, as a crack swimmer.

The effect of our original EPISODES (I and II) cannot be recovered from its present truncated version. Not only was Graham's realization memorable, but the occasion itself—her unique symbolic association with the traditional academic dance—provided an ephemeral piquancy not to be repeated. Balanchine's furiously contorted solo variation for Paul Taylor was a statement of such extreme virtuosic perversity in its angular deformation that it almost seemed an insult to a splendid physique. Not only was the dance, and Paul's performance, outlandishly violent—a prolonged acrobatic motor sequence of anguished sound strung on negative gesture ranging from purr to scratch or buzz to strangle —but it prefaced, in dramatic reversal of mood and meaning, the ballet's finale, changing from his extended solo to our full company. The last part of EPISODES II is still danced to Webern's praise of Johann Sebastian Bach, in the "Ricercata for Six Voices from Bach's *Musical Offering.*"It is an elaborate structure of elevation and grandeur, wholly divested of deformation or commentary, simply expressing the noblest progression in formal dynamics, a sort of *heilige Dankgesang*, a sacred danced song ending with a tremendous organ chord supported by cymbals. It was an assertion—particularly after Paul

Balanchine's New Complete Stories of the Great Ballets, p. 134.

Taylor's long preface of madly tortured, whimsically anxious, captiously awkward movement—of rational wholeness and humane order.

Predictably, there were passionate partisans of both persuasions, one group vowing that Balanchine should never have worked alongside Graham and another, even more loyal, grieving that she had betrayed nonconformism by permitting herself commerce with the enemy. Actually there was no formal contact between the two sections. A stage was shared; an orchestra offered a bridge for the passage of two disparate visions, one plastically dramatic, the other plastically musical. An event took place which could not have been achieved without the contact or juxtaposition of such discrete elements. There was no lessening of integrity or intensity in either partner, nor was there the least intimation of competition or comparison. Two teams mutually respected their totally opposed disciplines, and an audience shared the incandescent integrity of a peculiar but satisfactory proposal.

DECEMBER, 1959: NEW YORK

To Morton Baum's with Betty Cage, to convince him we were about to receive (as of January, 1960) a subvention from the Shah of Iran toward THE FIGURE IN THE CARPET. Again Baum brought up the possibility of Brahms's Liebeslieder Walzer. We couldn't produce the Shah or any cash. Short of either, he was unenthusiastic, more interested in PANAMERICA; Brazil and Cuba are closer to home.

Since she had fallen ill and required Colorado's high air, Frances Hawkins had ceased to be our general manager. Her friend and apprentice Betty Cage took on the protean task of being at once labor negotiator, certified public accountant, legal expert, mother superior, confessor, psychiatrist, and practicing witch (white magic). In New York she had worked for Miss Steloff of the Gotham Book Mart. Hence she had come to us well-schooled in handling problems of production which involved ideas, artists, money and the lack of it, excess temperament, and hysteria. While not a trained dancer, she was expert in the classical Chinese discipline of Tai-chi and wrote an excellent manual of its exercises. She had more than casual knowledge of I-Ching, the Tarot pack, and other arcane aids for the fate and facts of life. We despaired

when Frances Hawkins was forced to leave, since her contacts with Morton Baum had been breezy, close, and tidy. She was parsimonious of time and funds, while keeping Balanchine busy producing as much and as fast as conditions allowed. Now Morton Baum came to trust Betty Cage implicitly and tried not to threaten or trouble us with any more dire warnings than necessary, faced as he was with permanent crises. These were not precisely daily bankruptcies, but closely resembled them. Insistence on penurious budgets was something we'd come to live by after a decade of his sponsorship, but Baum was enough of an artist to know that constant poor-mouthing lessened scope in ingenuity and imagination.

Betty Cage came to us already skilled, and would become infinitely more proficient, in the science and pursuit of the possible and impossible. She was accessible, as was Baum, all day and far into the night. By nature taciturn, quizzical, detached, unflappable, she sensed tension before it flared and judged dressing-room gossip for precisely what it was worth. I might be upset by demonstrations of individual erratic behavior; she remained diagnostic, surgical, placatory. She had never seen a wholly "happy" performer, or any who, because of unhappiness, did less than his best in performance. "Happiness," at least in our odd family, was an ideal spread of milk and honey, a golden luxury we could never afford. She accepted strikes or threats of strikes with equanimity; they would pass, like worse disasters— important personal ones, like broken ankles and snapped Achilles' tendons, and collective ones, like the cancellation of promised patronage. As a substitute for applied "happiness," she offered a patient ear, lively mind, dispassionate style, and rational belief in powers superior to the fevers and complaints of lawyers, bankers, and dancers.

The Fourth International Congress of Iranian Art and Archaeology was to be held in Manhattan in April, 1960, under the high auspices of the Shahinshah of Iran and the President of the United States. In 1934, as our final gesture for *Hound & Horn*, we had issued a plump homage to Henry James, reviving a lapsed interest in the intricate patterns of his fiction. His phrase "the figure in the carpet" was a resonant metaphor which stuck in the memory, to serve now as a possible rallying cry for a demon-

THE FIGURE IN THE CARPET

Betty Cage

stration of the mystery of design, at least in one important visual sector.

I had long ago encountered Dr. Arthur Upham Pope, the dean of American scholars in the field of Iranian culture, and fallen victim to his subtle and persuasive enthusiasm. Years before, he had guided Edward Warburg through Persia, so I caught a sense of his fantastic gifts in "seduction" and thereby obtaining subvention for his encyclopedic publications on ancient Persian monuments.

Now Dr. Pope showed us an extraordinary construct laid out on a big table. At first sight it appeared to be a scrupulously rendered reduction of the interlace of a famous Ardabil rug. However, it was not painted on a single surface, but rather on half a dozen transparent plastic sheets. Each represented a separate system in the design, and when they were placed in the combined order of the rug's all-but-illegible intricacy, they vibrated as a single rich whole. A map of warp and woof, when "the figure in the carpet" was thus analyzed and demonstrated, it no longer seemed a confused vibration of quivering fields of color on one plane, but a chart in dimensional depth of a formal garden which supported a life of its own. The silk plush calligraphy of symbolic clouds, birds, streams, trees was arranged in a tufted mosaic governing a visionary oasis. Carpets laid down on desert sands were originally fictive gardens; their threaded paths and pools wove pleasure and relief from fatigue and heat. The diagrammatic carpet which Dr. Pope demonstrated to our designer, Esteban Francés, was transformed into dances framed as a Franco-Persian court fete. They suggested the age in which the arabesque of Islamic ornament wove itself into Western European fashion and design, just as the *arabesque*, our ballet position, fixed the place of Islam in a royal academy of dancing at Versailles.

The accompaniment was Handel's *Royal Fireworks* and *Water Music* suites. In a prologue, "The Sands of the Desert," Balanchine visualized shifting dunes, before rain transformed dead sand into live gardens. "The Weaving of the Carpet" was a *pas d'action* in which nomad tribesmen shuttled strands in a metaphor of long, multicolored ribbons weaving back and forth to fill the stage like a huge loom. "The Building of the Palace" framed an imperial reception for foreign ambassadors, including those from Scotland, France, Peru, Spain, and Africa, fitting écossaise, rigaudon, chaconne, bourrée, and other forms loosely and fancifully based on folk material in Handel's time. After this parade of national entries, the Prince and Princess of Persia, heirs of the Great Sophy, performed their stylized *pas de deux*. The evening's *raison d'être* was a demonstration of the carpet's figuration in its structural overlays, realized as a sequence of pierced and painted drops which descended, one after the other, to majestic strains which may first have been heard behind a royal barge on the Thames. The audience was instructed, as from a gigantic blackboard, in how carpets were woven in the logical design of their symbolic ornament. For a final *bonne bouche*, in "The Fountains of Heaven" there was a Persian garden, inspired by a miniature from a manuscript *Book of Kings*, with a real fountain from whose multiple jets spouted streams which splashed into a tank (weighing tons). Although the Shah-

inshah's subsidy never arrived, an assemblage of Iranian scholars were happy for an evening. But the ballet was too unwieldy to maintain. Costumes were cannibalized for other more useful divertissements. While we sometimes spoke of revival, THE FIGURE IN THE CARPET too soon became a wistful memory.

At this time we also busied ourselves, under the guidance of Maestro Carlos Chávez, Mexico's senior composer and symphonic organizer, with an evening of Pan-American dancing and orchestral music, including six representative scores. Balanchine shared choreographic obligations with Gloria Contreras, a Mexican dancer and student at our school. Francisco Moncion, who was born in the Dominican Republic, produced a piece by Villa-Lobos. In 1941 in Buenos Aires, we had commissioned ESTANCIA from young Alberto Ginastera, but war had intervened to prevent its production. John Taras, who had been on tour with us at the time, now took music by Ginastera for the basis of a ballet which was perhaps the most convincing of the evening. Jacques d'Amboise used a suite by the Uruguayan Héctor Tosar Errecart; Balanchine chose music from Cuba and Colombia by Julián Orbón and Luis Antonio Escobar. We handed out pretty programs in accordion pleats, printed on brightly colored tissues like those for fiestas and bullfights; but one can hardly pretend that such occasional events are viable for very long after their introduction. However, our attempt to explore new music of quality, with the aid of so capable an authority as Carlos Chávez, had some justification, while it indicated to Governor Rockefeller that we had not forgotten provinces south of the border. Although the scores selected had small staying power, a pleasing variety sprang from valid indigenous material orchestrated with tact, if without commanding theatricality. The experiment was worth pursuing, but it also reinforced the statistics showing that of all the novelties we introduced from whatever source, less than a third stayed in repertory past three seasons; and that of those that stuck, a majority were by Balanchine. Yet novelty did spice our seasons. Increasingly we came to provide liveliness and interest which attracted and held a growing public.

JANUARY, 1960: ALBANY, NEW YORK

Special train at Grand Central to bring company to Albany for Nelson Rockefeller's inauguration. Rehearsal of STARS AND STRIPES on a miserable stage in the state armory, accompanied by hammering, bunting, balloons, etc. Nelson looked in to see if all was well; ordered more lights. Spoke briefly to him on need for proper space for state occasions. His ideas for the construction of an enormous complex of government buildings. Program ran late, but the train to New York was held.

It seemed suitable that we appear at his inaugural when Nelson Rockefeller was first elected governor. We performed a similar service, also in an armory, for President Kennedy and later in tribute to Lyndon Johnson. Maria Tallchief and André Eglevsky had danced in the White House for General Eisenhower in 1953; later Melissa Hayden, Patricia McBride, and Edward Villella would entertain Mr. and Mrs. Nixon in the same big room.

On a high political level, the arts in this country have intermittently enjoyed the status of adornment, if never that of a national institution. Jefferson was an amateur of music, Lincoln an acute critic of Shakespearean acting. Mr. Truman, on occasion, played the piano, and he, like Mr. Nixon, enjoyed historical films with military pretexts. The Kennedys graced their entourage with celebrated performers, and in one of Mrs. Kennedy's early official engagements she had Balanchine to tea in the White House. But Nelson Rockefeller constantly built and pared his own collections, realizing that objects have a life of their own, independent of transient "owners," who are bound by a responsibility of present arrangement and ultimate disposition. While he had always taken advice from experts—notably René d'Harnoncourt, Robert Goldwater, Alfred H. Barr, Jr., and Dorothy Miller—it was his personal preference which guided his

Diana Adams,
Suzanne Farrell,
Gelsey Kirkland

MONUMENTUM PRO GESUALDO

first choice, and usually those secondary ones, which are more revelatory, secure, and final. Some of this collector's attention he allocated to Balanchine, and through him, to our school, dancers, and audiences, in ways which he's never cared to claim. However, he put us on paths of public acceptance and provided a chance for finding our permanent home. He appreciated what our special or immediate situation merited, just as he understood differences between Sèvres and Chinese export porcelain, or masks used in the Sepik valley or on a Noh stage.

Balanchine was reared as a cadet attached to an imperial household. The czar in person gave presents to the younger students in the ballet school at Christmas parties. Hence Balanchine found the profession of courtier easy to practice when he became attached to Diaghilev — who in his own youth had served as *chambellan de la cour* and knew from experience the hopes and hazards of court life. In the United States, ensigns of power support a "democratic" style, but behavior in the vicinity of potentates is often more servile, insecure, and frightened than it is under the symbolic authority of two purely honorific climates: the lapsed divine rights of the Court of St. James and those of Kyoto and Edo — where tradition is still strong, succession is by birth rather than election, and each hierarchical and historical level is defined. In America, presidents are only private persons before election and become so again after their brief exercise of authority. Thus a president's encouragement of anything as ephemeral or occasional as art in performance is often capricious, cosmetic, or compassionate, reflecting what is, at best, loose taste on a level of domestic, intermittent, and lightly prized populist entertainment. In America we often congratulate ourselves that art patronage is a private function whose exercise is personal, an evidence mainly of the patron's current affluence. Often as not it has been neither discriminating nor far-reaching.

Institutional theater in particular, including the musical theater, is a living organism which needs nurture from the hearts and minds of qualified authorities for deployment to people who require such skilled and disciplined service. The accelerating permanent crisis of privately (under-) endowed, charitable tax-exempt agencies, whether these be museums, repertory theaters, symphony orchestras, operas, or ballet companies, can no longer in the last quarter of the twentieth century be supported or even alleviated by systems which suited patronage throughout the nineteenth. Government must eventually presuppose that these arts and skills are no less redundant than other necessaries for the public weal. What Europe with its hereditary and hierarchical precedents offers by way of models is less quality in arts, which one way or another produce themselves come what may, than chances resident in continuity. This only means an advance over accident or improvisation, a degree of security and a decency of social recognition which permits performing artists the minimal but basic status of civil servants. For performers are indeed in public service, working for a large audience and utilized as well for political duty past their own borders.

With our company, a sense of paternal, possibly paternalistic, responsibility and consideration has been as strong as conditions allow, given the economy or society in which we exist. To make attractive or impose what must be an aristocratic, elitist discipline upon an anarchic, permissive, heterogeneous source of material has been one of our school's chief problems and accomplishments. Such arbitrary powers emanating from a central authority separate the goats from the sheep, men from boys, ordinary girls from ballerinas. It is not a position or attitude which accommodates facile affection, mass popularity, or much comprehension from the multitude. It is not at all "democratic," but it has its own electorate, and candidates inclined toward the profession nominate themselves without a constituency other than that proposed by individual temperament and capacity.

Through hundreds of years in which order, security, stability, identity were expressed in a criterion of excellence maintained through the paradigm of public gardens, building, singing, dancing, standards were proclaimed by the location of peak excellence under peak patronage. The product was sometimes inferior to the symbol, but nowhere and at no time during social or political revolution, when the ostensible villains were tyrants or crowned heads, did schools or theaters manifesting art in performance stay shut for long. Lyric theater has been constantly carried as one more blazing decoration contributing to the visible glory of common wealth. In the process, the courtier's skill is no less necessary than it has always been. A consciousness of its proper exercise can be gained through the pages of Machiavelli's *Prince*. A far more useful current guide is offered by the Jesuit Baltasar Gracián, theologian of Tarragona, whose *Truthtelling Manual and Art of Worldly Wisdom* dates from 1653:

Of Cultivated Taste. It can be cultivated even as the intelligence: the better the appreciation, the greater the appetite, and when fulfilled, the greater the enjoyment. Greatness of spirit is known by the richness of the things needed to gratify it; for it takes much to satisfy a great capacity; just as much food is required for great hunger: even so does the sublime in spirit demand the sublime in matter. The boldest objects of nature fear this judgment of taste; and the finest in art trembles before it: few are the stars of the first magnitude, let appreciation of them be equally choice. Taste and contract have a way of going together, and the inheritance is in line: wherefore he is fortunate who may consort with those who have taste at its best. But neither should a trade be made of dissatisfaction with everything, for that is the extreme of fools, and odious in proportion to its affectation, and its intemperateness. Some would wish God to create another world, and of wholly different ideals, in order to satisfy their crazy phantasies.*

APRIL, 1960: NEW YORK

Meeting at the Century Club to discuss possibilities of Lincoln Center for Music, Inc. Overwhelming representation of interlocking directorate from Met and Philharmonic. I suggested that a representative of organized labor be elected to the board; also that the name be Lincoln Center for the Performing Arts, since dance and perhaps film would ultimately be constituents; seconded by Anthony Bliss. Conversation with Bliss about future position of City Center of Music & Drama at Lincoln Center.

The Metropolitan Opera Association had long needed a new home. No one knew better than we the inconvenience and dangers of the appealing old palace on 39th Street. In its last days, we joined with others to try to

* Baltasar Gracián, *Truthtelling Manual and Art of Worldly Wisdom* (translated by Martin Fisher), Charles C. Thomas, Springfield, Ill., 1934, p. 67.

MONUMENTUM PRO GESUALDO

the New York City Ballet

previous page: The Snow Scene
top: Shaun O'Brien as Drosselmeyer
bottom: Allegra Kent and Conrad Ludlow
as the Sugarplum Fairy and her Cavalier

top: Soldiers and mice
bottom: Melissa Hayden and Jacques d'Amboise
as the Sugarplum Fairy and her Cavalier

above: Robert Weiss as Candy Cane

top left: Waltz of the Flowers — Kay Mazzo
middle left: Tea — Deni Lamont
bottom left: Finale — Patricia Wilde, Conrad Ludlow
above: Melissa Hayden, Christopher d'Amboise

above: Mother Ginger and her polichinelles
next page: Farewell

prevent its demolition. Odds were against preservation or conversion to other use, for good enough reasons. The cost of restoring the structure to conditions which would conform to rudimentary fire department regulations would have been more than half enough to build a new house. If it was converted, by some off chance, it might conceivably have been turned over to a troublesome poor relation (like the New York City Opera Company) which hardly deserved such grandeur. And in some vague future, such a poor relation might pose a threat to the Metropolitan Opera's absolute control similar to that which the Met faced when it suppressed Oscar Hammerstein's insurgent Manhattan Company in 1910.

If the Met by itself could have built a new home, it would surely have done so, and there would have been no great need or even excuse for Lincoln Center. The Met had never pretended to be a people's theater; its public ensign was a diamond horseshoe which scintillated on the bosoms of hereditary boxholders whose shares controlled the corporation. However, it was now willing to make common cause with the Philharmonic Society, which could afford to be tired of shabbiness at Carnegie Hall. Like the Met, Carnegie Hall was also ripe for destruction, and likewise faced a spectral threat from some competitive agency if there should be a vacuum left to fill in a big empty hall on 57th Street and Seventh Avenue.

There were, however, minds at work sensible of contemporary social and economic realities, which had changed radically over half a century and two world wars. Otto Kahn, Enrico Caruso, Guilio Gatti-Casazza were gone; no triumvirate of such capacity was likely to appear to command a new Puccini. Opera was maintained, but the Met's leadership had proven more custodial than inspired. Policy was perfunctory, although the need for a new face was admitted. The custodians were forced to consider several new aspects of deficit support for a permanently luxurious operation. Great corporations and their subsidiary charitable foundations gave evidence of interest. In such a shift of basis even an institution from the very wrong side of the tracks like City Center, improvisatory as it was and unlicensed by legitimized status or hereditary prestige, intruded to propose a

possible service in combination with older and firmer establishments.

Among other unrelated factors, our association with Nelson Rockefeller, his long and understanding help to Balanchine and me, enabled us to nominate our personal architect for a putative theater which might house "The Dance," at least as so specified in promissory brochures. However, there was no specific mention of any permanent controlling inhabitant, other than the parent corporation. But imminent threats of still another World's Fair, again on Flushing Meadow, offered the governor opportunity to appropriate funds to erect a State Theater in the metropolis itself as Albany's permanent contribution to, and memorial of, an otherwise redundant celebration.

One could have hoped that Lincoln Center, Inc., would have commanded a coordinated plan from one single masterful hand, eye, and brain, whosoever that might be. By any European scale the site was not vast or impressive. But a coherent design would, in the opinion of many, have more chance for an achievement of genuine quality than dispersed notions among fatally divided, haphazard, or competitive talents, each of whom might feel compromised or frustrated by subservience to an inevitably lowest common denominator. Michelangelo's Roman Campidoglio, for example, was approximately the same size as Lincoln Center's plot. So were Jones's and Wren's Greenwich Hospital, the city center of Nancy in Lorraine, and Sir Edwin Lutyen's magnificent solution of the government complex at New Delhi. This is no place to detail the gestation or construction of Lincoln Center, but it is appropriate to mention a few of the salient conditions governing Philip Johnson's accomplishment in realizing his State Theater.

Morton Baum was wary of Lincoln Center, Inc., and with good reason. He had been tossed off the Met board for bad manners in talking out of turn (or talking at all). He knew that a struggle for the ultimate control of the State Theater by City Center would be a battle which could cost much. In an important sense it cost his life, and for this he was ready. It was hardly that Lincoln

Center would know how to manage any new theater once they owned it, except to exploit it commercially to the hilt by allowing whatever impresario who might rent it to scale ticket prices as high as possible. Baum acted by fiat, as if he had no board; later he consoled his colleagues by his energy and authority, as he stood almost single-handed against the strongest alliance of social prestige and economic power New York might offer.

Tension that was engendered in the grim fight to save the State Theater for the people of New York (city as well as state), precipitated bitterness which may be forgiven, since one is forced to learn that rage only feeds self-destruction. However, it is scarcely forgotten. One must be thankful for what was finally gained, or rather enforced, by Baum's resilience and wisdom, plus the skill, persistence, and integrity of Betty Cage in the actual formulation of an ultimate contract. Few can be comforted, however, by the graceless facade and awkward interior of the Met, the waste involved in multiple corrections of acoustical faults in Philharmonic Hall, or the manipulation of the repertory theater. Had Lincoln Center been a profit-sharing concern, like those other more important ones controlled by its board members, the shareholders could have called them to strict account. The least I could do was to resign, and with the information I had absorbed, struggle as I might for the autonomy of the State Theater. That we were successful, that Lincoln Center stands and operates, that it has found itself a median populist stance and has come to be accepted as a law-abiding and useful citizen in the community, obviates further repining except possibly by impartial historians of architecture or a society whose time is yet to come.

As for the design of the State Theater, we knew we could never aspire to an "ideal" house, and since we were not footing the bills, must obtain what we could by patience, connivance, and ingenuity. We did hold some important advantages. For one, as far as stylistic or elementary aspects of the new building were concerned, we were our architect's single client. The lawyers, bankers, and realtors of Met and Philharmonic

New York State Theater

were content to have building committees relieve them of the necessity for reading blueprints and for standing firm on whatever particular hopes they may have had. Apart from technical considerations—which were hardly masterfully handled, in view of the redundancy of glass at the back and sides of Philharmonic Hall, the dubious sufficiency of its acoustics, the pitiful lack of public space acknowledged by the Met, and its failure with mechanical devices such as turntables on its opening—the architects of these edifices were in fact virtually their own clients. A vacuum in their patrons' taste is represented by the cramped and confusing foyers of the Met and the entrance which forces Philharmonic subscribers to crowd narrowly past two sides of a restaurant.

Balanchine and I, on the other hand, knew precisely what we wanted and had no one's objections to overcome. Our taste coincided with Philip Johnson's to the smallest detail, and in details, according to Johnson's master, Mies van der Rohe, lie truth, rightness, splendor. Gadgetry was out; technically ours would be a minimally equipped stage. There would be no hydraulic lifts, no turntables, no elaborate trapping, and only minimal electronic circuits (which so far, except for switchboards, have scarcely proved to have any advantage over manual operation). There would be no glaring glass surfaces on three blind exteriors to increase maintenance and illuminate nothing. There would be an auditorium seating some 3,200, with the least possible number of the partial-view seats which must invariably exist in every theater seating over 1,000. However, there would be "continental" seating: aisles, which contain much of the best viewing space, were eliminated; the space between rows of seats would be ample for passage. A double wall would serve as the auditorium's sound-lock against street and foyer noises. Backstage space was sacrificed, but fairly generous onstage side storage was provided. Although not lavish, the rehearsal rooms and practice studios, with pine floors woven in a system developed by Balanchine, were superior to

any theater on this continent. We deliberately deprived ourselves of many desirable amenities, even necessities, toward one positive purpose.

New York in the early sixties possessed no space suitable for welcoming heads of state, conquering heroes, astronauts, and international cultural ambassadors. It had made do with state armories or hotel ballrooms. If the city (and state) were provided with an appropriate space to serve as parlor for the metropolis, the municipality could be justified in contributing to its perpetual upkeep, thereby reducing maintenance costs for City Center. Philip Johnson proceeded to envision the most splendid interior our city possessed since the great waiting rooms of Grand Central and Pennsylvania railroad stations, now defaced or doomed. Plans for the State Theater's promenade went through innumerable changes. In Japan, both Johnson and I had been attracted by the Japanese rectilinear modular systems; thin, beveled supports, rhythmically syncopated; and slender balconies, unrelieved by adornment except for the elegance of their structural materials. Johnson prepared several models, one of which even flaunted a fanciful polychromy inspired by the Momoyama baroque and the lacquered glories of Nikko's shrines and Kyoto's Nijo Palace. Finally, under the lean Miesian aesthetic of "less is more," he reduced the structural elements and their chromatics to champagne-colored travertine, gilt bronze, rose marble, a fourteen-carat-gold ceiling, and gilt anodized bead curtains for the large front windows. Two heroic twin figures, the largest marble pieces ever cut in Carrara to be shipped overseas, were based on life-sized figures by the sculptor Elie Nadelman, of which Governor Rockefeller had long owned bronze replicas. These gigantic lady acrobats or dancers in repose were set as the sole decoration in the foyer to give it scale and polarize its space. There would be no crystal chandeliers; instead of a single grand staircase which, as in the Met, led nowhere and did nothing except to confuse or further frustrate the flow of people on narrow overhanging balconies, there

were two boldly hand-carved stone staircases which permitted the huge unimpeded areas of the foyer to serve as a festive visual fanfare for whatever spectacle was held within.

Certainly there were problems—practical, financial, aesthetic. In order to procure gilt-bronze railings for the open balconies cantilevered out from the curved bearing wall, a shop had to be set up which for a year and a half constructed individual hand-forged panels, each different, in patterns roughly deriving from Jackson Pollock's aleatory "drip" technique. The Nadelman marbles in their glowing metaphorical nudity exacerbated a small but influential group in the Lincoln Center management, at a time when ultimate control of the theater was still in doubt. A clutch of hard-hats made wisecracks about big bosoms, and there was even talk of their removal. However, the large hole in the building's exterior wall, which alone was wide enough to admit them to a floor above the street, had been sealed on schedule, and the figures were safe. And over our protest, an orchestra pit had been imposed that would seat only thirty-five contract musicians. This is the number which customarily accompanies Broadway musicals, the brand of entertainment which most cost-conscious realtors, lawyers, and bankers relish. Concrete had been poured, but early one morning Balanchine chanced into the auditorium, crowded with forests of scaffolding, to stage one of the most moving and effective solos of his career. After his immediate threat to withdraw our company from further tenancy if the orchestra pit remained straitjacketed, power drills were brought in to double the space, so that it can now, with discomfort, hold some seventy men. This is about two-thirds the size of the orchestra in any fair-sized European opera house that produces Wagner, Verdi, or Strauss, to say nothing of other "grand" opera. And by this time it was apparent that the State Theater would be shared by the New York City Opera Company, under the direction of Morton Baum's dedicated protégés, Julius Rudel and John White.

REVERIES: Conrad Ludlow, Sara Leland, Kay Mazzo, Anthony Blum

RAYMONDA VARIATIONS

the New York City Ballet

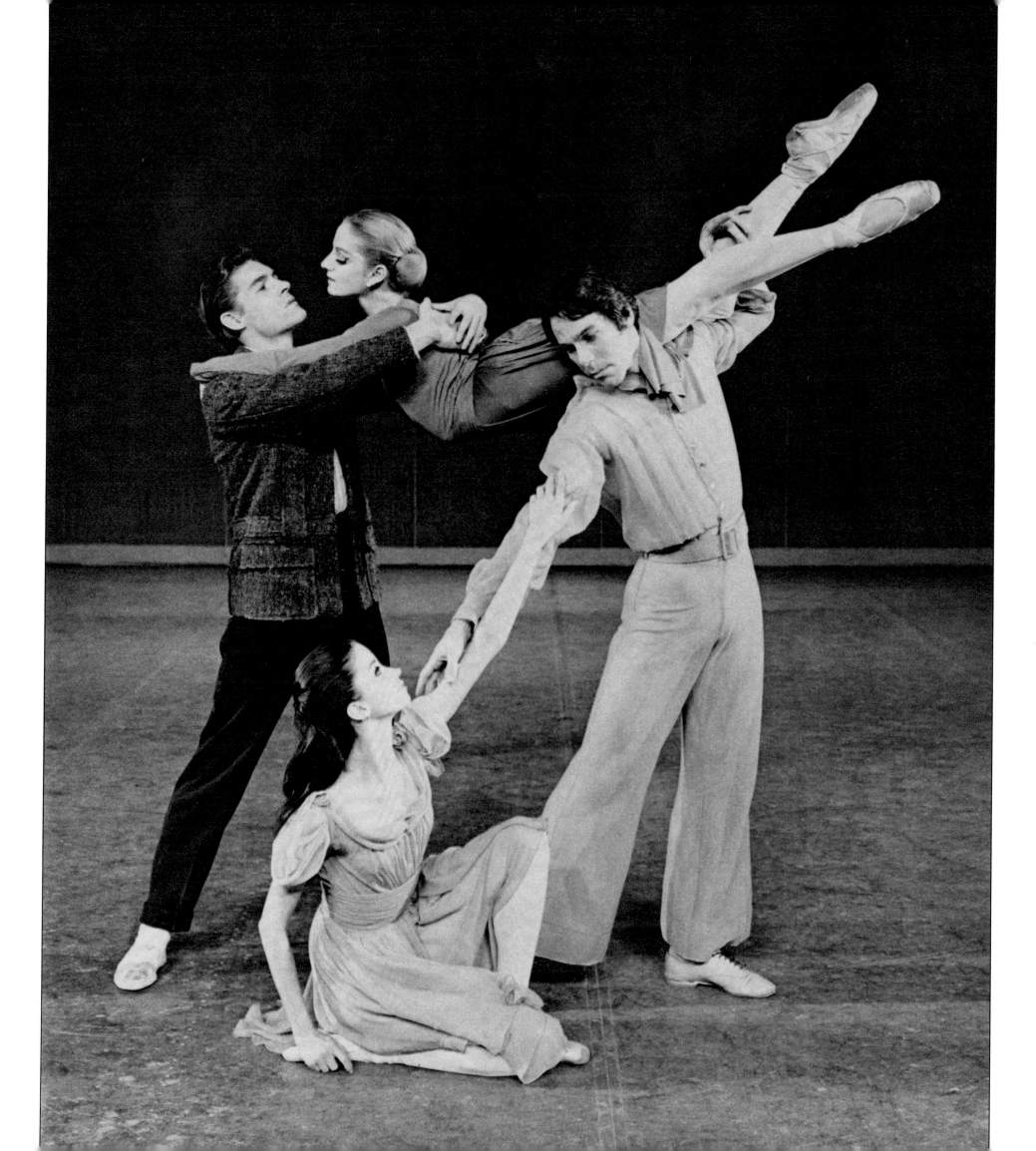

JANUARY, 1961: NEW YORK

Lunch with General Maxwell D. Taylor, U.S.A. (ret.), newly appointed director, Lincoln Center for the Performing Arts, Inc. Tried to explain our intransigence relative to autonomy for the State Theater, as well as differences between City Center and Lincoln Center in socioeconomic terms. Failed. The field he now commands is in contest, not in tension; but how to make this clear?

As a constituent in occupancy of a projected performing arts center, it was appropriate that a new full-time director should meet with representative participants. By temperament and experience, I was much attracted to professional soldiers. During the war I'd been on detached duty at West Point and was made to feel wholly at home, lodged with a delightful Engineering Corps officer, whose wayward daughter was a gifted artist and confirmed Marxist. His tolerance of her young pacifist companions, his taste in music and painting, demonstrated that traditional authoritarian discipline was elastic enough, off the field of combat, to accommodate freedom of imagination. Also, I had thoroughly enjoyed myself in the Army; in my hagiology, George Patton replaced T. E. Lawrence. My predeliction for histrionics predisposed me to embrace a military ethos, even as ploughshares were forged into swords, or vice versa. And through my West Point contacts, we arranged for deputations of cadets to attend our performances at the State Theater on free weekends. They adorned our theater with immaculate dash and courtesy, like *chevaliers gardes* off duty, waiting on ballerinas at the Maryinsky.

Hence I was charmed and flattered to sit, *à deux*, with General Taylor, expressing admiration for his career and profession as well as anxiety and fear in our present situation. In semiretirement he directed a Mexican light and power company. He had been superintendent of West Point, would become Army chief of staff; chairman, Joint Chiefs of Staff; adviser to Presidents Eisenhower, Kennedy, and Johnson; finally ambassador to South Vietnam. Why, with such credentials, should he not also be coordinator, developer, public relations officer, indeed, director of Lincoln Center? Perhaps he came to ask himself that insignificant question between bad nights and worse days in Southeast Asia; it was possibly a mercy that he soon took refuge in fields more furious.

General Taylor's appointment was a sterling and characteristic and inevitable response on the part of Lincoln Center's board. It offers a classic example of the behavior of responsible Philistines when they think to take over a province of Israel. Responsible General Taylor was; Philistine he was not. For reasons doubtless dictated by his selfless sense of service, and at the moment lacking a sword, he was called to do what should be done about a situation which was increasingly disorderly and promised worse. The gentlemen who nominated him had no clear idea of such development in its particulars, except that it was damnably untidy. To these trustees, the cost of untidiness leads to iniquity deeper than perdition. Their unique talent fosters control, which is what others might name neatness. Neatness means "success"; waste means "failure."

Apart from managing their own business, they handle the trusteeships of hospitals, museums, or schools, considered as obligatory services, in approximately the same fashion. Under them, professionals, doctors, scholars, teachers learn to know their place and proceed, as they

can, according to guidelines of certified public accountancy which characterize no-nonsense control, efficiency experts, cutbacks, etc. But when it comes to "art," beyond those objects which are inert, negotiable, real property—or worse, when it comes to the immeasurable and unpriceable arts of performance—it is almost impossible for them to translate "entertainment" which spells "amusement" into "service." Money is always to be "lost" rather than "spent." If it is "lost," loss spells waste and failure threatens, naturally in the form of bankruptcy.

From a wide experience, Stravinsky had many observations on patronage which those burdened with a disposition of funds to our fifty states might consider:

Art, to middle-class millionaire politicians, is something to be collected and dowered. And this is part of the reason why our yachting millionaires and racehorse millionaires include so many French Impressionist millionaires but so few musical millionaires: the resalable musical artifacts are comparatively insignificant.

Nor are the cultural economics of other societies more instructive, except for drawing still more invidious comparisons. We can learn from them that musicians have not always been starvelings or in such undemanded supply as they are now. In Sophoclean Greece, for example, musicians' salaries were fixed by law. . . . And in Greece, as well as at Mantua, and Esterház, and Monticello (Virginia), they seem to have been regulated by merit. . . . Jefferson was musically cultivated, by the way, and though he was probably a difficult source of income to his orchestra players, demanding that they should also be gardeners, and so forth, he spent a far greater share of his money on music than the "eleven cents out of every hundred dollars of disposable income" . . . that his fellow countrymen are now squandering on the "performing arts."[*]

What our nation needs is not a plethora of bronze and travertine art centers, nor concentrations of facilities serving communities which can't recruit subscription audiences sizable enough to support the buildings' heat or electricity. If the federal government is finally brought to support the performing arts with a modicum of the money spent annually on West Point, Annapolis, and the Air Force Academy, one might hope that directors of these three facilities will stay where they are and not be purloined to guarantee a tidy lack of waste in theaters, museums, studios, and opera houses. Ex-performing artists, indeed, may be forced to assume the managerial role of soldier, which is no easy impersonation. A time may come when bankers, realtors, lawyers can no longer offer themselves as convenient bullies or scapegoats. In Britain a sense of civil service has not vanished with imperial shrinkage. Lessons learned in the Indian

*Igor Stravinsky and Robert Craft, *Retrospectives and Conclusions*, Alfred A. Knopf, New York, 1969, p. 61.

civil service have profited custodial precedents for many present programs. May our operators benefit from the lightened weight of Vietnam.

Arnold Goodman represents a type of public servant which, alas, the United States has found it rarely possible to train or support. Apart from his qualities as man of affairs and diplomat, he is a critic with erudition and cultivation. Lord Goodman's tenure in the bureaucracy of the Arts Council spelled a new period of stability, sensitivity, and service. He has something to say for state subsidy (in Britain, a smallish island):

It does insulate cultural organizations against the totally untrammeled concern of the wealthy or busybodying amateur. The Arts Council—blessed be the name—whatever its shortcomings has from the day of its establishment maintained the principle of subsidy without interference. This is not a doctrine of timidity but a doctrine of sense. Its duty is to consider worthy recipients, confirm their worthiness, and bestow this financial assistance. Whatever the problems and shortcomings of this system, it shines with splendor by the side of a system of wholly private contributions from people who think that on that account they have a right to a voice and a judgment on subjects where a lifetime of knowledge is required to express any valid view.[*]

OCTOBER, 1962: MOSCOW

Rocky Staples, cultural attaché, informed us that the embassy takes no responsibility for dancers, that we cannot charter a private plane from Helsinki or Warsaw, and that in case of our internment, he has no authority to intervene. In the Kremlin at the Palace of Soviets, brilliant performance of AGON, with the crowd cheering Arthur Mitchell ("Meech-elle, Meech-elle"). On the way to the hotel, rumbling tanks in back streets. The kitchen made a special effort to provide a feast; the maids frighteningly sympathetic. Betty Cage and I in silent cold sweats. Balanchine cheerful: "I've never been to Siberia." From various correspondents (Time, N.Y. Times, Paris Soir), rumors of a military putsch within the Kremlin.

The first Soviet tour of the New York City Ballet in 1962 was preceded by Stravinsky's own triumphal return, which he has intimately and precisely recorded through Bob Craft. When Balanchine arrived in Russia after an absence of thirty-eight years, he usually behaved with mannerly irony and casual *politesse*, but did not make it easy for apparatchiks or hack journalists to claim him as a repentant prodigal. Now an American citizen of a quarter century's standing, he affected the stance of a stranger not simply from another country, but from another century. Although he had left Russia at nineteen, he behaved as if he could recall only prerevolutionary Petersburg before 1914, when he was

* Arnold Goodman, *New Statesman*, Nov. 24, 1972, p. 770 *et seq.*

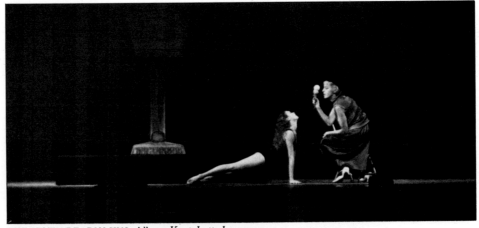

THE SEVEN DEADLY SINS: Allegra Kent, Lotte Lenya

ten. His brother Andrei Balanchivadze, like their father an honored nationalist composer, was at the airport to greet him. There were touching if crass efforts to involve Balanchine in the historical texture of his origins. A reporter found that Balanchine in his youth had once been in the same room with the eminent poet and suicide Vladimir Mayakovsky, although no word had passed between them. Asked his opinion of Anna Pavlova, Balanchine had to admit he'd never seen her, since she had left Petrograd and performed only abroad during his youth. However, *Pravda* ("The Truth") reported that Mayakovsky had encouraged and influenced the budding choreographer, who had first been inspired to dance by the mysterious feminine soul of Pavlova. Resisting such coloration, Balanchine adopted a slyly antiquated manner of speech, patiently answering hack journalists as if he had difficulty with a barbarous vocabulary or jargon. Postrevolutionary portmanteau words and agitprop slang had indeed penetrated the idiom, but they are no more difficult to decipher than captions on a cartoon.

As for impressions, favorable or otherwise, which our repertory may have made, it is impossible to reconcile what we heard and saw of the response with what could be read in newspapers. Official Marxist dialectic transformed original impulse or personal intention into something which, if not particularly rich, at least was passing strange. In AGON, for example, Arthur Mitchell, our elegant black soloist, performed the crucial *pas de deux*, cool as spring water in its dispassionately erotic acrobatics. When Arthur first came to our school nearly twenty years before, a furious father full of antebellum prejudice threatened to withdraw his (pinko-gray, ungifted) daughter if this (black, gifted) boy was allowed to "handle" her—in adagio class. In the AGON *pas de deux* Balanchine had arranged one of his most ingenious serpentine, linked patterns in equal balance between partners of opposite sexes. In certain passages Mitchell's pantherine sinuosity tended to swing the combination into approximately a star turn. In the Muscovite press, however, Balanchine's expression of Stravinsky's mutations of Mersenne and de Lauze's Renaissance dances was interpreted as a Negro slave's submission to the tyranny of an ardent white mistress. Andrei Balanchivadze, in conversation, at least, expressed admiration for his brother's tact, daring, and taste in presenting a white girl and a black boy in such an implicit and prolonged

Back from Russia at City Hall. *Front row:* Jillana, Hayden, McBride, Kent, Cage, Adams

design. This element had caused no comment at home in the five years of its existence.

Naturally the townscape of Leningrad made its hypnotic impression. One's sense of the present was almost obliterated by the treasures of the Hermitage: the cabinet of Scythian gold, the felt tapestry hangings recovered from Altai permafrost, Rembrandt's *Danaë and the Golden Shower*, the twin galleries of military portraits of commanders in the alliance that defeated Napoleon, the massive but exquisitely cut vases of semiprecious stone demonstrating the mineral richness of the Urals. Rossi's lovely small theater, linked by a bridge from the museum palace, was particularly impressive, for here Diaghilev, on a stage identical with the Maryinsky's, had rehearsed his dancers for the 1909 Paris season. Suddenly his foreign office subsidy was withdrawn, and he was forced to continue for the moment entirely on his own.

From my attachment to Nijinsky's memoirs and from Balanchine's school-day recollections, we approached the Kirov Theater as a shrine. We appeared there for a few performances before transferring to a huge, relentlessly unglamorous sports arena, but the former imperial opera house presently appeared as a pretty enough, small nineteenth-century theater. But with shabby draperies, it was musty and sad, particularly in comparison with Philadelphia's Academy of Music, built in 1859, which was at the moment being superbly restored by Philip Johnson as self-instruction preparatory to planning our own State Theater.

Differences between Soviet and American ambience and possibility were sharply illuminated, particularly in theater. At the Maly there was a magnificent revival of Meyerhold's thirty-year-old production of Lermontov's MASQUERADE, with its astonishing prologue. On big double turntables, revolving against each other, an entire pack of personified playing cards danced Khachaturian's polonaise. The pack vanished; from the center of the stage rose a huge gaming table, its green baize lit by a single overhead lamp, throwing in dazzling relief a crowd of officers and dandies against whom the opening dialogue was now heard. There was also a splendid performance of Chekhov's early THAT FOOL IVANOV, played according to the author's intention (generally ignored in the West) as a tragic rather than comic melodrama. I was assigned a formidable companion, whom I was told held the rank of colonel in the political police. She took me to any play I wished to see. At a dreary, perfunctory delivery of THE WINTER'S TALE at the Moscow Art Theater, then passing through a drab period, her eyes filled with tears which flowed steadily from the first declaration of Hermione's innocence. I stayed stubbornly dry-eyed, impatient, only willing to stick it out since she was so obviously moved. As we left, she turned on me like a tigress: "Do you know why you didn't weep?" I risked faint criticism. "No!" she snapped: "It's because you're so *rich!*"

We were permitted to attend classes in the ballet schools, a sobering and instructive experience. In Leningrad we found much what one might expect—strong discipline, expert acrobatic partnering, rather blunt and slow bodies. A frontal static correctness in basic positions of arms and feet governed a lack of plastic fluency; the rigor in constant returns to an initial rigid anchorage in the canonical five positions robbed many sequences of uninterrupted flow. We saw group photographs of

graduating classes from the early nineties. Portraits of prizewinners included those of Pierre Vladimirov, Felia Doubrovska, and Anatole Oboukhoff, who at that moment were teaching in our own Manhattan classrooms. There was a charcoal sketch of Georgei Balanchivadze, aged thirteen, costumed as a cupid. The school in Moscow was even more physically impressive, but stylistically the instruction was less to our taste. It was more a national than a municipal institution; we had learned (although this was officially denied) that the best provincial students were siphoned into classes preparing the Bolshoi company, which, while not highest in prestige abroad, is politically more powerful at home.

A remarkable class of Central Asians was filled with extraordinarily supple and handsome boys, twelve to fifteen years of age, strong and Mongol in cheekbone, tawny skin, and black hair. They'd come to Moscow speaking no word of Russian and susceptible to pulmonary disease in city air vastly different from their native steppes. The Asian students had their personal tutors, nurses, doctors, infirmary, and were cared for with the attention we give only to prize athletes or champion colts, which they proudly resembled. It would seem that, out of a class of fifteen or twenty, there must emerge at least half a dozen splendid male soloists, and that over a five-year period, on the basis of such material and conditions, the Soviet Union would be gaining regiments of unparalleled stars. But considering the mass (one-sixth of the world's land) and extent of the Union of Soviet Socialist Republics, and the prestige of classic ballet for both home consumption and diplomatic export, it is notable that Russia has produced comparatively few prime male dancers since the Revolution. In the past, Chabukiani and Messerer; more recently Vas-

IRISH FANTASY: Melissa Hayden

siliev, Solovyov, and now Barashnikoff are at the peak of their profession, along with Leningrad's defector, Nureyev. It is curious that the astonishingly numerous and promising aspirants in the lower grades of Russia's ballet schools result in so few finished artists, either men or women, of the first rank.

The one sad and implacable cause seems to lie with music: a lack of variety and scope in training, not the somatic body, but the ear; a lack in developing aural capacity as trigger, not alone of bones and muscles, but of imagination, mind, spirit, and governing philosophy as well. While jazz, moderate rock, and other international popular forms were permitted in social clubs and even some public concerts, there was an absolute division in academic instruction between the variety of rhythmic metric which has dominated Western music since 1917, and that which governed the generation of the great Five, Balakirev, Borodin, Cui, Moussorgsky, Rimski-Korsakov, and their succession. The pervasive transformation of Western audition, deriving on one hand from improvisational forms originating in New Orleans, Kansas City, and Chicago, and on the other from the progressive methods of Stravinsky, Schoenberg, Webern, Varèse, Ives, and Alban Berg, had not been licensed to inform the apparatus or legitimate production of Soviet musicians. We did meet a few "underground" composers who, secluded in their apartments, might have bootlegged scores or tapes, and who wrote, for themselves alone, in an arrested idiom wanly following the bourgeois pioneers of the West.

The experiments of a loyal Soviet artist, however, must be governed by ethical optimism, local ethnic melodic material, academic modalities, and supercharged heroics. No deviations from elementary tonality or primary rhythms were permitted to sully rigid habit, either in music or in movement which depended on it. Hence gifted young aspirants from Uzbekistan, Georgia, or the Ukraine were condemned in class and onstage to waltz, two-step, and fox-trot, their feet and bodies chained to 3/4, 2/4, or 4/4 measures. Thus in choreography there was absolutely nothing new in our understanding of the term, past the nineteenth-century repertory, except massive physical parade and prowess. The governing orchestration, with the remote exception of the early, now vaguely licensed Shostakovich, or the broken if unregenerate Prokofiev, was as bland and hygienic and "positive" as graduation exercises.

Any probing on our part into aesthetics, which are an important element in mechanics, was taken as unfriendly disapprobation. There were countercomplaints that Americans moved too fast, that we could not "interpret" Tchaikovsky; that our beat was heartlessly computerized, percussive, eccentric; in fact, that we had no "soul." No use to claim that our soul, while ticking, was not the same as others ticking to more syncopated tunes. While it was generally agreed (in private) that our training and equipment were "technically" accomplished, the concession was tempered by a tone implying that this quality was mechanistic, dictated by

an impersonal, inhuman, or decadent formalistic servility. Our spareness in decoration and costume was hapless formalism; our androgynous lack of polarization between musculated males and bosomy females was the result of a fatal absence of Socialist health and psyche. Such was the verdict of a large portion of printed opinion, yet certainly not of a vocative public which actually saw what we danced. Nor was it the judgment of that daring band of hopeless enthusiasts who followed our appearances from Leningrad to Tbilisi and Baku, back to Moscow and Kiev, who could hardly see enough of the novelty, strangeness, or freshness of a wholly alien vision and philosophy.

Our season in Moscow, which opened at the Bolshoi and continued in the Palace of the Soviets, one of the world's largest and most comfortable theaters, coincided with President Kennedy's Cuban missile crisis. The tension, indeed the terror, of those few days and nights, without a blow ever being struck in anger, were more demoralizing to me than anything I had encountered from the invasion of Normandy through the capture of Munich. Through it all, Betty Cage and Balanchine cushioned the brunt of unimaginable possibilities with such tact and skill that the danger of our situation hardly percolated down to the dancers, who night after night within the Kremlin's walls heard six thousand voices yell for fifteen minutes after every performance: "Bal-an-chin, Bal-an-chin!"

Among many distinguished guests after our opening at the Bolshoi at an elaborate party held in Spaso House, the splendid residence of the American ambassador, was

THE NUTCRACKER:
Waltz of the Flowers led by Jillana

Khrushchev's son-in-law Adzhubei, at the moment an all-powerful newspaper publisher. He placed himself by Balanchine's elbow apparently eager to offer formal felicitations. Balanchine, seated casually, continued a concentrated conversation with a girl and a boy, two of our youngest dancers. One became nervous in the heat of a human situation within a tense political atmosphere. Balanchine had long complained that we have no one to teach pantomime in our school, whereas Russian students constantly enact roles in dumb show along with their earliest dance training. I began to realize that he was now giving a lesson in advanced pantomime. Evidently Adzhubei recognized this also, for with a wry smile of comprehension he turned away. Balanchine had been so attentive to his two dancers that he could never have been charged with discourtesy.

I had known Sergei Eisenstein, the film director, in New York at the climax of his worst catastrophe. He was unable to retain his right to cut footage of QUE VIVA MEXICO! against Upton Sinclair (who had raised the necessary money) and was faced with the horrid prospect of returning to Moscow with nothing to show for months of willful absence. I now became friends with Pera Atasheva, his widow, in a whirlwind intimacy. Every morning after breakfast I'd walk to our embassy to hook whatever rumors were running, then go to her tiny apartment in the back courtyard of a ruinous block of fallen plaster and cracked concrete. Her sitting room was crammed with mementos of Eisenstein, circus days with Meyerhold, Noh masks, Aztec skulls, photographs of Cocteau and Charlie Chaplin, Gide and Dreiser. From her files she extracted my letters dating from the early thirties.

She and I shared crystallized nuts and fruit, herring and eel, during the fear, menace, and excitement of those threatening hours. On the worst morning, opening her door, she asked in a voice drained of sarcasm or irony: "Are we friends or enemies?" I had just passed by an aborted "spontaneous demonstration" organized to splash paint and rotten cabbages against the fortress walls of our embassy's chancery. Crowds, marshaled as far back along the wide avenue as the Borodinsky Bridge, had assembled with sloganed banners, eggs, bottles, moving-picture cameras, and sound trucks. But the weather would not cooperate; there was not

Rehearsal, d'Amboise and Farrell

enough light for decent filming, so the protest was spontaneously rescheduled to take place the following day. Pera Atasheva and a few of Eisenstein's young followers, who were now editing his theoretical prose in six volumes, could laugh at what would have been his opinion of such grotesque child's play. It was he who had foreseen the most breathlessly inventive ciné-vérité; he who had organized the entire city of Petrograd to shoot TEN DAYS THAT SHOOK THE WORLD (portions of which are filed in archives from Leningrad to Washington as authentic films of the 1917 Revolution). In farewell, Madame Eisenstein gave me his wicked sketches of Nijinsky and Diaghilev, which are now in the dance collection at Lincoln Center.

Performance of music and dancing aside, the atmosphere of this tour was fixed most fiercely and emotionally at our final performance in the Lensoviet sports palace, across the Neva in an almost suburban outpost of Leningrad. All our appearances had been sold out; the large trade-union syndicates had been assigned the distribution of tickets; there were none to be had for many young students and older artists. Therefore Balanchine announced an additional free, open performance—first come, first served—for the dancers, musicians, painters, and poets of his city. After the final ballet, a delegation from these workers of mind, fancy, and heart marched onto the stage, their leader bearing an ivory-handled silver samovar filled with red roses. I sat with a conservator from the Hermitage who spoke excellent French and English and had often traveled West. The delegation's captain, dancers clustered around him, began a speech to Balanchine. The Cuban crisis had passed, but its menace hung in the air like a faint scent of sulphur. The audience was charged with inchoate emotion, a mixture of warmth, regret, and that vague hope in delinquent brotherhood which men feel when mutual terror fuses common anxieties for a brief thrilling moment.

The speech in Russian went on, emotionally and at length. The audience grew impatient; it was late and rainy; the evening should have ended more aptly. Finally Balanchine was presented with the silver and ivory urn. He handed it to one of our girls. For a long half minute he stared at the floor, his silence covered by a solid burst of applause. After he'd raised his hand to stop it, he spoke, very clearly, one sentence in Russian which I could not follow. It caused an absolute blanketing of every cough and breath. Nervously I asked my friend from the Hermitage what Balanchine had said. "C'était assez triste," she said. "It was simply, Thank you: in troubling times which we may share in time to come, try to think of us as we are tonight; we'll try to think of you as you are tonight!"

There had been lighter moments. At a cocktail party given by Ambassador Foy Kohler on our departure, the guest of honor was Madame Ekaterina Furtseva, the cultural commissar. Mr. Kohler, who had been a rock for us and his country, complimented our company on their exemplary behavior over their weeks in the Soviet Union, during which cultural exchange and even diplomacy had trembled on the brink of what one dared not risk. He raised his glass: "To the dancers of the New York City Ballet who, through thick and thin, on good stages or bad, made no false step."

MAY, 1963: NEW YORK
Stravinsky on Balanchine's arrangement of
MOVEMENTS FOR PIANO AND ORCHESTRA:

To see Balanchine's choreography of the MOVEMENTS is to hear the music with one's eyes; and this visual hearing has been a greater revelation to me, I think, than to anyone else. The choreography emphasizes relationships of which I had hardly been aware—in the same way—and the performance was like a tour of a building for which I had drawn the plans but never explored the result. Balanchine approached the music by identifying some of the more familiar marks of my style, and as I heard him fastening on my tiniest repeated rhythm or sustaining group, I knew he had joined the work to the corpus of my music, at the same time probably reducing the time lag of its general acceptability by as much as a decade. I owe him even more for another aspect of the revelation: his discovery of the music's essential lyricism. I gather that his dramatic point is a love parable—in which ballet is it not?—but the coda had a suggestion of myth that reminded me of the ending of APOLLO.

The ballet, which might also have been called ELECTRIC CURRENTS, is a double concerto for male and female solo dancers, both identified with the piano solo. The choric group is spare—none of Balanchine's usual attendant caryatids this time but only a hexachord of those beelike little girls (big thighs, nipped-in waists, pin-heads) who seem to be bred to the eminent choreographer's specifications. The full dancing sextet is identified as a unit only in the Interludes, an idea which projects the shape of the entire piece with great clarity.*

In November, 1960, Balanchine introduced Stravinsky's MONUMENTUM PRO GESUALDO, which had had its orchestral premiere in Venice two months before. Accompanying the atmosphere of this earlier piece, Balanchine evoked the deliberate, almost sinister gravity and fatality shadowing court dances performed in the lifetime of this prince of madrigalists and murderers. MOVEMENTS FOR PIANO AND ORCHESTRA, with which it would come to be paired in repertory, was first played in New York in April, 1963. Choreographically it is even more compact, relentless, spare—a comment on one of the most complex of Stravinsky's later statements. The special quality of a "late" manner, the terminal florescence of an old artist's expression, has often been analyzed relative to Beethoven, Titian, or Rembrandt. Edgar Wind, a provocative historian lecturing on the "old age" of Raphael, who died at thirty-seven, produced an ingenious exposition of this painter's metaphysical and even biological maturation, considering the age and perfection of his early work and the expansion of its sequence. Stravinsky made sharp distinctions between ordinary clock time and other dimensions of encapsulated or concentrated temporal metrics through an imploded intensity of musical ideas which permitted no fat or rhetoric upon the fluid structure of his motor process. His constant shift in interests, musical or worldly, kept him lean, active, and full of youthful thought as he progressed through calender time during nine decades.

It was our great fortune that Stravinsky honored us as a virtual partner in many important orchestrations from 1937 through 1972. He enforced the unique responsibility or opportunity of making our ears, minds, and bodies stretch to the limits of his elastic achievement. While it was obvious that Balanchine benefited directly and

* Igor Stravinsky and Robert Craft, *Themes and Episodes*, pp. 24–5.

the New York City Ballet

it was obvious that Balanchine benefited directly and immediately from successive analyses of his scores, it is often overlooked that our dancers also learned new means of thinking and counting, and thereby moved to measures that were physically and theatrically unprecedented. A synthesized syncopation of sound and silence, the torque and break of symmetrical or asymmetrical balance and imbalance, the ability to follow and encompass modalities in motion as if they were tonally dictated—these contributed to the kinetic sophistication of performers whose apparatus would not be limited by a past academy or middlebrow music of dubious quality.

Stravinsky also educated our audience and our orchestra, for Robert Irving, who had cast his lot with us after our first Covent Garden season, embraced this strange and wonderful repertory as a true *maître d'orchestre*, as comrade in arms and legs of *maîtres de ballet*. Stravinsky wrote ruefully of his MOVEMENTS that Balanchine "has joined the score to the body of my music far faster than it could ever get there by way of the concert hall—where in fact it has not yet arrived." Ten years later this was still true. Irving built an orchestral group into a coherent instrument which would become recognized, before and during the Stravinsky Festival of 1972, as unequaled anywhere. It was accustomed to play difficult orchestrations, and whether a novelty was by Toshiro Mayuzumi, Iannis Xenakis, Morton Feldman, Morton Gould, or Robert Russell Bennett (for Richard Rodgers), it was given the preparation and performance of full symphonic exposition. Part of this came from the knowledge that Balanchine, as musician, knew exactly what he was doing when making dances for music. Having himself extracted piano versions of new pieces for himself and rehearsalists, he showed little fumbling, waste, or indecision. He could start composition and his orchestra could start reading, with ingredients already laid out, prepared in order and quantity, and waiting, like fresh uncooked food on a kitchen table, to be combined into an appetizing dish.

NOVEMBER, 1963: NEW YORK

Conference with W. McNeil Lowry, Marcia Thompson, his deputy, and Eugenie Ouroussow, director, School of American Ballet, at the Ford Foundation concerning survey made and submitted by Ballet Society, Inc., relative to a national program for the support of ballet, its education and production. A ten-year schedule is blocked out, encouraging general regional growth as well as aid to specific companies across the country.

The concept of an American national ballet institution on the model of the French, British, Canadian, or Russian systems would appear to be logical, but local conditions in the United States make such parallels impractical. The Comédie Française, the Royal Shakespeare Company, the Bolshoi Ballet, the Scala Opera have been formed to suit local social, political, and artistic climates which have little resemblance to those on this side of the Atlantic. After we had made a year-long study, backed by testimony from a majority of the interested teachers and producers, the Ford Foundation granted the School of American Ballet funds to support itself on a stricter and more secure basis—and to aid tax-exempt schools all over the continent both through subsidies and through scholarship grants. But profit-making schools were perforce excluded. Grants-in-aid to individual regional companies for production and development were handled directly by the foundation, not through us.

The program, a pioneering effort in the United States, was neither easy to organize nor simple to administer. Its very announcement provoked a wild storm of waspish protest, presupposing that Balanchine had been granted hegemony over world dance. While he had been only indirectly involved, since he was managing our company and continually composing new works (and not for us alone), it was natural that his advice would be followed. Persons in whom he had confidence would implement the planning, since the program was focused entirely on classic academic traditional ballet, of which he had been undisputed leader for half a century. A famous figure in the "modern dance" called me at home one night around midnight, furious at what she felt was our takeover, and said, "You're nothing but a common thief." Journalists reacted virulently on the part of those who were not included in the Ford Foundation's program—those who by definition had rejected any contact with the classic discipline as an infringement on their inviolate and fractional idiosyncrasy.

But in this scheme, individuals were not being promoted, whatever their individual talent. The program was designed to support regional education—schools and civic companies which shared a common idiom and in many cases had the same repertory works as well as dancers with identical training. For all its presumably regressive structure, the academic dance possessed a popular legible language and was taught from about the same syllabus all over the world, while the "modernists," from whom most of the indignation sprang, had in half a century never armored themselves with a coherent or collective expression. They had no more than a dozen self-canonizing idioms, whose energetic and aggressive characteristics prevented them from making any impact as a group with a common agreement for joint preparation or performance, and they had been unable to cooperate in the practical economy of repertory performance. Also, with the inevitable disappearance of first-generation founding figures, any succession was fragmentary. Works once framing these individuals were of necessity abandoned, although many were of historical interest. The Ford Foundation, the School of American Ballet, and various beneficiaries weathered the storm of disapproval. It was ill-tempered, ill-founded, but bearable, dissipating itself soon enough.

But in the aim to raise the national level of practice and performance, there were inherent problems which can never be solved by subsidy, direct or indirect, however generous. For example, suppose that an ambitious and talented girl or boy, educated on the Pacific Coast and given good basic training there, joins a local company. How much does the dancer owe to the company which grants him a start or even an early reputation? Is he condemned by loyalty to remain forever where he commenced by circumstance? What are the feelings of directors of regional companies who find their best dancers dazzled and seduced by the concentrated glamour of the Atlantic Seaboard? As for the New York City Ballet, we can satisfy conscience that we never approach any individual who is under contract to another company, nor do we discuss contracts with dancers who have not already terminated a previous association. Dancers who come East and join us often return to their parent group for guest appearances. Local teachers, however loath they may be to let their most hopeful students leave, can boast of their future development.

But while it is true that New York is not America it is equally obvious that ambitious kids know where the action is. Since Hollywood is no longer much of a focus or magnet, Manhattan has more to offer than less noisy, anarchic, or chaotic capitals. Along the East Coast, in the South and Southwest, and on the Pacific Coast, we enjoyed excellent relations with both teachers and companies and gratefully accepted scholarship students sent us with the highest qualifications. Balanchine has always been generous in giving ballets without charge to regional groups who desired them. Levels of local training and performance were certainly raised, as had been the intention of the Ford program. In the most populous area of the Middle West, however, it had no effect. Chicago remained in splendid isolation, despite the long and consistent pioneering of Ruth Page over half a century. Unlike Boston, Philadelphia, Washington, and San Francisco (to say nothing of Vancouver, Toronto, Winnipeg, and Montreal, which had their own excellent Arts Council program), Chicago was the single American metropolis which, after innumerable tentative efforts, would build no representative company, despite the continuous local vitality of its opera, symphony, museums, and libraries.

BALLET IMPERIAL: Suzanne Farrell, Jacques d'Amboise, Patricia Neary

APRIL, 1964: NEW YORK

Checking the almost completed State Theater with Philip Johnson. Central chandelier still not winched to rise and lower with the curtain. The gilt-bronze proscenium frame, pierced for lights, will not be lit—yet. Installation of sculptures by Lipchitz, Reuben Nakian, Jasper Johns, etc. Tastefully placed, not one was intended for its present location. Brass stair rails delayed. Dressing rooms comfortable; practice room as big as the stage floor. We have to be thankful for the best theater for dance in America (the world?).

The State Theater at Lincoln Center opened on schedule, with few gross overages, disasters, or corrections necessary. At the opening Governor Rockefeller, through whom it had come into being, said cheerfully to Balanchine: "It's all yours, George. Take it from here." Such continuing largesse was not within the capacity of any donor, however grateful we may have been for his generosity or initiative. The battle for the control of a popularly priced house under our autonomy was by no means over; in fact, the worst of the war was still to be fought. It would end only in 1968 with a truly Pyrrhic victory. Through thick and thin Morton Baum fought the brutally high-handed attempts to contravene the rights of City Center. Finally, with the aid of Betty Cage's powerful legal and extralegal intelligence, he did indeed gain control, for our city and the City Center of Music and Drama, as well as for the New York City Opera and New York City Ballet. Then at a tragically early age, he died.

The transfer from Mecca Temple on West 55th Street to the State Theater at Lincoln Center Plaza was inevitably awkward and costly. What scenery we had hardly fitted the much higher, larger, and deeper new stage. We had commissioned no novelty to serve as an appropriate launching of the occasion, but Stravinsky sent us a delightful surprise—a twelve-tone fractured fanfare which trumpets sounded from the top balcony of the

promenade to send people from the foyer into the auditorium. The City Center in such palatial premises would no longer be able to present itself uniquely as a poor man's facility. Our format was now irrevocably on a grand scale; in some eyes, it was the Big Time. Among those rendered nostalgically disconsolate by our change of venue was Wystan Auden who, allowing *Es muss sein*, was unreconciled to rose marble and gilt bronze, regretting a comfy shabbiness and familial warmth at Mecca Temple, with its cozy Italian bar across the street. Such regrets were shared by few singers or dancers, who could now be sure of hot showers and decent dressing rooms, to say nothing of breadth and possibility in expanded performing space. The State Theater magnetized new audiences. At first they came from curiosity to judge the bright building, but they soon returned to see performances they had ignored in the gloomy old one. At the prompting of the Ford Foundation, we introduced a subscription system which guaranteed moderate security from advance payments so that we could plan rather than, as so often before, merely improvise. There were, of course, complaints that those who had not taken the trouble to subscribe were "never" able to buy seats. This was rarely true, but absolved people whose interest was only cursory.

Our big full-length MIDSUMMER NIGHT'S DREAM was revised for the new frame. Balanchine continued to alter details, and never seemed satisfied with the processional based on Mendelssohn's "Wedding March." However, its narrative exposition was clear as could be, and Arthur Mitchell as a dusky Puck, Edward Villella as a bouncy, bejeweled Emperor of Faery, seemed even more magical in a far taller forest. THE NUTCRACKER, aided by Lincoln Center's production fund, was given its present embellishment by Rouben Ter-Arutunian, who also redesigned SWAN LAKE and BALLET IMPERIAL (now called TCHAIKOVSKY CONCERTO NO. 2). From memories of his youth at the Maryinsky, Balanchine now animated Petipa's HARLE-

QUINADE (called THE MILLIONS OF HARLEQUIN in 1900). From the New York City Opera Company we borrowed Ter-Arutunian's settings for Rossini's LA CENERENTOLA with its "penny-plain, tuppence-colored" enlargement of a Pollock Victorian toy theater. In this Villella disported himself like a true jumping jack in the multicolored patches of Bergamo, while Patricia McBride danced an angelic Columbine. Antony Tudor introduced his wistful and passionate DIM LUSTRE from 1943, with new watercolor-and-ink cloths by Beni Montresor. Sir Frederick Ashton now saw an accurate revival of Britten's ILLUMINATIONS, which had been out of repertory for many years, performed to his satisfaction with a younger cast.

Our sensitive and skillful ballet master, John Taras, set Aaron Copland's *Dance Panels* (1962) as SHADOW'D GROUND. He had wished for the collaboration of a young poet, and at his behest, Scott Burton invented a series of rhymed epitaphs as inscriptions on stones slanted in a burying ground. It took its tone from rural New England, a boating party ending in disaster, the fateful adventure of a volunteer who joined the Lafayette Escadrille—the ordinary individual mortality defined in a country graveyard. John Braden's surround was an ingenious series of interlocking overhead panels on which were projected Kodachrome landscapes, unpeopled but suggesting sites where action took place below on the plane of the stage floor. It was a conscious attempt to explore our new facilities. Richard Buckle, who had flown from London to see Taras's charming work said: "A big company in a big house has a right to a big failure." Failure, or the accusation of it, always rankles. For me, SHADOW'D GROUND did not fail; what was attempted succeeded on its own terms. However, its quiet discretion in so large a frame seemed discrepant. Its failure was in the assertion of so somber and elusive an ambience at a moment which seemed to call for brighter colors, louder noises, and more jovial action.

JEUX D'ENFANTS: Roy Tobias,
Allegra Kent

RAYMONDA VARIATIONS: Melissa Hayden,
Jacques d'Amboise

THE CHASE: Jacques d'Amboise,
Suki Schorer

Looking at Gustave Doré's illustrations in his <u>Spain</u> and <u>Don Quixote</u> for ideas and style. Nicolas Nabokov's historical analysis of <u>Hispanidad</u>, the concept of grandee and hidalgo. Balanchine's memories of Petipa-Minkus version of 1869, which he danced at the Maryinsky in 1916. Unanimous decision to avoid folkloristic dance forms. Esteban Francés—palette for the piece: grays, brown, black-and-gold armor of El Greco's <u>Burial of Count Orgaz</u>; the Escorial, not the bullring or <u>feria</u>.

Some artists with innate energy beyond the strict realms of their profession at times utilize an acute political instinct, an exemplary general education, and a worldly experience to pursue extramusical careers. This tends to remove them from serious consideration by colleagues and critics as legitimate participants in a puritanical advance guard. Apart from his acute intelligence and devotion to the promulgation of the arts through international festivals and conferences, Nicolas Nabokov is one of the few current composers who possess a melodic gift in an epoch when melody is condemned as the resort of the ostentatious lowbrow or reactionary coward. As a protégé of Diaghilev's he began his career in 1928 by collaborating with Tchelitchev and Massine on ODE. He has since pursued a lonely path on which persistence in harmonious, tonal expression has caused his more perfunctory contemporaries to ignore his work.

Twenty years ago, Nabokov had written an orchestral suite portraying Dulcinea's attachment to the Knight of the Doleful Countenance. Balanchine had admired it, and they spoke of an expanded dance-drama. It was Nabokov's special lyric gift, not his comic, grotesque, or ironic commentary on Don Quixote's character, that appealed to Balanchine. The notion of this subject resurfaced over the years. Tchelitchev in 1937 had proposed the Don as the first in his projected EPISODES balancing Hamlet and Don Juan. Morton Baum had even asked Balanchine to choreograph Richard Strauss's tone poem *Don Quixote* of 1897, but the scale of the orchestration was too large for our pits.

Balanchine and Nabokov, with considerable aid from Esteban Francés, painter and Catalan, not from La Mancha, fashioned a skeletal structure which offered the atmosphere of Cervantes' Spain as the source of the Don's character, which would display his overwrought fantasy as more real, logical, and appealing. Even in a three-act ballet there is opportunity to suggest only a fraction of the novel's incidents, and even less of the preposterous delusions which Gustave Doré so precisely delineated.

DON QUIXOTE: Balanchine bowing at the premiere

Cervantes transcends nationalism, and it is vain for a non-Spanish company to aim at much indication of "authentic" Iberian folk forms. As far as local color went, however, we had in Francés a powerful partner. Trained as an architect, he is a master of illusory perspective and an easel painter of merit. After Tchelitchev, Eugene Berman, and Noguchi, he has been our most satisfactory collaborator in the line of Diaghilev's use of artists whose preoccupations are not primarily theatrical. In his textured impasto, illusionism, and rich chromatics, he had absorbed and would re-create the mineral climate of a barren landscape relieved by spatters of crimson, gold, and bronze. His elegantly detailed costume designs, executed by Karinska, were visions prompted by Zurbarán and El Greco, combining the chivalric rigidity of velvet on armor, starched lace against satin with sackcloth and rags, which clothed court, church, and countryside in the late medieval sunset just before Velázquez.

However, in many ways the ballet never had a chance to be completed. Since we could not afford to shut the theater, it was prepared, in spite of a multitude of technical problems, within the ordinary schedules of one repertory season. We should have had extended rehearsals, with the auditorium closed to the public. The premiere was a gala benefit to help pay for the production. Mechanically it was more or less viable, but the complexity of the spectacle and its governing ideas had no time for maturation. Over the next half-dozen years Balanchine made numerous piecemeal changes, retaining the obvious high points, eliminating what seemed less efficient, transposing the order of whole scenes. In the process he cut many precious fragments. But the strength of the concept, the haunting opulence of Nabokov's melodies, the splendor of Francés's decorations, the nightmare of storm-blown windmills, giants, and monsters have always interested audiences, no matter what changes were interposed. At the start, but less frequently now, Balanchine himself took over the role of the Don. When he performed, as in the first seasons, with Suzanne Farrell as Dulcinea, it was the most compelling realization since Chaliapin's filmed version. In various revisions the synthetic folk dances gave trouble, and secondary incidents were replaced by new music and more formal dances in the style of Petipa and Ivanov. Nevertheless, the Iberian Catholicism of the basic concept—Dulcinea as Ideal Woman, Repentant Magdalen, Innocent Shepherdess, Virgin of Seven Dolors, paired with the Don as Man of Sorrows, Fool of God, Idealist, and Tragic Hero, were powerful metaphors, touchingly visualized in performance.

As for "success," again, the word taunts; the achievement is intangible. The magic and scale of the scenic devices, the handling of children as Moors and Crusaders in the puppet show, the imperious pageantry and ritual sadism of the court ball, above all, Balanchine's extended classic dances at the commencement of the third act—these never failed to delight. The expansive serenity of the ending in its grisaille sobriety, against which passes a parade of ecclesiastical princes, religious orders, cross-bearing flagellants, is strongly supported by Nabokov's cathedral bourdons. But we always hoped for concentrated weeks of undivided study and rehearsal which would have welded a dispersed spectacle into the compactness, intensity, and wholeness it deserved.

Bob Craft, with Balanchine, discussing unplayed music suitable for dancing. Schubert's incidental music? Scriabin—present unpopularity, inevitable revival? Boulez, <u>Le marteau sans maître</u>? Carlos Chávez's <u>Toccata for Percussion</u>? Chamber music? Brahms's LIEBESLIEDER WALZER transferred well from City Center to State Theater's big stage. Bob suggested Schoenberg's orchestration of Brahms's <u>Piano Quartet in G Minor</u> (Opus 25, 1861), which sounds, he says like a "fifth" Brahms symphony.

Balanchine's BRAHMS-SCHOENBERG QUARTET was first danced in April, 1966. It was the initial "abstract" work designed for a new space and the larger scope of a considerably enlarged company. None of the dancers in any of its four movements appeared twice. Balanchine had often said that chamber music (particularly string quartets) is not suitable for supporting big ballets, since chamber music pieces are "too long, with too many repeats and are meant for small rooms." Schoenberg himself was reproved for his elaborate orchestration of this particular piece. He wrote his reasons to Dr. Alfred Frankenstein, the distinguished critic, when it was first played in California: "1. I love the music. 2. It is seldom played. 3. It is always very badly played, as the better the pianist, the louder he plays and one hears nothing of the strings. I wanted for once to hear everything and this I have achieved."

Karinska's ball dresses, court uniforms, and gypsy regalia are in a range of autumnal reds and browns, dusty rose, silvery pink, maroon. The dances seem steeped in the apprehension and change permeating the sunset of the Austro-Hungarian monarchy. They suggest a world drunk on "wine and roses" which consoles itself with the anxious gallantry of hussars on palace duty and the intrusion of gypsies in a Hofburg ballroom. A dusky vision, the ballet has a texture that is acid and sweet, serene, noble, and violent. Certainly its music may not have been planned for theater, but its use corroborates suspicion or hope that a vast unread literature hides innumerable possibilities which only require suspension of prejudice, the flouting of fashion, and relentless curiosity to uncover and utilize.

A MIDSUMMER NIGHT'S DREAM: Suzanne Farrell

A MIDSUMMER NIGHT'S DREAM: Arthur Mitchell

JULY, 1966: SARATOGA SPRINGS, NEW YORK

Preparation for opening new Performing Arts Center. Despite 17-week construction strike, the theater is complete, landscaping laid out, parking lot lit. Eugene Ormandy, conductor, the Philadelphia Symphony, objects to noise from adjacent waterfall, which will be tunneled for silence. Enormous acoustical reflector above the proscenium mouth, like a Medusa's mask. The acoustical engineers consider it a sculptural masterpiece and insist that muting its light color will kill the sound projection.

Diaghilev had been granted Charles Garnier's beautiful miniature opera house in Monte Carlo by the hereditary prince of Monaco, as an adjunct to roulette, *chemin de fer*, and baccarat tables. There, new seasons of the Ballets Russes were prepared following the company's return to France after the First World War. We had long hoped for a similar facility, half vacation spot, half workshop, where in unhurried calm we might test future dances without the customary urban pressure. We had played previous summer engagements in Ellenville (New York), Los Angeles, Washington, Red Rocks (Colorado), Ravinia (Chicago), and St. Louis, but never over an extended period or with much continuity. Richard Leach had managed summer festivals at Aspen, Colorado, before leaving the direction of planning for Lincoln Center to plan Saratoga's ambitious July and August programs. He invited us to play there every July, while the Philadelphia Orchestra would play every August. In the thirties, Franklin Roosevelt's Works Progress Administration aided the depressed economy of the "Capital Area" around Albany by erecting an elaborate complex of neocolonial brick-and-limestone buildings in a dense pine woods. There were halls for mineral-water fountains, a hotel, a bottling plant, restaurants, and a small, intimate theater. Attached to this state reservation was an enormous public swimming pool and a vast plant nursery which stocked the state park systems. In the sixties the community was again suffering from bad business. In an imaginative pump-priming operation, Governor Rockefeller and his Park Commission authorized the design and construction of an auditorium seating some five thousand persons under cover, while as many more could be accommodated on the graded grass lawns beyond.

John MacFadyen, architect of the open-air theater, in collaboration with engineers, acousticians, and landscape gardeners, devised an ingenious solution for access to a very large free-hanging balcony. Three walkways lead directly from the top of a natural amphitheater into the hall, with no need to climb stairs. A soundproofed roof protects the public from mountain weather, which the Adirondack foothills sometimes breed, while the sides are left open to spectacular sunsets and starry skies. There are stage facilities based on the scale and proportions of our State Theater, practice and rehearsal rooms, a generous orchestra pit, and good dressing rooms.

The dancers at first took over an unfinished motel, consisting of cottages in a settlement beyond the town, commonly known as The Dustbowl, or Kibbutz. But it soon became clear that there would be little time available for preparation of new ballets, although Jerome Robbins's GOLDBERG VARIATIONS received its roughing out in the summer of 1970. Current repertory was maintained with efficiency, but swimming pools, horse racing, and Lake George were relaxations too powerful to resist. Our workweeks had much increased over the years; the dancers needed rest. In the exuberance of enjoyment there were hazards—broken toes from soccer games played recklessly in bare feet; ferocious sunburn; too much dosing with mineral water.

I had known Saratoga in the early thirties with Walker Evans, the photographer who made brilliant and valuable records of the vast mid-nineteenth-century wooden resort hotels. Now the Grand Union and the United States had been torn down for parking lot or supermarket. Skidmore College was building a handsome new campus on the outskirts of town, and the new dormitories provided housing for our musicians. While the prime month for horse racing is August (when seasonal rentals triple), we associated ourselves in July with the American Dressage Institute, which enjoyed the instruction of principal riders from the Viennese *Spanische Hofreitschule*—in 1972 celebrating its four hundredth anniversary. This unique performing arts institution has made a true ballet company out of generations of white Lipizzaner stallions. It is a living exemplar of baroque equestrian art, as perfect in its archaeological purity as Gagaku or Noh. Balanchine spent two weeks learning to ride a retired veteran Lipizzaner. Demonstrations of *haute école* equestrian disciplines by Austrian and American riders were held before the ballet performances, to the music of Handel, Haydn, Mozart, and Lanner.

In alternate years, we opened Saratoga with a week of A MIDSUMMER NIGHT'S DREAM, in which painted scenery blended imperceptibly into the surrounding woodland, or THE NUTCRACKER, when July heat magically produced a snowstorm. Dozens of children from local dancing teachers replaced the small students from our New York school. A number of our dancers bought summer cottages of their own and identified themselves with the Saratoga community. However agreeable the atmosphere, the net result as far as our institutional existence went was merely four weeks of steady work; not one new ballet would be introduced for its world premiere. It became only too clear that a semivacation engagement is not a situation which lends itself to experiments or to a true "festival," in the European meaning of Salzburg, Spoleto, Aldeburgh, or Edinburgh. While any progressive company depends on novelty for existence, and while money is often available for costumes and scenery, the element of time is at once the most costly and least available ingredient of a new production. And time is unappealing as a focus of patronage; a closed theater "loses" money. In countries with standard subsidies from arts councils or propaganda ministries, this is considered money spent, not "lost." In America, hospitals, museums, libraries, and schools are necessities in which loss is basic, however grudgingly recognized. But in theater, particularly in lyric theater, of which ballet and opera are the main categories, deficits are so large that a proposal to shut an auditorium for preparatory experiment seems to be the straw that breaks the camel's back.

DECEMBER, 1966: NEW YORK

In our costume shop, Madame Karinska's first models and samples of appliquéd plastic gems lighter than glass, glued or sewn to supple bases on velvet and brocade. Problem of creating glitter without wiping out face and form. Choice of "jewels." Pearls also? No; too close to flesh color, and nonreflective.

As a demi-oriental boy from the Caucasus, Balanchine had always been fascinated by the irreducible mineral treasure of mine and mountain. Some of the most impressive artifacts in Leningrad's Hermitage are huge vases turned from great hunks of Ural semiprecious stones, porphyry, malachite, sardonyx, and basalt. His friend the violinist Nathan Milstein had introduced him to the jeweler Claude Arpels, who allowed Balanchine to fondle a splendid collection of gems. A metaphor to demonstrate perfection, emeralds, rubies, diamonds are the residual matter of aeons, consummately shaped and faceted as an incarnate mathematical paradigm of price, preciousness, luxury; hence of luck or fortune. They are lavish paradoxes of high cost and small size, unbreakable durability against soft mortal flesh, cool fire flashing from some self-generating eternal source. In 1947 for Balanchine's original Paris choreography to Bizet's long-lost and recently recovered Symphony in C (which Stravinsky first told him about), then entitled LE PALAIS DE CRISTAL, he assigned jewel colors to the four movements. When our SYMPHONY IN C (the identical dances) was introduced in New York the next year, it held no gemlike connotation. However, the notion stuck in Balanchine's memory.

JEWELS is a "full-length" ballet without a plot. Karinska's taste and ingenuity robed it in a sightly cohesion appropriate to its flashing pretexts. Dresses and tailoring were fitted and blazoned with lapidary skill. Some cost-conscious carpers questioned the need for consummate attention to needlework which is so delicate between the fingers that the detail is bound to be lost on the far side of the footlights. But Karinska declared: "I sew for girls and boys who make my costumes dance; their bodies deserve my clothes." Karinska's attitude toward thread, needle, and tissue is different in kind from the commercial costumier, as *cordon bleu* cooking differs from home fries in a hash house. Her insistence on an absolute criterion is not reckless extravagance but a practical approach based on the chemistry of the human lymphatic system. Dancers sweat; sweat is as corrosive an acid as exists this side of hydrochloric. Karinska's underpinnings are built like a bridge, cost hours to construct, and endure for many seasons. The caution in her craft inspires a like pride in the wearing by, and bearing of, dancers. As partner to music and choreography, her stitchery of galloon, rhinestone, sequin, and tinsel contributes to the general dazzle.

the New York City Ballet

HARLEQUINADE

BRAHMS/SCHOENBERG QUARTET

JEWELS

Tchaikovsky Suite No.3

Metastaseis & Pithoprakta

Slaughter on Tenth Avenue

TCHAIKOVSKY SUITE NO. 2

LA SOURCE

DANCES AT A

GATHERING

CONCERTO
FOR
2
SOLO
PIANOS

4
—
LAST
SONGS

CHOPINIANA

Who Cares?

PAS DE DEUX & DIVERTISSEMENT

Balanchine had considered some orchestral music of Schoenberg's for a sapphire section, but blues command an awkward range of gelatines for stage illumination. And in combination with rubies and diamonds, the blue stones take on a patriotic tinge already accommodated in STARS AND STRIPES.

Contrast of musical coloration was considerable. The translucent serenity and transparent shimmer of Gabriel Fauré's pieces from his PELLÉAS ET MÉLISANDE suite (1898) and his incidental music for SHYLOCK (1889) suggested a submarine summer-green garden of moss, lime, and—Emeralds. Rubies—Stravinsky's Capriccio for Piano and Orchestra (1929)—dictated an ironic speed and lyric humor for dashing variations by Edward Villella and Patricia McBride. A platoon of pony jockeys and filly ballerinas danced in oxblood or crimson epaulettes and belts. Diamonds used Tchaikovsky's Third Symphony (the *Polish,* 1875, less its first movement) —two scherzi, a grand adagio, and a big polonaise, seeming to employ the entire company of ninety and fill the stage to surfeit, although only thirty-four dancers are used. This is one of the best examples of Balanchine's applause-machines, different in style but similar in effect to the finales to the other Tchaikovsky scores for SUITE NO. 3 and CONCERTO NO. 2, the Gounod and Bizet symphonies in stimulating climactic excitement and response. Minutes before the end, the fluid collective organism drives toward a sumptuous peak. The audience's empathy and instinctive appetite for block-busting muscular effects devours a big crescendo, gulping at a stage crammed with uniform, symmetrical, head-on movement, and firm primary gesture while the big orchestra builds to a smashing curtain tableau. JEWELS has been an unequivocal and rapturous "success" since its introduction; the very title sounds expensive before a step is seen. But some who watch it frequently find that Emeralds rather than the bouncier Rubies or the panache of Diamonds are indeed the most exquisitely set gems in this particular *parure.*

APRIL, 1969: NEW YORK

Listening to pianos onstage and off for Jerome Robbins's new Chopin. Neither Gordon Boelzner, our solo pianist, nor Balanchine wishes the piano amplified, but its presence onstage is limiting and has been used before in Jerry's comic ballet THE CONCERT (1956) which is to be revived. Balanchine suggested a platform over an end of the orchestra pit, unless the balcony's overhang smothers sound.

Robbins had turned his energy to Hollywood films and Broadway musicals, notably WEST SIDE STORY and FIDLER ON THE ROOF, after his earlier ON THE TOWN, which he derived from his ballet FANCY FREE of 1944. Possessing an analytical method and choreographic authority second only to Balanchine's, he naturally wished to exercise personal possibilities unhampered by conditions which our schedule imposed. He proceeded to an impressive and fruitful career with his own troupe and later, through aid from the National Endowment, experimented with dancers of his choosing, on his own time, with no need to produce a definite piece by a given date. His quasi-religious treatment of Stravinsky's LES NOCES for Ballet Theater, while diametrically opposite to Bronislava Nijinska's masterpiece of 1923 for Diaghilev (now admirably danced by the Royal Ballet), had its own massive if wrongheaded integrity. However, he admitted afterward that he preferred Nijinska's version, which was characteristic of his basic objectivity and clear eye. After years of independent labor, he gave evidence of interest in our enterprise.

Balanchine has always wished for someone, almost anyone beside himself, to share the pressure of continuous composition and production. Out of any three novelties, only one has much chance of remaining in repertory after two seasons. His own work dominates almost by default. This is naturally irritating to everyone who chooses to believe that Balanchine tyrannizes over other ballet masters and that they are prevented from working with him only by his jealous fear of some poten-

tial competitor. Alas, one hunts in vain for so lucky a find, although journalists have kept themselves busy and proud year after year discovering dozens. Balanchine had long acknowledged Robbins as the native-born choreographer with the strongest structural and musical sense.

We had attempted many times to broaden our base. Frederick Ashton, working with Cecil Beaton, had given us two successes: ILLUMINATIONS of 1950 and PICNIC AT TINTAGEL (Sir Arnold Bax's *Garden of Fand*) of 1952. However, with Ninette de Valois's retirement as director of the Royal Ballet and Fred's logical succession, he had his own big garden to cultivate, and he was by temperament happiest on the far side of the Atlantic. As for Antony Tudor, perhaps we failed to find him a comfortable frame. Of our five ballets from him, only a revival of DIM LUSTRE (1964) was retained, although our LILAC GARDEN (1951), in the lush shrubbery which Horace Armistead took from Fragonard's panels in the Frick Collection, had one of its strongest presentations anywhere, with an exceptional cast (Nora Kaye, Tanaquil LeClercq, Hugh Laing, Tudor himself). It is not simply for choreographers schooled in climates other than our own to arrive cold, as it were, and warm up impassive if not faintly hostile dancers who are slow to change habits of acceptance or resistance.

In rehearsal Robbins drives, and displays himself as driven. He appears more instinctive, less analytical than Balanchine, at least in the immediacy of composition. When he returned to us, Balanchine assigned him most of his own rehearsal time for some four seasons, from 1969 through 1972, during the preparation of DANCES AT A GATHERING and THE GOLDBERG VARIATIONS. There was no reluctance in this temporary abdication, either in New York's winter or Saratoga's summer. A painter aims at perfection far more easily than a choreographer, for the painter works at his own pace. Although external compulsions of one-man shows or private commissions may prod him, time is his own. But ballet masters must reckon by the union scale, union conditions, and time-and-a-half

Balanchine rehearsing Shaun O'Brien

Balanchine rehearsing Michael Arshansky

Robbins rehearsing Blum

for overtime, to say nothing of allowing for daily rehearsals to maintain a current repertory and adjusting to the injuries and replacements inevitable for any company that dances hard eight times a week. Nor is it easy for a tightly bonded family of performers accustomed to one type of domination or obedience to embrace or even submit to another entirely different personal method. Our dancers were developed on Balanchine's systems, which are fantastically rapid, whatever their immediate form or subsequent alterations.

Robbins's choice of Chopin's piano pieces was dictated by affection and at the risk of self-repetition. His CONCERT amounted to a comic masterpiece in its parodies of the classic academic idiom. While it often used identical musical material, italicized by sections of a thumping orchestration, within its format, the figure of the solo pianist is as important as any of the dancers. After Fokine's LES SYLPHIDES, which we would revive as CHOPINIANA (without costumes or decor), complacent critics might consider that nothing further should hack at the already eroded monument of Chopin. Robbins worked against, and overcame, varieties of doubt, since his instinct for an intrinsic quality in pianistic vocalism, the haunting echoes of folk sources in their lyric tenderness, enabled him to evoke a vision which was without precedent, one which he magically extracted from the resonance of a grand piano.

DANCES AT A GATHERING places five girls and five young men on some ambiguously native earth, far, yet not too far, from Chopin's own ground. Minimal costumes suggest, mainly through blouse and boot, that the men are neither princes nor peasants, although gently born. The girls wear filmy shifts and are clearly dancing out-of-doors, but as neither countesses nor shepherdesses. They are charming, well-bred young women. The time is possibly past midsummer, fading into autumn, the year perhaps closer to today than to any "romantic" past. The tone of movement proposes mutations of national dancing which, a century ago, adapted themselves to big ballrooms, but which still are infused with earthy vigor and informal courtesy. The men belong to some confraternity; the girls might be cousins; their contacts are more familial or tribal than passionate. Robbins empowered his dancers with so strong a personal flavor of homage to Chopin's spirit that the sequence of duets, trios, quartets, quintets, and their combination expanded into a kind of formal drama, although there was an almost total absence of personalizing characterization, except in the exquisite palette of Joe Eula's costumes. There is no narrative except in a contrast of musical mood, no marked climax, but rather a series of crescendi or diminuendi, which fill metaphorical incident with suave fun, sweet games, and the hint or threat of violence. As a finale, there's an elegaic, offbeat processional, a progressive thanksgiving or hymn to native soil. No exact reference is ever given, however; the processional may apply to the ages of man rather than the map of a nation.

Robbins and Balanchine work as a duet in tandem. Both are too secure in endowment and practice to compete where there is no need for competition. They are separated by nearly twenty years, yet their joint respect for music as a floor for dancing can forge no firmer bond. For thirty years Robbins has watched Balanchine more closely, with more benefit, than any other ballet master.

While it is impossible to imagine THE CAGE without a double image of the bacchantes' final fury in ORPHEUS, the metrical division which Robbins gave his hive of horrid creatures is due as much to Stravinsky's syncopation as to Balanchine's structure. Similarly, the lovely finale of DANCES AT A GATHERING derives from the last three minutes of NIGHT SHADOW, but now with the dancers turned to the front to face the audience. It is so astutely adapted that few audiences are conscious of the conversion.

It is not alone from Balanchine that Robbins has borrowed or digested, just as Balanchine himself has rifled the whole range of gesture and movement from well-known repertory "classics," circus, music-hall, film, and memories of which only he can identify the original source. However, digestion, assimilation, absorption amount to much more than "being influenced by." Stravinsky said that no artist is more himself than when he imitates somebody else, for it is personal choice or taste that counts. Think of Rimski-Korsakov in FIREBIRD, Pergolesi in PULCINELLA, Delibes in APOLLO, Handel in OEDIPUS REX, Gesualdo in MONUMENTUM. Robbins wanders far, works hard in many companies, is not attached to any for long, has seen and read a multitude of pictures and books. What he notes and hears continually strikes sparks in his mind's tinder, which is always ready to take fire. What he possesses to a surpassing degree is the gift for shock, for conscious eruption, for an attack by novelty in broad, legible statements.

SEPTEMBER, 1969: NEW YORK

To the Juilliard School, Claremont Avenue. Peter Mennin, the director, invited me to meet Norman Singer, in charge of musical attractions at Hunter College. Discussed the Platonic Ideal of an executive manager for City Center. Memories of Morton Baum; the good old, bad old days, beyond recall. Nervousness about a musicians' strike.

Morton Baum's death in February, 1968, was a paralyzing blow. It removed an anchor on reality. For some anxious months we carried on as we might, acting more or less autonomously if automatically, although token control naturally remained with our central authority. The City Center on 55th Street, the State Theater at Lincoln Center, each has its problems. The State Theater was an added burden to Baum; we were only beginning to make a new facility function. We managed to stumble on as if there were no possible replacement for Baum, while realizing that eventually we'd be forced to find one. However, the battle with Lincoln Center, Inc., had been won by Baum, assisted by the intransigent strategy of Betty Cage, the resolute support of the New York City Opera, and unyielding loyalty from Baum's associates. Control of the State Theater would rest in our hands, with no latent threat of exploitation by any high-bidding impresario or agency that could charge whatever prices "special" attractions might be made to justify. The house we had jointly conceived and fought for would remain a permanent, populist home for singing and dancing. This was Baum's victory and legacy.

Without Baum's political sense, honesty, empirical method, and courage, we were confused and in shock. No one else could run the City Center the way he did. His procedure and attitude were attached to a definite historical epoch—from Fiorello La Guardia through Robert Moses to John Lindsay. With his passing, a chap-

ter was over. Our scale of operation was completely changed; City Center was now the arena of a multitude of added activities. It needed direction for increasingly broad and varied programs and service on an international as well as a national basis. Its program would continue to compete with commercial concert-managements, manipulated directly or indirectly by television or the subsidiaries of banks. City Center would continue to provide interesting foreign and native attractions at low prices. Performing-arts agencies in America have always been greedy and monopolistic. Now a number of hopelessly unprofitable adventures, from home and abroad, found a haven in the nooks and crannies of Mecca Temple. Meanwhile, even the larger managements needed to book houses smaller than Madison Square Garden, in those months when the Metropolitan Opera operated its own subscription series.

Providentially, circumstances brought us Norman Singer, who then controlled concerts at Hunter College, whose philosophy of programs complemented and supplemented the City Center's. There he had managed a large hall and smaller theater (where both American Ballet Caravan and Ballet Society, Inc., had danced). His programs were no less distinguished, the artists he presented no less renowned, than those appearing at Carnegie Hall at twice the price. He was both an educator and an impresario familiar with world markets. He had also worked at summer festivals in Aspen, Colorado, and possessed a general experience and catholic taste which recommended him on every level.

Nor was he naïve. The necessary intransigence of opera and ballet, our prickliness, irritability, or independence, had lit a couple of candles which were not hidden under any bushel. On our first meeting, he asked what would be the gravest fears relative to our autonomy. Apart from the fact that Baum had always recognized Balanchine and Rudel as laws unto themselves, we pic-

SLAUGHTER ON TENTH AVENUE: Suzanne Farrell

tured ourselves as rational brigands whose motto was: "A little too much is just enough for us." This did not daunt Singer. We told him we feared "efficiency" in any form. On any board of directors like Lincoln Center's, overwhelming sorrow came over finance committees at each manifestation of rising costs (less of materials than of labor; less of construction than of performers or performances). The affluent realtors, lawyers, brokers who charge themselves with the promulgation of art in performance naturally turn to efficiency experts to propose how costs can be cut. They crave the impervious wisdom of computers, time clocks, cost accountancy, and personal reformation. The efficiency experts are presumably hired because they have no knowledge of the special climate of theater and will be properly horrified at the looseness, changeability, fantasy, and hysteria of professional behavior. They know how a corporation should be run, profit or no profit, whether it be a bank, hospital, museum, or library. Losses should be modestly predicated, with every inch of planning spelled out, and no further problems. As for isolated personalities and their pretensions to unique service, isn't everyone replaceable and expendable?

Singer knew exactly what we were trying to tell him. What few realize who have not survived in theatrical wonderlands is that there is an elixir without which no performance has a chance of persuading the public (for long) that what is performed is worth the price of admission. This magic has little to do with good taste, intrinsic aesthetic values, advertising, an honest box office, a pretty theater, and a fair reputation. It is hysteria. Distinctions can, of course, be made. Hysteria in the performing arts is not (necessarily) neurotic, although it may show itself in the more spectacular masks of schizophrenia, paranoia, or other poisonous egocentric manias. Freud, faced with the genius or pathology of Dostoevski, said that when confronted with the artist, psychoanalysis must lay down its tools. Not all performers are hysterics, although all are continually under psychic stress, since they risk what they may make from their private psyches for public judgment. Unless they possess that excess of electrical energy which is easily confused with aberration, it is unlikely that they will overcome the essential shyness of every rational self-doubter to project themselves past the footlights. Offstage, except in transient lucid moments, the conduct of many theatrical artists can be read as irrational, untidy, wasteful, unjusti-

fiable, and exasperating. Why can't these folk behave like other folk? Because they are not like other folk.

Norman Singer was accustomed to the climate of hysteria, which breeds many viruses of treachery, loyalty, excitement, and brilliance; but this was exactly what fascinated him. In our stews and swamps, his job was to clear a place where artists in their best minds and moments could use onstage what might be dismay, high spirits, self-indulgence, or practical joking offstage.

OCTOBER, 1969: NEW YORK

With Balanchine and Hershy Kay leafing through George and Ira Gershwin's collected songs: "'s wonderful! 's marvelous (That you should care for me!)" "Do, do, do what you've done, done, done, before—(Baby!)" "I'm bidin' my time, 'cause that's the kinda guy I'm." "Who cares? (If the sky cares to fall in the sea?)" Hershy knows of a tape recording of George Gershwin playing his own arrangements; it can be inserted as a cadenza in a suite of dances which he'll arrange for large orchestra.

When George Gershwin died of a brain tumor in Hollywood on July 11, 1937, the master of dodecaphony, Arnold Schoenberg, said the next day in a radio broadcast of the memorial service: "Music was to George Gershwin not a matter of ability. It was the air he breathed, the dream he dreamed. I grieve over the deplorable loss of music, for there is no doubt that he was a great composer."

Music written for light opera or social dancing provides a wealth of diverting scores which corroborate our nostalgia for a not too remote past. Stephen Foster, Offenbach, Gilbert and Sullivan, Irving Berlin, Cole Porter all wrote very singable songs which make danceable tunes, and these tickle aural and visual reminders of our parents' youth or our own. But when Balanchine, after three decades, took Gershwin's songs, he had no thought of basing a ballet on a synthetic revival of the taste of the twenties or thirties, no intention of presenting an affectionate pastiche of Fred and Adele Astaire or Ginger Rogers. He had no interest in musical-comedy hoofing or tap dancing as such. What he wished to demonstrate was the intrinsic wit, polyrhythmic genius, and melodic beauty of Gershwin as a propellant of motor metric, impelling the use of his tempi and tunes toward the classic dance. There would be side glances at Broadway musicals, while Jo Mielziner's metamorphic skyscraper and Central Park South–scape might have served well as an early *New Yorker* cover.

Balanchine had been set to work with Gershwin on THE GOLDWYN FOLLIES in his last summer. I had met him through Eddie Warburg's friendship with Kay Swift, whom Gershwin had proposed for ALMA MATER, our first "American" ballet. Gershwin and I once had a talk when during a penthouse party we took refuge in the pantry. He'd been hunting for a subject for an opera, not at all like PORGY AND BESS, but something with a chance to use black singers, not alone in solo voices but for massed choral effects. He rejected *Uncle Tom's Cabin*, although, as he said, there were the canonical roles: Little Eva (soprano), Simon Legree (basso), St. Clare (baritone), Topsy (falsetto!). He could not imagine an audience —half of which having been brought up seeing the local "Tom-shows"—accepting the pretext as much beyond parody. Our hope for e. e. cummings's *Tom* had proved impossible or implausible for the opposite reason: it was overheroicized.

I suggested the figure of Toussaint l'Ouverture or Christophe and later gave Gershwin John Vandercook's *Black Majesty*, a sketch of the rebellion in Haiti against the French. Orson Welles and John Houseman had recently had a triumph in Harlem with the Federal Theater project, transposing MACBETH from Dunsinane to somewhere near Port-au-Prince. Gershwin seemed bemused by the proposal, but hesitated at the demands of a piece attached to a past epoch, the need to pay some attention

REQUIEM CANTICLES: performed as a tribute to Martin Luther King, Jr.

JEUX: Allegra Kent, Edward Villella

BRAHMS-SCHOENBERG QUARTET: Conrad Ludlow, Patricia McBride

to minuets, waltzes, polkas. Did I think William Faulkner could write a libretto? He wrote films, after all. The perfect librettist for him, he had in his pocket: Ira! Yes, for songs; none better; but to construct three acts . . . like Da Ponte, Ghislanzoni, Boito, Illica, or Giacosa. The pictorial possibilities appealed to him: uniforms, the Duke of Marmalade, the Duchess of Orangeade, jungle, voodoo.

Gershwin was also a painter, like Schoenberg and cummings, but rather more professional than either. His was a translucently sunny spirit; so natural a cheerfulness, such impersonal good humor in so powerful and focused a talent are rare. None of it was saccharine or affected; he had none of the "famous personality's" compulsive self-framed mannerism. The quality of light irony, sage humor, sweetness, and delight radiated from George's presence and saturates the lyrics and music of the brothers Gershwin.

Balanchine has always been preoccupied with popular idioms, the argot of every language, popular musical theater, and films. The first work of his I ever saw was a *pas de deux* in an American tour of Nikita Baliev's Chauve-Souris in 1925. This talented troupe of White Russian singers and dancers gathered from Paris night clubs, where they earned a living in exile by their wits and skills. They had as impresario or emcee a big apple of a man. Baliev bore an astonishing resemblance to my father, who much admired him; by some chance symbiosis they became friends. My father, as master of ceremonies, would give fairly convincing imitations of Baliev for amateur nights at his country club; the Russian visited us in Boston when he came through on tour. Balanchine as a young boy had married Tamara Gevergeva, a student in the Leningrad Academy. They left Russia together, and later they both joined Diaghilev. Balanchivadze turned into "Balanchine," she into "Geva." Tamara quit the Bal-

Left to right:
George Balanchine, Eugenie Ouroussow, Lincoln Kirstein, Natasha Molostwoff

lets Russes to join the Chauve-Souris, and for her Balanchine made an "Etruscan" *pas de deux* which seemed to me, in Boston's old Wilbur Theater, perverse, pornographic, and passionately interesting.

Before the curtain, Baliev appeared to describe the next number. He poked snide fun at Balanchine's choreography before anyone had a chance to see it. I had the nerve to ask him why, if he included it on his program, did he run it down? He said he was, like my father, a merchant and not a crusader ("like your fraynd, Mees-taire Dee-awg-ee-leff"); that he depended on no patronage save his public; that he introduced such *avant-gardisme* as the "Etruscan" duet just as he would offer a novel soap or perfume. The Ballets Russes had begun to have a certain trans-Atlantic chic. Also, he thought the duet funny and sexy and even rather liked it. However, one must consider saving the public's face if it is not smart enough to accept novelty on first sight. Before this, I'd not considered that theater might possess a pragmatic or commercial side. I had thought that all works passing within a proscenium must perforce be "art" — some possibly better than others, but as much "art" as architecture, sculpture, or painting, in whose holy provinces commerce need never intrude. Baliev was a stateless exile, the first of many I would meet. From him I discovered that performing artists were also declassed gypsies who not only, in his words, sang "sahd sonks" but who had nothing to protect them but a scrap of paper labeled a Nansen passport. This a few immigration officials might accept while

Alexandra Danilova teaching

others would not, just as some audiences would be pleased enough to enable the artists to eat better, or even oftener, than others.

When Balanchine landed in New York he was paid a pittance. He never asked us for a binding contract, nor was he given one. Within a year, however, he was approached to make dances for the "final" edition of a Ziegfeld Follies, and soon afterward he began his partnership with Lorenz Hart and Richard Rodgers. After Gershwin died, he worked with Vernon Duke, who in 1924, under his own name of Vladimir Dukelsky, composed ZÉPHIRE ET FLORE (Massine–Georges Braque) for Diaghilev. Balanchine was the first to insist on the word "choreography" as applied to invention of dances on programs and posters for Broadway musicals. His extended sequences in BABES IN ARMS, I MARRIED AN ANGEL, ON YOUR TOES, CABIN IN THE SKY, LOUISIANA PURCHASE, and other commercial successes raised the level of dancing in the eyes of both performers and public. In 1968, after we moved into the State Theater, he revived SLAUGHTER ON TENTH AVENUE, Richard Rodgers's number originally invented for Tamara Geva and Ray Bolger, while Jo Mielziner enlarged his cerise and maroon honky-tonk bar from I MARRIED AN ANGEL of 1938. But now, restudying George Gershwin's songs, which he prized for their great residual value, Balanchine anthologized the most compelling and seductive songs as a symphonic suite.

Like many of our new ballets at their first appearance, it was presented with simple dresses and rudimentary scenery—projected blowups of skyscrapers at night. But WHO CARES? found favor, at home and abroad, and nowhere more warmly than throughout the Soviet Union in 1972 on our second tour.

Balanchine rehearsing Farrell

Balanchine and Karinska with dancer

the New York City Ballet

206

THE SONG OF THE NIGHTINGALE: Gelsey Kirkland, Francisco Moncion

SCHERZO FANTASTIQUE: (previous page) Gelsey Kirkland; (above) Victor Castelli, Bryan Pitts, Stephen Caras

FIREBIRD: Gelsey Kirkland

ORPHEUS: Francisco Moncion, Jean-Pierre Bonnefous, Melissa Hayden

REQUIEM CANTICLES: Company

FIREBIRD (next page): Jacques d'Amboise, Gloria Govrin

JUNE, 1970: NEW YORK

Annual stage performance by students of the School of American Ballet at the State Theater, for subscribers and Friends of the City Center. Program, KONSERVATORIET (Act II, 1849), by August Bournonville, staged by Stanley Williams, and COPPELIA selections (1870), arranged by Alexandra Danilova, after Arthur Saint-Léon. The Friends filled the theater twice.

Our School of American Ballet was newly installed in handsome quarters on the third floor of the splendid complex of theaters, concert halls, studios, and classrooms which constitute the Juilliard School, only a long block from the State Theater at Lincoln Center. Designed to our specifications by the architects and engineers Belluschi, Catalano, and Westermann, the space assigned was the result of years of consideration and negotiation. While our school has no legal connection with Juilliard's corporation, we were enabled through the patronage of the Ford Foundation to lease space for our perpetual use.

Studios were as large as the performing area of the State Theater's stage, well-lit by high windows of uninterrupted glass. (We had, with considerable difficulty, managed to perforate the back and side walls of our State Theater offices with mean slits, inserted almost as an afterthought. Air conditioning supposedly obviates any need for daylight, since windows must be sealed, but the psychological effect of hermetically sealed rooms is depressing.) Balanchine now restudied the systems of the studio floors to provide more spring than those in the theater. An interlace of pine slats, thinner, but laid in more depth, covered with battleship linoleum, provides what might seem to measure as a minuscule lift. But it spares knees and ankles in the skeletons of bipeds who were not structured to compete with birds or kangaroos. The school's foyers were hung with a pictorial history of the development of stage dancing, old color prints of Petersburg's palaces, and George Platt Lynes's photographic record of our early years.

The conveniences for teachers and students that are needed in a ballet school do not sound glamorous, but a generous supply of brightly tiled showers and commodious lockers is more welcome than any luxury. Anyone inspecting the recently erected buildings in Kiev, Leningrad, or Moscow must be deeply impressed by the Soviet's concern for its patrimony of aspirants to its ballet companies. While no American school, however fortunate, can compete with such massive subvention, we now enjoyed vast improvements over anything obtainable on the corner of 59th Street and Madison, or later at Broadway and 83rd. There are separate dressing rooms for both young and more advanced children; teachers have their own space for robing and relaxation; there is even room for a Ping-Pong table. The administrative offices are bright and comfortable, overlooking a panorama of Broadway traffic. Considering the prevailing conditions in this country, and our desperate absence of dormitory space with the supervision required for young students from outside New York, the situation at Juilliard is realistic and efficient.

While our first generation of masters continued with the lively instruction of Felia Doubrovska and Muriel Stuart, our early stalwarts Pierre Vladimirov and Anatole Oboukhoff were gone. From the Royal Danish Ballet, Stanley Williams, dancer, ballet master, and teacher with a world reputation, brought us his experience of tradition, teaching, and performance that are parallel to but quite different from our predominantly Russian academy. He taught the style and steps of August Bournonville, Scandinavia's contemporary of Petipa and Ivanov, who put the emphasis on strength in male soloists. Madame Alexandra Danilova, who was trained with Balanchine and Doubrovska in the old imperial and state schools and who danced with them under Diaghilev, provided her arcana of stage behavior and technique to our students. Dancers who had been in our school and company for years, and who now no longer performed, also joined the faculty—among them Elise Reiman, Richard Rapp, and Suki Schorer. Dancers who are continuing to perform, yet who have a definite predilection for teaching, also began to master the difficult skills of instruction. These represent a new generation, with a philosophy of performance gained from Balanchine's repertory. We were fortunate in finding two teachers who continued the traditions of instruction formulated in Russia. Helene Dudin, who graduated from the Kiev Choreographic Academy and danced in Leningrad and Moscow, left during the Second World War. Antonina Tumkovsky, who had similar training and experience and studied under Vaganova in Leningrad, came to New York in 1949.

Anatole Oboukhoff teaching

Balanchine

Muriel Stuart teaching

Felia Doubrovska teaching

Pierre Vladimirov

Ballet schools are little vineyards with aging racks and bottling plants. Some years provide prime vintages; others are less generous with the juice of the grape. While we have always attracted long-legged, promising girls in quantity, more boys with more promise have now begun to come. From 1963, two separate grants from the Ford Foundation Division of Humanities enabled us to expand and develop. Because of the cautious interest and courageous wisdom of W. McNeil Lowry and Marcia Thompson, his deputy, we now stood in a fair way to become a service school on a national scale, although scarcely on the Soviet level comparable to a West Point or Annapolis. Our Ford program presupposed a highly selective policy in which we cooperated with affiliated regional schools. Continental tours of inspection by members of our faculty corroborated the opinions of those teaching at the grass roots and enabled local schools to send talented students for advanced study and later employment past local possibilities. Scholarships for training by hometown teachers are awarded gifted teen-agers for whom the extended cost of serious instruction is often impossible. Beginner groups are sponsored in regional schools as testing grounds and additional sources of talent for eight- to fourteen-year-olds who (for economic or environmental reasons) would not ordinarily enroll in a ballet school. These young people receive free instruction from one to three years; then the more promising may continue on local scholarships. Such students may find employment in the community, or go on to advanced schools of their own choice in some of the larger centers. They may also be awarded full scholarships and modest maintenance at our own school, with the prospect of eventually joining our company.

In addition, Balanchine conducted advanced seminars for teachers who came from all over the Americas, while our instructors visit widely scattered schools for repeated periods of concentrated teaching. Several of our former dancers have become responsible for schools and companies of their own. Balanchine's repertory is extensively performed by regional companies. It is also taught all over the globe by ballet masters and mistresses trained in it, as well as by the dancers who continue to appear in these works. While our school has no civic, state, or federal support, and while our company is far more representative of a metropolis than of a nation, the School of American Ballet has indeed set a standard for the country, and is recognized internationally for doing so. Not only are our dancers increasingly called to perform or teach in Germany, Holland, Switzerland, and Japan, but the school attracts foreign soloists and teachers to New York. The rationale of its leadership and instruction under the long-term guidance of Eugenie Ouroussow, Natasha Molostwoff, and Natasha Gleboff is recognized throughout the world, as it was recently in the *London Times*, as a "star factory."

OCTOBER, 1971: NEW YORK

With Balanchine to see Richard Clurman, Time-Life Building, with budget of Stravinsky Festival. Tried to persuade Balanchine to insert one ballet a week into repertory, during twelve weeks of spring season. He refused, insisted on one concentrated week. However, if all thirty ballets are produced at once, the State Theater must be shut in midseason for one week, adding $100,000 to costs. Clurman "sympathetic," which Balanchine took for assent.

Stravinsky's death the previous April meant both the end of an epoch and the entrance of a number of new ballets to his music, sparked by a mammoth celebration of his achievement in June, 1972. Counting by sundial or clock time, he was surely an ancient. By the metric of art and spirit, he was much in the running and would remain so as long as our dancers could count. Even before his mortality was fact, Balanchine had proposed a lively homage, not so much in praise as in gratitude for his gifts, which could best be expressed by their public demonstration. The expense involved in money, mind, and muscle would be considerable. We were prepared to commit production capital for three years to budget the single week, assuming the likelihood that we could gain as many additions to repertory at once as over the longer period. However, this meant an outright involvement of money that we did not, or in all probability would not, have to spend.

Norman Singer had already assumed the day-to-day business of ensuring our survival, but he was scarcely permitted to plan ahead on such a scale against the pressure of imminent schedules. Long-range programming deep into the seventies was necessary. With its two permanent theaters and rental of others, City Center's civic and national programs had so expanded that it was now the largest public performing-arts service in the world. Annual expenditures were some ten million dollars, of which a third was deficit. Fresh sources of support would have to be found from state and federal agencies, while big business corporations showed more interest in committing themselves for further tax-exempt contributions. Educational and charitable foundations had been generous, but with their fixed policy of terminal grants, their support was always limited in duration. The problem was to find a successor to Morton Baum.

The solution seemed strange. A man was chosen who, while recognized in the confines of his profession, had even less of a public face than Baum had had. Unlike Baum, however, his successor did not even have the reputation of an amateur in the performing arts. For some decades Richard Clurman had been an executive in the publishing empire of Henry Luce; he had been charged most recently with coordinating the worldwide bureaus of Time-Life's national and international news gatherers. He was at home equally in Saigon or Seattle; his continual physical contact with global action gave him access to any office and to most persons who could possibly be useful in collecting world information. He had no special interest in opera or ballet; opera was something of a blank book; ballet, he might guess, was about dancing. He liked games, however—those performed publicly and others conducted otherwise. He had an expert's understanding of the personal performance of men in power, and of the people they manipulated. To him as a journalist, life in the raw and *Life* in print, time as history and *Time* the weekly news capsule, were spec-

tator sports, whether in Moscow, Miami, Madrid, or Manhattan. More important, he was accustomed to star performers, although a proscenium did not frame their stage. He had experience in judging the unique value of reckless reporters, intrepid and passionate foreign correspondents, and prima donna photographers. Stress and extremity were familiar in his world; emergency, accident, replacement, and catastrophe were normal.

When Clurman explained to Julius Rudel, John White, Betty Cage, Balanchine, and me his doubts about being responsible for opera singers and ballet dancers, he hardly had to be told that, on a human level, there would be no surprises. One way or another, he'd heard it all before, with a different cast of characters, on a broader scale. However, principles of excellence in performance, and in breadth and quality of service, amounted to a similar expenditure of energy. What doubts we had concerning inroads on our autonomy, such as the chance interjection of Time-Life efficiency experts, reorganization, or office reform, were quickly dispelled. Dick Clurman said firmly, and meant it, that he was incapable of accepting the job unless we continued as if Morton Baum still sat at the desk where the buck stopped. He agreed to hold the handle of the umbrella over City Center, and we were to proceed much as before.

Our proposal for the Stravinsky Festival was a first big test. In our eagerness to make the complexity of the operation absolutely clear, it was not necessary to exaggerate the costs or difficulties. Nothing had ever been attempted on such a scale in this country before. When Diaghilev proposed his invasion of Western Europe in 1909, he had the advantages of a czar's privy purse, Russian Foreign Office propaganda for the Entente Cordiale, and later, an international committee of patrons—Polignacs, Murats, Rothschilds, the Aga Khan—implemented as much by cash as by a coherence of class. In New York there was none of this. Clurman estimated the challenge rather like a pianist strumming chords or a painter laying out a palette. It was not that some sounds or colors were preferable, but that each had its own tones in combination. Had we offered him only custodial supervision of our maintenance or survival, then other theaters of war or peace would have been more attractive to him. Nevertheless, to embrace

WATERMILL:
Penny Dudleston

the New York City Ballet

WATERMILL: Edward Villella

huge deficit financing with open eyes as a virtual introduction into an enchanted jungle, whatever the attraction or justification, may be taken as foolhardy. Anyone seeking ease or comfort in the vicinity of theaters is ill-advised—something Clurman did not need to be told. So the ballet and opera were licensed to proceed. But now we viewed in a different light our lists of the works we wanted to produce to demonstrate Stravinsky's long career from Opus 1 through his last years. Previously, we had thought that anything, everything, or nothing might be possible. Now with tangible proposals and a budget accepted, we could figure realistically what might be produced at the State Theater in the months, weeks, days, hours, and minutes until 7:30 P.M., June 18, 1972.

JANUARY, 1972: NEW YORK

Ronnie Bates has received and hung the "moon" for Jerry Robbins's new WATERMILL. It is not a film projection but half a plastic globe, lit from within, with a shutter which changes it from thinnest sickle to full moon. Teiji Ito's small band of musicians rehearses onstage—a Bugaku-gamelan combo. Barking dogs, sea-gull cries, wind and jet plane noises, over-and-under, on tape.

After DANCES AT A GATHERING, Robbins felt compelled to design still another work to Chopin's piano pieces. IN THE NIGHT was a nocturnal encounter, its ambience more of ballroom than of open field. There was little repetition of motive or movement from the earlier DANCES; while shorter and less expansive, it satisfied. He had also been considering the entire series of thirty variations composed in 1736 by Johann Sebastian Bach for the harpsichordist Johann Goldberg. In 1938, during a third and final tour of Ballet Caravan, William Dollar had set a third of the series to attractive choreography. His dancers wore costumes having no bearing on any historic epoch; their tights were marbleized in veins of black, white, and gold, under the influence of Tchelitchev's then-current fascination with the striations in marble. Robbins used the complete suite of variations originally composed for Count Kayserling, a sleepless nobleman, so that Goldberg, his court musician, might alleviate his insomnia.

Experiments were made with an actual harpsichord, but its sound did not carry in Saratoga's huge auditorium, while amplification altered its timbre. An unamplified concert grand was preferable. GOLDBERG VARIATIONS lasts considerably over an hour, and was originally performed with no intermission. Its demands on both dancers and audience are not light. Our subscribers in New York and our captive audience in Saratoga have, over the years, accustomed themselves to our insistence on making them listen hard at the same moments when they look with attention. A minimum of visual adornment and emphasis on unfamiliar rhythms and sonorities demand a concentration which is willing to accept a certain didactic tyranny. This has been taken as arbitrary or even tiring. While our decorative or cosmetic style has been visually meager or underprivileged, it has had compensations in the aural element. Close listening is different from loose hearing; hard looking is not the same as easy viewing. In GOLDBERG VARIATIONS there is little adornment to distract from a density of formal structure. Drama and decor are inherent in contrasts of tempi or accentual movement, made kinetically plastic by metric and melody rather than painted color. In such a context it has a deliberate intensity unique in our repertory.

Its "theme" is gravely declared by two dancers uniformed in an adaptation of court dress worn in Bach's day. Having stated this as a basis for subsequent deployment, the pair disappear while their companions appear in contemporary classroom practice dress. During a complex progress through thirty variations, bits and pieces of costumes are acquired, so that by the complicated combinations of the final *quodlibet*, the entire large cast is clad in the discreet festive apparel of some provincial baroque court. To reaffirm the entire musical exposition, the two figures of the introduction now reappear alone on an empty stage, in the resumed simplicity but equal formality of their own practice uniforms. The ballet has turned itself inside out, like a superbly fashioned glove, embroidered on both sides in changeable silk. GOLDBERG VARIATIONS concerns dancing in "time," Bach's as well as ours, as well as the time it takes dancers to measure and encapsulate a historical past within a historical present. Robbins's demonstration of the composer's formal patterns is exhaustive instruction in hearing and seeing, relieved by memorable vignettes of abrupt action, acrobatic amusement, generous invention, and fine dancing. His was a daring intellectual concept and, in its own terms of taste and format, well-risked.

When Robbins was pondering yet another novelty, he remained reluctant to use the weighty sonorities of a symphonic orchestra. However, he had now achieved four works based on an unaccompanied piano, and they all stayed in repertory. Still fascinated by the exploitation of altered, expanded, or mutated elements in unsuspected temporal duration, the extension of possible measurings beyond clock time, he dispensed with a fixed or concrete timetable in WATERMILL. It is laid out as metrically unstructured, except by impositions of mood through visual short circuits and atmospheric poetics. The musical partnering by Teiji Ito and his group of exotic instrumentalists sounds as quaintly appropriate interjection, punctuation, or aural italics. What Robbins now proposed was tantamount to repudiating Bach's insistent arithmetical beat—and abandoning all classical geometric movement and gesture such as have been prompted by occidental music inherited from dance suite through the sonata form to the symphony and beyond. Music for WATERMILL was reduced to the service of a superexistential sound track, fragmented, spiky, wispy—the cursive trilling of birds or insects through rasping reeds on some imperturbable inland sea.

Measurement or expansion of ordinary passing time and division of space are two factors upon which our most characteristic and enduring works have been based. Most of these works are densely compacted of movement, attached by invisible sewing-machined stitches to a musical lining or substructure. WATERMILL, on the other hand, is a loosely woven translucent tapestry within which passes a linear three-dimensional procession. Time stands still; it does not pass; but figures proceed through its element circuitously without progress, like fish in a bowl. The units are bipeds who are also numbers on a planetary moondial. The work can be taken both as timepiece and space clock. The visual surround, suggesting a monochrome brush-and-ink scroll, is lightly fondled by barely perceptible breezes which rub dry sheaves of grass, rustle fallen leaves, toss about a few early flakes of snow. In it a single male human enjoys, endures, combats times of day, seasons of years, asleep or awake, meditating and remembering, acting or dreaming. He recalls childhood, adolescence, and in present manhood foresees senility. The moonlamp waxes and wanes, from cuticle to pale celadon fullness, fixing its mean or noble scale against the reflection of some sister planet. Added piquancy was gained by casting Edward Villella, whose phenomenal acrobacy, speed, and muscular power are famous, in the role of a monumentally static Hamletlike protagonist. His physical control makes him capable of sustaining such relentless slow motion. The tempo of the ballet is, in all truth, fiendishly slow. At first it seems slower than a normal heartbeat, than systole or diastole. One intelligent critic confessed that she began to feel as if she might go mad from a dislocation in her ordinary habits of sensing a passage of what we commonly take to be "time." WATERMILL is also a race against anxiety which endurance temporarily wins.

Sun Eve June **18**	GREETING PRELUDE (HAPPY BIRTHDAY) FIREWORKS SCHERZO FANTASTIQUE SYMPHONY IN THREE MOVEMENTS VIOLIN CONCERTO FIREBIRD
Tues Eve June **20**	SYMPHONY IN E FLAT CONCERTO IN D FOR STRINGS ("THE CAGE") CONCERTO FOR PIANO AND WINDS DANSES CONCERTANTES
Wed Eve June **21**	OCTUOR SERENADE IN A THE FAUN AND THE SHEPHERDESS DIVERTIMENTO FROM "LE BAISER DE LA FEE" EBONY CONCERTO SCHERZO A LA RUSSE CIRCUS POLKA
Thurs Eve June **22**	CAPRICCIO ("RUBIES" FROM "JEWELS") DUO CONCERTANT THE SONG OF THE NIGHTINGALE SCENES DE BALLET
Fri Eve June **23**	CONCERTO FOR TWO SOLO PIANOS PIANO-RAG-MUSIC DUMBARTON OAKS ODE PULCINELLA
Sat Eve June **24**	APOLLO ORPHEUS AGON
Sun Eve June **25**	Choral Variations on BACH'S "VOM HIMMEL HOCH" MONUMENTUM PRO GESUALDO MOVEMENTS FOR PIANO AND ORCHESTRA REQUIEM CANTICLES SYMPHONY OF PSALMS

the
New York
City Ballet

214

JUNE, 1972: NEW YORK

Stravinsky Festival. Dress rehearsal for PULCINELLA; singers and orchestra; tons of scenery, trick effects; dozens of children, incomplete choreography, lumped together in organized chaos. Not enough spaghetti; masks don't fit; however, as with other rehearsals in this effort, no tempers lost; cheerfulness, no forebodings of disaster.

Our ambition was to display a panoply of Stravinsky's representative scores, some without staging; from first to last recognizing his entire range in one compact, monumental week. Some of us had hoped, for ease, economy, and a lighter load on performances, to distribute it all over three months, our twelve weeks of a normal spring season. However, Balanchine insisted on the imploded fusion of one big bang. The point of a feast was to gorge, not nibble; this was no simple *zakuska* but a state banquet in a State Theater. If each new ballet was scheduled with a week between, the whole impression would be diluted. Subscribers might pick only works which by chance, in advance, they considered amusing. He was, of course, correct; the festival as planned and produced had the air of a holiday, with crowds embarked on a luxurious cruise, crossing an ocean for a gala vacation. Over the one crammed week, from Sunday to Sunday, unfamiliar faces grew friendlier in the climate of a common excursion. The concentration of premieres and music unheard before generated its own enthusiasm. Yet all passed so quickly that at the end one wondered how, or indeed if, it had really taken place. There was scarcely a sense of daylight spent outside the theater; everyone seemed constantly congregating at an al fresco picnic or birthday party. As for the procession of performances onstage, they tended to blur in their current immediacy. Their memory was revived later when they took their place, revised and refined past the first festival occasion, in our permanent programs. Then great peaks of sound, sight-and-sound, or sights alone could be savored anew.

Kirstein and Balanchine at opening of Stravinsky Festival

Although some thirty works were performed in the seven days, many pieces which had musical importance were omitted after due deliberation. Balanchine always considered the tremendous orchestration of LE SACRE DU PRINTEMPS beyond a choreographer's capacity to compete with, although this by no means deterred the Royal Ballet, La Scala, the Paris Opéra, or other companies from attempting it. LES NOCES is visible in Madame Nijinska's original version of 1923, beautifully performed in London, as well as on tour, by the Royal Ballet. Jerome Robbins's recension is active with Ballet Theater. OEDIPUS REX, although intentionally static, has received impressive presentations, notably by Michel Saint-Denis for the Sadler's Wells Company; it is in repertory with the New York City Opera. Balanchine wished to stage THE FLOOD again, since its initial presentation had been a disaster because of a television corruption rather than any shortcomings of the piece itself or its production. This was too costly for the festival; in time it must be done. RENARD and MAVRA were too small in format for revival on a big stage. PERSÉPHONE is declamatory, although this beautiful score is grateful for a visual frame; but we reserved the fullest choral effect for the benediction of SYMPHONY OF PSALMS, which only angels should dare to dance. Our final choices were a matter of agreement between Balanchine, Madame Stravinsky, Nicolas Nabokov, Goddard Lieberson, Robert Irving, and Robert Craft—friends, associates, historians, and preservers of his music in memorials, recordings, or continual performance.

Planning for the many onstage rehearsals was in the hands of Ronald Bates, our executive stage manager, and his capable staff. Ronnie came to us after the Army from apprenticeship at the American Shakespeare Festival. Over the years he joined our family by marrying into it. He and the lovely dancer Diana Adams would have a daughter named, inevitably, Georgina. Part master electrician, part master sergeant, he is also a poet and inventor of stage illumination. His sleight of hand in making time when there was no time, of inserting extra rehearsals when there were overwhelming demands from equally justifiable calls, the drain on tact, nerves and intelligence with no sleep for three weeks except snatched naps on an offstage cot—these accomplished the Stravinsky Festival. His taciturnity, lack of waste motion, appreciation and achievement of the preposterous or impossible are too often taken for granted.

Ronnie's ordinary climate is emergency—replacement, improvisation, quick choice of substitutes. His daily duties require him to maintain high operating averages despite inevitable if unforeseeable accidents arising from the nature of a hydra-headed beast: dancers' injuries; failures of fingers on levers, ropes, or buttons; fatigue in electronic circuits; Jerry Robbins's indecision; Balanchine's caprice; mutual changes of mind; drastic

alterations needed when costumes and scenery are viewed under stage lights for the first time. For the Stravinsky week, Bates laid out scheduling a month before as if he were a junior Eisenhower preparing mini-Operation Overlord. He captained his own general staff, but also under his single command were Balanchine, Robbins, John Taras, the younger ballet masters, the dancers, and a large crew of stagehands who were as sensitive to their conductor as Robert Irving's musicians were to him. Far above the auditorium, in the light booth topping the highest balcony, were the highly strung quartet operating two dyna-beams and twin xenon special-throw lamps, which vignetted individual soloists as they moved across the stage. In such carefully modulated movement as that to be framed in Balanchine's DUO CONCERTANT, their pinpointing of isolated arms, hands, fingers would participate in the choreography itself.

Over the years before and after we moved into the State Theater, Robert Irving, our musical director, forged a band of instrumentalists which by now is recognized as the peer of the major symphonic orchestras. He could have become permanent conductor to half a dozen civic orchestras in Britain or the United States, but his temperament and talents were suited to work with dancers. When he returned to New York with us after an engagement at Covent Garden, there were plaintive protests at his seduction and loss to the Royal Ballet. But he turned into a New Yorker, and later in Saratoga, he was as passionate a racer of horses as before he had been an ardent mountain climber. In variety and quality, the repertory he could offer his orchestra was superior to any other in the same category. It was he who was responsible for the choice of soloists, singers, and chorus for the vocal parts in Britten, Brahms, Kurt Weill, and Stravinsky.

As for the public's reception of our Stravinsky Festival, it was everything we had hoped. All critical judgment apart, the *New York Times* covered the event as news on its front page, as well as in special features and editorials. The weeklies followed suit, and a flock of foreign correspondents flew across the Atlantic to spread the word throughout Britain and the Continent, and as far as Japan. While some of the new works would be more complete later, and although the percentage of anticipated casualties met its quota, the event, both in immediacy and increment, justified itself.

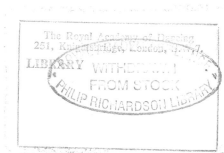
the New York City Ballet

From the souvenir program published for the Stravinsky Festival, June 18, 1972:

I must leave it to others, better professionally qualified than I, to estimate Stravinsky's achievement as a composer. I can, however, I think, speak with some authority about Stravinsky as a paradigm of the creative artist, a model and example from whom younger men, be they composers, painters, or writers, can derive counsel and courage in an age when the threats to their integrity seem to be greater than ever before.

First, let them pay attention to his conception of artistic fabrication. "I am not," he said, "a mirror struck by my mental functions. My interest passes entirely to the object, the thing made." An artist, that is to say, should think of himself primarily as a craftsman, a "maker," not as an "inspired" genius. When we call a work "inspired," all we mean is that it is better, more beautiful, than we could have possibly hoped for. — *W. H. Auden*

Of course, *Petrushka, Sacre, Oedipus,* were and are great beauties, but for Stravinsky, they were his past, well beloved and well remembered. It was his fantastic output of new ideas at a period of his life which many would have considered a time for consolidation, rest, and (alas, with many artists) repetition, which made him, right up to the end, the most contemporaneous of men. Yet, it was this quality that irritated so many. Just as a child wants his parents or grandparents to look and act their age, so Stravinsky was expected to act the respectable old master in his carpet slippers, rewriting all of his now famous music. This, of course, didn't suit him. And he entered new worlds. — *Goddard Lieberson*

In cleaving to free-will he refused to frame his self as a romantic agonist — self-serving, self-indulgent, self-slaying, a role adored by flashier tragedians of the era. Unfashionable except for a few ferocious friends after his initial notoriety, he was firm in a faith towards formal wholeness. Abstraction, fragmentation, self-expressionism was the order of the day, canny hysteria canonized as idiosyncratic revelation. He credited concreteness, stricture and structure, inherited objective disciplines, for responsible collaboration with dozens of patrons and publishers, hundreds of performers serving a multitude of audiences in an elevated social context. He never let fractional means, sound as sound, color as color, artifice for artifice's sake with their inflated partialities satisfy him as interesting or worthy ends. Stylization is formula, not method. Personalism is a nosegay of accidental cullings, freezing talent at one lone repetitive peak. The person of sure practice proceeds by an ever-developing potential. His whole work, over seventy years, came to command a world of witnesses. — *L.K.*

The festival opened formally with the fanfare which Stravinsky had written for the State Theater's inauguration April 19, 1964. It was sounded from the top ring of the promenade. When the audience was seated within, Bob Irving's fine orchestra played the "Greeting Prelude," an arrangement of "Happy Birthday (to *You*, dear 'Eager')." This was composed in 1955 as a singing telegram to Pierre Monteux, conductor of the tempestuous premiere of LE SACRE DU PRINTEMPS in 1913, on his eightieth birthday. It was described by its composer as "a half-minute primer of canonic art." Then Balanchine appeared before the curtain to welcome assembled guests and to present them with an unannounced miniature gift in the form of a single movement, the scherzo (all that was recoverable) of Stravinsky's Opus 1, which Madeleine Malraux, the pianist, had been able to transcribe from the manuscript of a lost Sonata in F Sharp Minor written in 1902 at the age of twenty, even before Stravinsky sought advice from Rimski-Korsakov. Madame Malraux's continuous exquisite performances were one of the week's chief delights. This fragment was followed by the orchestra alone presenting *Feu d'Artifice* (*Fireworks*, 1909), the morsel which magnetized Diaghilev's first curiosity. Then Jerry Robbins tossed across the stage a stylish, delicate, and witty version of SCHERZO FANTASTIQUE (1908), made more vivid by the kaleidoscopic dancing of four young boys, all quite new to the company, with Gelsey Kirkland, a recent and electrifying soloist.

The opening pieces were followed by two Balanchine blockbusters: SYMPHONY IN THREE MOVEMENTS (1946) and VIOLIN CONCERTO (1931), magnificently rendered by Joseph Silverstein, first violin of the Boston Symphony. These novelties could have been enough to distinguish two ordinary seasons. Coming as they did, head-on at the very start of the celebration, they served as vindication not alone of the festival's pretensions, but of the powers of its progenitor. Balanchine had achieved an age and status when it had become profitable, and in a sense mandatory, to proclaim his talent desiccated, his authority dubious. The attention paid to, and deserved by, Jerome Robbins's four recent triumphs, three on a big scale, gave credence to hopes that his senior might now be discounted, and someone (anyone) introduced to crack the monotony of hearing Balanchine spoken of as being on the same level as Picasso or Stravinsky.

However, the present breathless constructs of fresh rhythmic response and gestural complexity in two large ballets were a devastating demonstration of augmented capacity. They were startling innovations — as far ahead of AGON as AGON had been of ORPHEUS or APOLLON at the midpoint and debut of Balanchine's career. Thus abruptly were introduced the most startling results of a partnership which had begun nearly half a century before. This astonishing evening concluded with Marc Chagall's de luxe illustrations of FIREBIRD which, perhaps more transparently than any choreography by Balanchine or Robbins, made visible its famous orchestral irridescence.

In the ensuing six performances some pieces were obviously less captivating or convincing than others. Opportunities given to younger choreographers were possibly daunting, since it put them on the line with their elders and betters. From the musical aspect, however, all the scores chosen were of the same quality as the "major" works. John Taras's handsome pageant of THE SONG OF THE NIGHTINGALE (1919) was particularly pleasing. Balanchine had restaged it for Diaghilev in 1925 with decor by Henri Matisse. Taras did without scenery, but Rouben Ter-Arutunian transformed his stage space into a black velour jewel box. There a begemmed nightingale and her sweet-songed but sadder-vested sister scintillated against the mandarin parade of a slipper-satined court and its gorgeous embassy from the Japanese emperor. Taras's SCÈNES DE BALLET (1944), which had been set by Frederick Ashton for the Royal Ballet in 1948, provided beautiful performances by Patricia McBride and Jean-Pierre Bonnefous, with a large and skillfully manipulated corps. Bonnefous as Orpheus, Francisco Moncion as the Dark Angel, and Melissa Hayden as Eurydice restored ORPHEUS (1948) to something above its initial beauty, for Isamu Noguchi had now enlarged and refined his elegantly sculptured objects and crocheted costumes to the scale of the State Theater's proscenium. ORPHEUS had been preceded by APOLLON (1928) and followed by AGON (1957). Arthur Mitchell, now director of his autonomous Dance Theater of Harlem and its school, danced his original part in AGON, superbly partnering Allegra Kent in her exceptional clarity and strength. These three masterpieces of the Balanchine-Stravinsky collaboration, bridging four decades, were thus seen and heard as often intended for the first time.

STRAVINSKY VIOLIN
CONCERTO: Kay Mazzo

An Evening's Waltzes

Cortège Hongrois

Stravinsky festival

Monumentum pro
Gesualdo

Requiem Canticles

Symphony of Psalms

The Cage

Concerto for Piano
and Winds

Ode

Octuor

Sonata

Scènes de Ballet

Circus Polka

Rubies

Movements for Piano
and Orchestra

firebird

Violin Concerto

Dumbarton Oaks

Danses Concertantes

Pulcinella

Symphony in E Flat

The Song
of the
Nightingale

Scherzo Fantastique

Ode

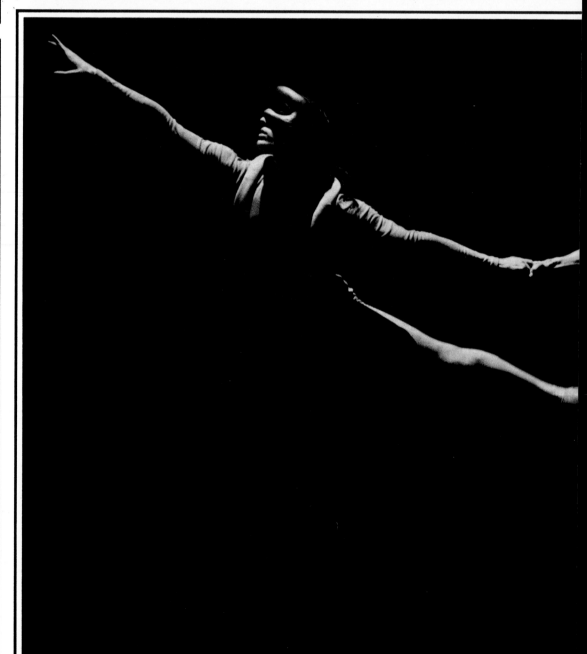

Concerto for 2 Solo Pianos

Orpheus

Ebony Concerto

Apollo

Choral Variations on Bach's "Vom Himmel Hoch"

Duo
Concertant

Scènes
de Ballet

235

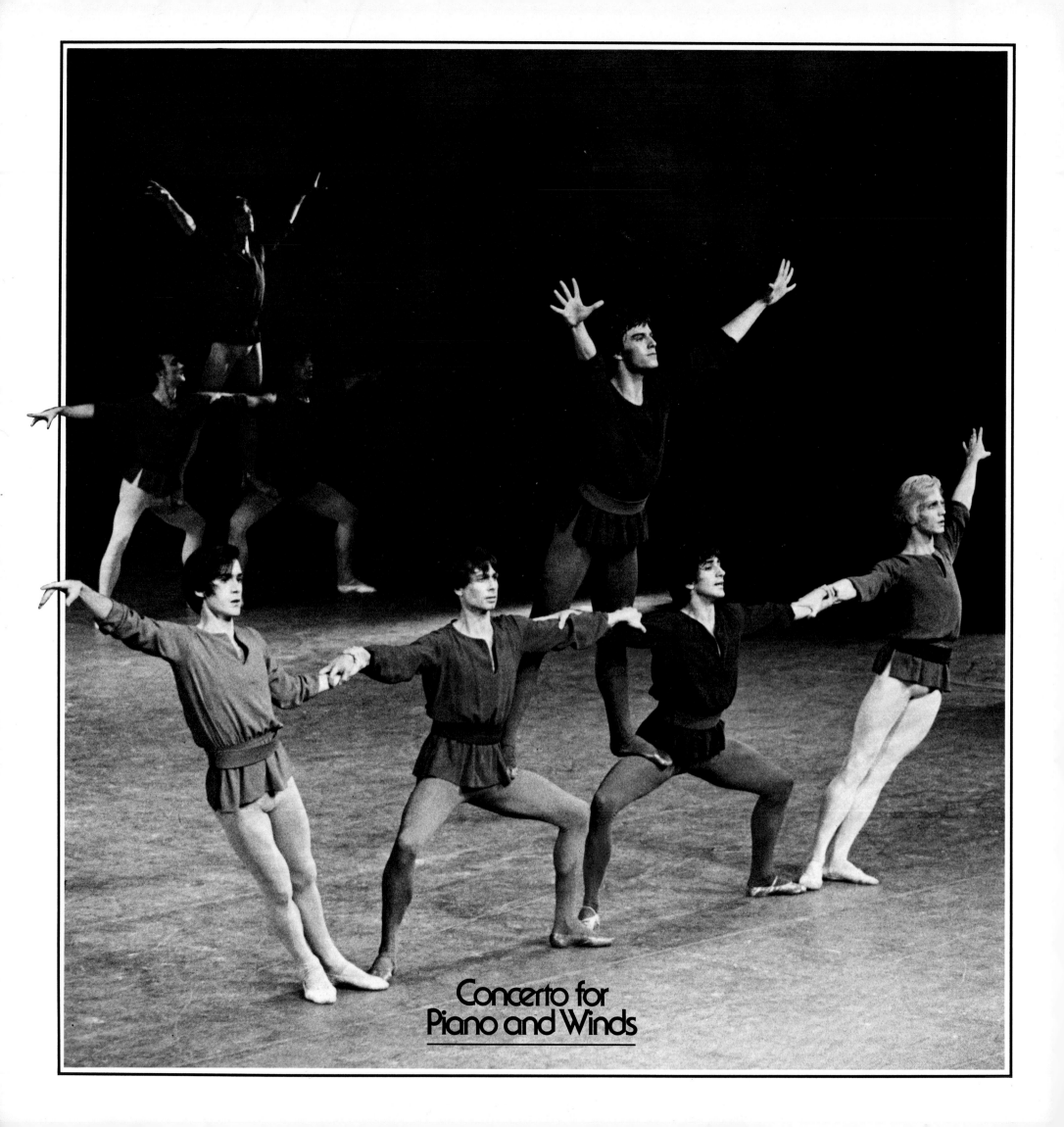

Concerto for
Piano and Winds

Le Baiser de la Fée

Sonata

Rubies

Agon

Piano-Rag-Music

Serenade in A

Movements
for Piano and
Orchestra

Monumentum
pro Gesualdo

Circus Polka

Symphony
of Psalms

The Cage

Robbins and Balanchine together worked out the raffish pantomime of PULCINELLA (1920), with Eugene Berman's stupendous evocation of a townscape for Neapolitan *commedia dell'arte* spectacle. There was not nearly enough time to present it with the finesse it merited, but Edward Villella's ithyphallic monster father-figure of all the world's Punches was a merrily ironic and acrobatic impersonation. Violette Verdy was perfectly tailored as a soubrette of surpassing elegance. With her Gallic savor, precision, waifish regret, and neat musicality, she served as his good fairy, mistress, partner. As a final fillip, Balanchine and Robbins appeared briefly as raggle-taggle beggars lambasting each other in a rub-a-dub duello. The stage was packed with the huge company, augmented by one dozen small Pulcinelli from our school. For once no one said we had stinted on the visual, for Genia Berman's monumentally rackety frame and masterfully delineated curtains were architectural delights. To be sure, there were those able to take pleasure in displeasure by lamenting the abandonment of our usual stripped and stoic format for such an unseemly burst of decorative extravagance. Stravinsky was used to this clan of critics; he had written:

Pulcinella was my discovery of the past, the epiphany through which the whole of my late work became possible. It was a backward look, of course—the first of many love affairs in that direction—but it was a look in the mirror, too. No critic understood this at the time, and I was therefore attacked for being a *pasticheur,* chided for composing "simple" music, blamed for deserting "modernism," accused of renouncing my "true Russian heritage." People who had never heard of, or cared about, the originals cried "sacrilege": "The classics are ours. Leave the classics alone." To them all my answer was and is the same: You "respect," but I love.*

CIRCUS POLKA (1942) involved fifty-four baby ballerinas from our school, organized into waves of *entrées* under a ringmaster in riding breeches, tailcoat, and top hat. This was the marshall of the rout, Jerome Robbins himself, snapping a whip, dragooning the children into enormous cursive initials signed on the stage floor: I. S., with two tots crouched into two dots. Robbins's REQUIEM CANTICLES (1966) was an austere abstraction of ritual lamentation, impersonally eccentric, but in an

* Igor Stravinsky and Robert Craft, *Expositions and Developments,* Doubleday & Co., Garden City, N.Y., pp. 128–9.

elevated range of invention in negative accents of inversion and fluttering deformation. It was a metaphor of the aberration or alienation from ordinary behavior which grief unlocks. Robbins's skill and experience in theatrical organization were a prime factor throughout the festival. He was aided by Tommy Abbott, once a student in our school, later Robbins's assistant in transferring his musicals from one company to another and from stage to film. For us Abbott facilitated the deployment of very young children in swift but deliberate regimentation, without which their presence would have been useless.

The finale of the festival began on a clear, early evening, an unsmogged azure June Sunday, with Balanchine's *grand défilé* of the entire company and the children, for Stravinsky's *Choral Variations on Johann Sebastian Bach's "Vom Himmel hoch da komm' ich her"* (1956). The original theme piece was written in 1747 as a "test" which would admit Bach (aged 62) into a "Society for Musical Knowledge." Balanchine took these canonic variations, with a choir (but without organ), and wove a processional tapestry in which orderly ranks of soloists and subordinate dancers were infiltrated by the youngest and smallest, shuttling through the cat's cradle of its web. First dancers, corps, young and more advanced students were paraded as if they were guardsmen changing their sentinel duty in dress (un-dress) uniform before a Palace of Music. This served as prelude, summation, and homage to the life work of a master of temporal dimension. In asymmetry and its resolution, balance and its upset, it was a didactic illustration of Stravinsky's dictum: "Music is the best means we have of digesting time."

The festival finished with an exalting and exalted offering of *Symphony of Psalms* (1930). It was not danced; our dancers, staff, ballet masters sat to listen on the stage floor encircling the orchestra, now set within the proscenium. Above them Rouben Ter-Arutunian had hung a glowing suggestion of silver and ivory organ pipes. Observed from the balconies, the dancers' bodies in hushed repose might have served Edgar Degas for a monument to the service which plastic stasis owes music. Robert Craft conducted *con amore;* sound seemed channeled toward Vera Stravinsky, seated serene and lovely in the first ring. The ultimate iteration of "Laudate" always makes a cathedral of whatever hall in which these psalms are sung. Stravinsky said that he

had been impelled by a vision of Elijah's chariot of fire ascending to the Godhead:

Never before had I written anything quite so literal as the triplets for horns and piano to suggest the horses and chariot [yet at the same time not literal at all. As for the] final hymn of praise. . . . I can say [that] one hopes to worship God with a little art if one has any, and if one hasn't, . . . then one can at least burn a little incense.*

From the first evening, Balanchine had insisted there should be no hint of mourning for a man whose absence was only physical. He recalled the custom of his native Georgian province, where raisins and grain are distributed at a graveside as evidence of the continual sowing and harvest of the human and the divine. So, after the swelling conclusion of the *Symphony,* a silent audience left the theater at the close of the grand affirmation of one enormous word. Its trisyllabic structure echoes the trinity of body, mind, and spirit which Stravinsky's genius praised. With the still resonant final DOM-I-NUM vibrating in ears and heart, every looker-and-listener was handed a slug of vodka to speed him on his way.

From the EVENING GAZETTE (Yuri Slonimsky), Leningrad, September, 1972:

In Stravinsky's VIOLIN CONCERTO (1931), Balanchine dons the full armor of "visible music" which, incidentally, the composer considered to be his partner's highest achievement. Balanchine consciously and wholeheartedly devotes himself and his performers to the fulfillment of this task which he considers the most important. In his devotion to it he occasionally transforms people on stage into graphically outlined symbols (could this account for the dancers' black outfits?), performing every zigzag of Stravinsky's thought, irony, joke, etc. No matter how unexpected, artful and complex the combinations of sound, Balanchine immediately responds by corresponding combinations of arms, legs, torso and head. There is food for thought here—occasionally dance becomes servant to music, and the human quality to the dancing. And at such times, it seems to me that the performers are like marionettes operated by an experienced puppeteer. Only in the two duets do the soloists, and in the *capriccio,* the corps de ballet, cease being the slaves of the interpretation of sound, acquire flesh and blood and indulge in human emotions.

* Igor Stravinsky and Robert Craft, *Dialogues and A Diary,* Doubleday & Co., Garden City, N.Y., 1963, pp. 78–9.

REQUIEM CANTICLES

SYMPHONY IN THREE MOVEMENTS: Sara Leland, John Clifford

The official Marxist aesthetic evoked by the second Soviet tour of the New York City Ballet was somewhat less strident than that precipitated by our visit ten years before. Now Balanchine's style was more familiar, and the political climate of Nixon's *détente* was far less ferocious than Kennedy's crisis over Krushchev and Cuba. With the exception of Baku, we revisited the same towns—Kiev, Leningrad, Tbilisi, Moscow. Every performance was sold out before the company arrived. The previous summer Madame Ekaterina Furtseva, Soviet Minister of Education and Culture, had dispatched Konstantin Sergeyev, her eminent ballet master, to Saratoga to choose from our repertory works which might meet with official approval. Sergeyev had known Balanchine from early days in the Leningrad school; they had remained in contact over the years. Now he spent ten days familiarizing himself with our repertory, dancers, and methods. He gave the company a class of his own, which vividly demonstrated differences in technique between the systems Balanchine had developed in the United States and those currently taught in the Russian state schools. Sergeyev viewed the new Stravinsky works, which were performed on a weekly basis in Saratoga. For the Russian season he chose ballets with music by three native composers—Tchaikovsky, Stravinsky, and George Gershwin (whose parents, at least, had been born in Russia).

On the tour the musical-comedy tone and style of WHO CARES? found particular favor. So did Robbins's two recent works to Chopin's and Bach's piano music, firmly executed by Gordon Boelzner, our indispensable staff soloist, who now was becoming an orchestral conductor as well. DANCES AT A GATHERING and GOLDBERG VARIATIONS were also happily received in Poland where, in handsomely restored theaters in Lodz and Warsaw, the tour ended.

The dancers had been performing without interruption for nearly a year. Following Saratoga, they had flown to Munich to represent the United States in the cultural division of the Olympic Games. Without respite they launched the fall-winter season of 1972–73, in which several ballets culled from the Stravinsky Festival would, after changes and revisions, enter permanent repertory. PULCINELLA received special attention. Eight white mice were added to the entourage of the Mouse King in NUTCRACKER. From the unused sections of Riccardo Drigo's charming score, considerable additions were made to HARLEQUINADE to show off the dazzling antics of Edward Villella, born to be both Arlechino and Pulcinella. Late in November the audience included a delegation of Peking diplomats from the United Nations. In January the magnificent Chinese acrobats attended performances and came backstage to meet the company. There were ripples of rumors which put our company dancing on the Great Wall in jig time. However, negotiations with the State Department over the second Russian tour had consumed months of triangulated maneuvering between Moscow, New York, and Washington, and by now we knew the difference between oriental and occidental estimates of time and money.

JANUARY, 1973: NEW YORK

Conference with Madame Karinska, Rouben Ter-Arutunian, and Balanchine over THE BIRDS OF AMERICA, anticipating bicentenniel celebrations of 1975–76. Karinska's sketches for apple festival, emceed by Johnny Appleseed, with entrées of pippins, Winesaps, Gravensteins. Audubon's birds, as painted by the "lost dauphin"; Indian sources in Catlin, Kane, and Buffalo Bill's Wild West Shows.

The proposal for a three-act heroic ballet based on an "American" subject had preoccupied us intermittently for three decades. The novelists Louis Bromfield and Glenway Wescott (and even Céline) had written extended libretti. But as with e. e. cummings's *Tom*, their narratives, while perhaps excellent for film or lyric biography, offered few pretexts for classic dancing. From 1965 Balanchine had discussed his requirements seriously and precisely with Morton Gould, who understood the demands of academic dancing transformed into a popular musical idiom with taste, celerity, and brilliance. His score for Jerome Robbins's INTERPLAY (1952) proved his capacity for stimulating dance steps. He now composed portions of a large score which suited Balanchine to perfection.

The demi-myth of John James Audubon, sensitively adumbrated by Constance Rourke, placed the great naturalist in the role of son to Louis XVI, come from the Antilles where he had been somehow spirited after the execution of his parents. In a quasi-Virginian forest, he met the birds whom he would later depict. We identified him with Johnny Appleseed, who strode across the Middle West sowing orchards and continued westward to the Golden Gate, where he married the daughter of Chief Thunderbird. At his wedding the various native strains which compose America would receive embassies from the rest of the world, in a setting recalling Audubon's legendary origin, and as well, the sources of classic dancing at the court of Versailles. The expense of such a work on the scale necessary would be high; hence from year to year we postponed any serious thought of scheduling

it. But the approach of the two-hundredth anniversary of our nation's founding seemed to indicate that, with the possible support of the National Endowment under the adroit manipulation of Miss Nancy Hanks, some federal funds might be forthcoming.

As for the constant proposals for new works, there would be a perennial oscillation of gain and loss. Robbins planned a dramatic abstraction of the tale of the Dybbuk, with a score by Leonard Bernstein. But his long-time collaborator accepted the Charles Eliot Norton chair of poetry at Harvard, where he would follow Stravinsky, T. S. Eliot, and his own master, Aaron Copland. From Iannis Xenakis, Balanchine commissioned a non-electronic score, for we have an orchestra eager to embark on any next step forward or backward from recent advance-guard sonorities. ANTI-EARTH is projected as a big science-fiction black joke, set for the spring of 1976. The bicentennial celebrations will doubtless precipitate other works on native themes.

The first "American" ballet I ever saw was on the stage of the Boston Opera House (built by Eben Jordan of Jordan Marsh, my father's rival in the department store business). It was Henry Gilbert's DANCE IN PLACE CONGO, performed in the season of 1919. Gilbert, a musicological pioneer in the material just preceding jazz, had been fascinated by the songs of descendants of African slaves. Of this work I recall only an enormous stage crammed with dancers in striped bandana kerchiefs. Whether they were in blackface or were indeed black I can't remember, but there was a knife fight, tides of motion, and a blackout finale. Dancers whirled madly; I was twelve years old.

Every so often Robert Irving, our musical director, leafs through stacks in the music library at Lincoln Center, researching an increasingly remote possibility of reviving forgotten American scores of the pre-Stravinsky epoch which made use of "Indian" or "Negro" or "folk" motifs. Most of Cadman, Chadwick, Converse, Hadley, Parker, or even Griffes sounds wanly naïve beside Charles Ives, who handled his indigenous material with a quirkier, more mordant touch. There were many other projects lying in abeyance for the right circumstances

APOLLO: Peter Martins

SYMPHONY IN THREE MOVEMENTS: Helgi Tomasson

Stravinsky Festival choreographers:
George Balanchine, Jerome Robbins, John Clifford,
Richard Tanner, Lorca Massine, John Taras,
Todd Bolender

to launch or resurrect. We thought of a ballet based on the lost glory of Saratoga's Grand Union colonnade and Colonel Canfield's gaming pavilion. We had spoken to Frederick Ashton about the notion of Newport as a surround for the sale of an American heiress to a British viscount, in the climate of Henry James. Balanchine dreamed of a SALOME to a score of Alban Berg, and of a non-Spanish set of dances to harpsichord music by Padre Antonio Soler, Scarlatti's pupil. There were Kurt Weill's powerful miniature Noh play, JASAGER (plus "neinsager"), and Reynaldo Hahn's FÊTE CHEZ THÉRÈSE. As for expressly advance-guard music, there have been few recent scores suitable for an orchestra of our quality and equipment which also serve for more than flashy *pièces d'occasion.* In 1960, Stravinsky met with a group of aleatory and electronic "young" composers in Buenos Aires. One of the disadvantages of a provincial situation is that it provokes in artists an eagerness to outdo the rest of the world in "experiment" or "creativity" at one remove, perhaps to compensate for their distance from world centers of international exchange. As Robert Craft has reported in *Dialogues and A Diary,* among the questions discussed were "the problems of trying to teach an 'integrated-traditional' as well as a 'mathematical-experimental' study of musical composition" (no conclusions), and the faults of *avant-gardisme,* which are "its dependence upon a superficial aspect of competition—the need to outdo the other at all costs—and its ignorance of music in the pre-electronic era (no remedy)."

There are, of course, complaints that the New York City Ballet has become conservative, "establishment." Since being established means having a chance to plan rather than improvise, to enjoy continuity and stability approaching the level of foreign state-supported institutions, we welcome the epithet. We have always been conservative, in the sense of preserving a traditional dance language, based on the music which most adroitly or capaciously subsumes it. With Stravinsky's disappearance, the self-appointed obligatory advance guard which he announced, led, and commanded for nearly sixty years assumes the taint of a disjunct, not very useful, self-serving closed fraternity, more interested in competitive shock in an area of sociopolitical happenings or put-ons than in servicing any ongoing repertories. The most for which one can hope from composers are useful scores of any source or coloration—ebony, bronze, or pinko-gray. What remains certain is that there are dancers capable of exposing both the virtues and the shortcomings of novel measurings of time and space. Over the last thirty-five years, where has the exposure of new or unfamiliar music been most transparently effective through the lens of classic dancing? In Paris? Moscow? Milan? London?

In New York!

Violette Verdy

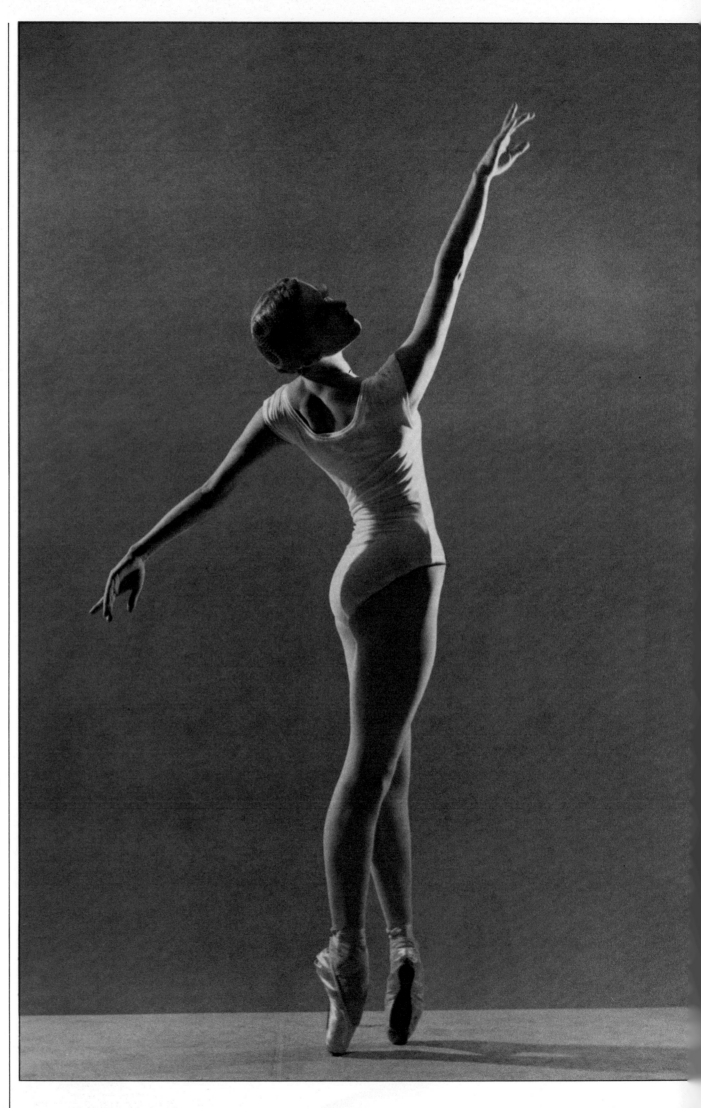

List of Premiere Performances

PRODUCED BY THE AMERICAN BALLET,
THE BALLET CARAVAN,
AMERICAN BALLET CARAVAN,
BALLET SOCIETY, AND THE
NEW YORK CITY BALLET,
FROM MARCH, 1935,
THROUGH MAY, 1973

THE AMERICAN BALLET

SERENADE
Choreography: George Balanchine
Music: Peter Ilyich Tchaikovsky
(Serenade for Strings in C major)
Decor: Gaston Longchamp
Costumes: Jean Lurçat
Premiere: March 1, 1935, Adelphi Theater, New York. (Prior to the official premiere, SERENADE was presented by the Producing Company of the School of American Ballet, June, 1934, at the Warburg estate in White Plains, New York, and December 6, 1934, at the Avery Memorial Theater, Hartford, Connecticut.)
Principal dancers: Leda Anchutina, Ruthanna Boris, Gisella Caccialanza, Kathryn Mullowney, William Dollar, Charles Laskey.

ALMA MATER
Choreography: George Balanchine
Music: Kay Swift
(arrangement by Morton Gould)
Decor: Eugene Dunkel
Costumes: John Held, Jr.
Book: Edward M. M. Warburg
Premiere: March 1, 1935, Adelphi Theater. New York. (Prior to the official premiere, ALMA MATER was presented by the Producing Company of the School of American Ballet, December 6, 1934, at the Avery Memorial Theater, Hartford, Connecticut.)
Principal dancers: Leda Anchutina, Ruthanna Boris, Gisella Gaccialanza, Kathryn Mullowney, Heidi Vosseler, William Dollar, Charles Laskey, Eugene Loring.

ERRANTE
Choreography: George Balanchine
Music: Franz Schubert (Wanderer Fantasy for piano, orchestrated by Charles Koechlin)
Costumes, lighting, and dramatic effects: Pavel Tchelitchev
Premiere: March 1, 1935, Adelphi Theater, New York. (Revival from the repertoire of Les Ballets 1933.)
Principal dancers: Tamara Geva, Charles Laskey, William Dollar.

REMINISCENCE
Choreography: George Balanchine
Music: Benjamin Godard
(orchestration by Henry Brant)
Decor and costumes: Sergei Soudeikine
Premiere: March 1, 1935, Adelphi Theater, New York.
Principal dancers: Leda Anchutina, Ruthanna Boris, Gisella Caccialanza, Elena de Rivas, Holly Howard, Annabelle Lyon, Elise Reiman, William Dollar, Paul Haakon, Joseph Levinoff.

MOZARTIANA
Choreography: George Balanchine
Music: Peter Ilyich Tchaikovsky
(Suite No. 4, Mozartiana)
Decor and costumes: Christian Bérard
Premiere: March 1, 1935, Adelphi Theater, New York. (Revival from Les Ballets, 1933. Prior to the official premiere, MOZARTIANA was presented by the Producing Company of the School of American Ballet, June, 1934, at the Warburg estate in White Plains, New York, and December 6, 1934, at the Avery Memorial Theater, Hartford, Connecticut.)
Principal dancers: Rabana Hasburgh, Holly Howard, Helen Leitch, Daphne Vane, Heidi Vosseler, Charles Laskey.

TRANSCENDENCE
Choreography: George Balanchine
Music: Franz Liszt
(orchestration by George Antheil)
Decor: Gaston Longchamp
Costumes: Franklin Watkins
Book: Lincoln Kirstein
Premiere: March 5, 1935, Adelphi Theater, New York. (Prior to the official premiere, TRANSCENDENCE was presented by the Producing Company of the School of American Ballet, December 6, 1934, at the Avery Memorial Theater, Hartford, Connecticut.)
Principal dancers: Elise Reiman, William Dollar.

DREAMS
(formerly called LES SONGES)
Choreography: George Balanchine
Music: George Antheil
Decor, costumes, and book: André Derain
Premiere: March 5, 1935, Adelphi Theater, New York. (Revival from Les Ballets 1933. Prior to the official premiere, LES SONGES was presented by the Producing Company of the School of American Ballet, June, 1934, at the Warburg estate in White Plains, New York.)
Principal dancers: Leda Anchutina, Ruthanna Boris, Paul Haakon.

THE BAT
Choreography: George Balanchine
Music: Johann Strauss
(Overture to DIE FLEDERMAUS)
Costumes: Keith Martin
Book: Lincoln Kirstein
Premiere: May 20, 1936, Metropolitan Opera House, New York.
Principal dancers: Leda Anchutina, Rabana Hasburgh, Annabelle Lyon, Lew Christensen, Charles Laskey.

ORPHEUS AND EURYDICE
Choreography: George Balanchine
Music: Christoph Willibald Gluck
(ORFEO ED EURIDICE, 1762)
Decor and costumes: Pavel Tchelitchev
Premiere: May 22, 1936, Metropolitan Opera House, New York.
Principal dancers: Lew Christensen (Orpheus), Daphne Vane (Eurydice), William Dollar (Amor).

APOLLON MUSAGÈTE
(Later called APOLLO, and APOLLO, LEADER OF THE MUSES)
Choreography: George Balanchine
Music: Igor Stravinsky
Decor and costumes: Stewart Chaney
Premiere: April 27, 1937, Metropolitan Opera House, New York. (Revival from the Diaghilev Ballets Russes.)
Dancers: Lew Christensen, Daphne Vane, Holly Howard, Elise Reiman, Kyra Blank, Rabana Hasburgh, Jane Burkhalter.

THE CARD PARTY
(Originally JEU DE CARTES; later called CARD GAME)
Choreography: George Balanchine
Music: Igor Stravinsky
Decor and costumes: Irene Sharaff
Book: Igor Stravinsky in collaboration with M. Malaieff
Premiere: April 27, 1937, Metropolitan Opera House, New York.
Principal dancers: William Dollar (The Joker); Ann Campbell, Jane Burkhalter, Lillian Moore, Vera Volkenau (Aces); Lew Christensen, Joseph Lane, Douglas Coudy, Erick Hawkins (Kings); Annabelle Lyon, Leda Anchutina, Ariel Lang, Hortense Kahrklin (Queens); Charles Laskey, Joseph Levinoff, Eugene Loring, Serge Temoff (Jacks).

LE BAISER DE LA FÉE
(Later called THE FAIRY'S KISS)
Choreography: George Balanchine
Music: Igor Stravinsky
Decor and costumes: Alice Halicka
Book: Igor Stravinsky, based on a story by Hans Christian Andersen
Premiere: April 27, 1937, Metropolitan Opera House, New York.
Principal dancers: Kathryn Mullowney (The Fairy), Rabana Hasburgh (Shadow), Gisella Caccialanza (Bride), Leda Anchutina (Friend), William Dollar (Bridegroom), Annabelle Lyon (Mother).

THE BALLET CARAVAN

ENCOUNTER
Choreography: Lew Christensen
Music: Wolfgang Amadeus Mozart
(Haffner Serenade)
Costumes: Forrest Thayr, Jr.
Premiere: July 17, 1936, Bennington College Theater, Bennington, Vermont.
Principal dancers: Annabelle Lyon, Ruby Asquith, Charles Laskey, Lew Christensen, Harold Christensen.

HARLEQUIN FOR PRESIDENT
Choreography: Eugene Loring
Music: Domenico Scarlatti
(orchestration by Ariadna Mikeshina)
Costumes: Keith Martin
Book: Lincoln Kirstein
Premiere: July 17, 1936, Bennington College Theater, Bennington, Vermont.
Principal dancers: Annabelle Lyon, Eugene Loring, Charles Laskey, Harold Christensen, Fred Danieli.

FOLK DANCE
Choreography: Douglas Coudy
Music: Emmanuel Chabrier
Costumes: Charles Rain
Premiere: July 17, 1936, Bennington College Theater, Bennington, Vermont.
Principal dancers: Ruthanna Boris, Lew Christensen.

PROMENADE
Choreography: William Dollar
Music: Maurice Ravel
(Valses nobles et sentimentales)
Costumes: after Horace Vernet
Premiere: July 17, 1936, Bennington College Theater, Bennington, Vermont.
Principal dancers: Annabelle Lyon, Ruthanna Boris, Charles Laskey, Erick Hawkins.

POCAHONTAS
Choreography: Lew Christensen
Music: Elliott Carter, Jr.
Costumes: Karl Free
Book: Lincoln Kirstein
Premiere: August 17, 1936, Colonial Theater, Keene, New Hampshire.
Principal dancers: Ruthanna Boris, Lew Christensen, Charles Laskey, Harold Christensen, Erick Hawkins.

YANKEE CLIPPER
Choreography: Eugene Loring
Music: Paul Bowles
Costumes: Charles Rain
Book: Lincoln Kirstein
Premiere: July 12, 1937, Town Hall, Saybrook, Connecticut.
Dancers: Eugene Loring and entire company.

SHOW PIECE
(BALLET WORK-OUT IN ONE ACT)
Choreography: Erick Hawkins
Music: Robert McBride
Costumes: Keith Martin
Premiere: August, 1937, Bar Harbor, Maine.
Principal dancers: Marie Jeanne Annabelle Lyon, Eugene Loring, Fred Danieli, Erick Hawkins.

FILLING STATION
Choreography: Lew Christensen
Music: Virgil Thomson
Decor and costumes: Paul Cadmus
Book: Lincoln Kirstein
Premiere: January 6, 1938, Avery Memorial Theater, Hartford, Connecticut.
Principal dancers: Jane Deering, Marie Jeanne, Marjorie Moore, Todd Bolender, Harold Christensen, Lew Christensen, Douglas Coudy, Fred Danieli, Erick Hawkins, Eugene Loring.

BILLY THE KID
Choreography: Eugene Loring
Music: Aaron Copland
Costumes: Jared French
Book: Lincoln Kirstein
Premiere: October 16, 1938, Chicago Opera House.
Principal dancers: Eugene Loring (Billy), Marie Jeanne (Mother and Sweetheart), Lew Christensen (Pat Garrett), Todd Bolender (Alias).

AIR AND VARIATIONS
Choreography: William Dollar
Music: Johann Sebastian Bach
(Goldberg Variations, arranged for two pianos by Trude Rittmann)
Costumes: Walter Gifford
Premiere: November, 1938, Athens, Georgia.
Dancers: The entire company.

CHARADE
(or THE DEBUTANTE)
Choreography: Lew Christensen
Music: American melodies, arranged by Trude Rittman
Costumes: Alvin Colt
Book: Lincoln Kirstein
Premiere: December 26, 1939, St. James Theater, New York.
Principal dancers: Gisella Caccialanza, Lew Christensen, Harold Christensen.

CITY PORTRAIT
Choreography: Eugene Loring
Music: Henry Brant
Decor: James Stewart Morcom
Book: Lincoln Kirstein
Premiere: December 28, 1939, St. James Theater, New York.
Dancers: Eugene Loring and entire company.

A THOUSAND TIMES NEIGH!
Choreography: William Dollar
Music: Tom Bennett
Decor: Alvin Colt
Book: Edward Mabley
General direction: Lincoln Kirstein
Premiere: May 11, 1940, Ford Pavilion Playhouse, World's Fair, Flushing Meadow, New York.
Dancers: Leda Anchutina, Mary Colbath, Peggy D'Arcy, Jean Davidson, Vera Bobitcheff, Betty Gilmore, Babs Heath, Jeanne Isaacs, Marie Jeanne, Margit de Kova, Peggy Noonan, Maria Quarequio, Pearl Schwarz, Mary Jane Shea, Barbara Stuart, Charlotte Sumner, Hilda Wagner, Anne Wiener, Virginia Wilcox, Anna Deere Wiman, Billie Wynn, Robert Armstrong, Todd Bolender, Douglas Coudy, Fred Danieli, Vladimir Dokoudovsky, William Dollar, John Duane, John Paul Dunphy, William Garrett, Kari Karnakoski, Alexis Kosloff, Nicholas Magallanes, Jay Martinez, Robert McVoy, Rem Olmstead, Newcomb Rice, John Schindehette, Serge Temoff, Nicholas Vasilieff, Ray Williams, and Robert Wolff.

AMERICAN BALLET CARAVAN

JUKE BOX
Choreography: William Dollar
Music: Alec Wilder
Decor and costumes: Tom Lee
Book: Lincoln Kirstein
Premiere: May 28, 1941, Hunter College Playhouse, New York.
Principal dancers: Yvonne Patterson, Rabana Hasburgh, Lew Christensen, William Dollar.

PASTORELA
Choreography: Lew Christensen and José Fernandez
Music: Paul Bowles
Decor and costumes: Alvin Colt
Book: José Martínez
Premiere: May 28, 1941, Hunter College Playhouse, New York.
Principal dancers: Gisella Caccialanza, Beatrice Tompkins, Lew Christensen, José Fernandez, Todd Bolender, Nicholas Magallanes, Charles Dickson, José Martínez.

CONCERTO BAROCCO
Choreography: George Balanchine
Music: Johann Sebastian Bach
(Double Violin Concerto in D minor)
Decor and costumes: Eugene Berman
Premiere: May 28, 1941, Hunter College Playhouse, New York.
Principal dancers: Marie Jeanne, Mary Jane Shea, William Dollar.

BALLET IMPERIAL (I)
Choreography: George Balanchine
Music: Peter Ilyich Tchaikovsky
(Piano Concerto in G major)
Decor and costumes: Mstislav Doboujinsky
Premiere: May 29, 1941, Hunter College Playhouse, New York.
Principal dancers: Marie Jeanne, Gisella Caccialanza, William Dollar, Nicholas Magallanes, Fred Danieli.

TIME TABLE
Choreography: Antony Tudor
Music: Aaron Copland
(Music for the Theater)
Decor and costumes: James Stewart Morcom
Premiere: May 29, 1941, Hunter College Playhouse, New York.
Principal dancers: Marie Jeanne, Gisella Caccialanza, Mary Jane Shea, Beatrice Tompkins, Lew Christensen, John Kriza.

BALLET SOCIETY

THE SPELLBOUND CHILD
Choreography: George Balanchine
Music: Maurice Ravel
(L'Enfant et les sortileges)
Decor and costumes: Aline Bernstein
Book: from a poem by Colette
Premiere: November 20, 1946, Central High School of Needle Trades, New York.
Principal dancers: Gisella Caccialanza, Ruth Gilbert, Georgia Hiden, Tanaquil LeClercq, Elise Reiman, Beatrice Tompkins, Paul d'Amboise, William Dollar (title role sung by Joseph Connoly).

THE FOUR TEMPERAMENTS
Choreography: George Balanchine
Music: Paul Hindemith
Decor and costumes: Kurt Seligmann
Premiere: November 20, 1946, Central High School of Needle Trades, New York.
Principal dancers: Gisella Caccialanza, Georgia Hiden, Rita Karlin, Tanaquil LeClercq, Mary Ellen Moylan, Elise Reiman, Beatrice Tompkins, Todd Bolender, Lew Christensen, Fred Danieli, William Dollar, José Martínez, Francisco Moncion.

RENARD
(THE FOX)
Choreography: George Balanchine
Music: Igor Stravinsky
Decor and costumes: Esteban Francés
Book: Igor Stravinsky
(English text by Harvey Officer)
Premiere: January 13, 1947, Hunter College Playhouse, New York.
Principal dancers: Todd Bolender (The Fox), Lew Christensen (The Rooster), Fred Danieli (The Cat), John Taras (The Ram).

DIVERTIMENTO
Choreography: George Balanchine
Music: Alexei Haieff
Premiere: January 13, 1947, Hunter College Playhouse, New York.
Dancers: Gisella Caccialanza, Tanaquil LeClercq, Mary Ellen Moylan, Elise Reiman, Beatrice Tompkins, Todd Bolender, Lew Christensen, Fred Danieli, Francisco Moncion, John Taras.

THE MINOTAUR
Choreography: John Taras
Music: Elliott Carter, Jr.
Decor and costumes: Joan Junyer
Book: Lincoln Kirstein and Joan Junyer
Premiere: March 26, 1947, Central High School of Needle Trades, New York.
Principal dancers: Elise Reiman (Pasiphaë, Queen of Crete), Edward Bigelow (Minos, King of Crete), Tanaquil LeClercq (Ariadne), John Taras (Theseus), Fred Danieli and Paul d'Amboise (Bulls).

ZODIAC
Choreography: Todd Bolender
Music: Rudi Revil
Decor and costumes: Esteban Francés
Premiere: March 26, 1947, Central High School of Needle Trades, New York.
Principal dancers: Virginia Barnes, William Dollar, Todd Bolender, Job Sanders, Pat McBride, Janice Roman, Ruth Sobotka, Jean Reeves, Irma Sandré, Joan Djorup, Marc Beaudet, John Scancarella, Betty Nichols, Gisella Caccialanza, Edward Bigelow, Gerard Leavitt.

HIGHLAND FLING
Choreography: William Dollar
Music: Stanley Bate
Decor and costumes: David Ffolkes
Premiere: March 26, 1947, Central High School of Needle Trades, New York.
Principal dancers: Gisella Caccialanza (Bride), Todd Bolender (Groom), Elise Reiman (Sylphide), Tanaquil LeClercq and Beatrice Tompkins (Bridesmaids), José Martínez (Minister).

THE SEASONS
Choreography: Merce Cunningham
Music: John Cage
Decor and costumes: Isamu Noguchi
Premiere: May 18, 1947, Ziegfeld Theater, New York.
Principal dancers: Gisella Caccialanza, Tanaquil LeClercq, Beatrice Tompkins, Merce Cunningham.

BLACKFACE
Choreography: Lew Christensen
Music: Carter Harman
Decor and costumes: Robert Drew
Premiere: May 18, 1947, Ziegfeld Theater, New York.
Principal dancers: Betty Nichols, Beatrice Tompkins, Talley Beatty, Marc Beaudet, Fred Danieli, Paul Godkin.

PUNCH AND THE CHILD
Choreography: Fred Danieli
Music: Richard Arnell
Decor and costumes: Horace Armistead
Premiere: November 12, 1947, City Center of Music and Drama, New York.
Principal dancers: Herbert Bliss (Father and Punch), Beatrice Tompkins (Mother and Judy), Judith Kursch (The Child), Gisella Caccialanza (Fishwife and Polly), Charles Laskey (Peg Leg and Constable), Lew Christensen (Puppeteer and Devil), Edward Bigelow (Musician and Doctor), Victor Duntiere (Street Cleaner and Hangman), Luis López (Professor).

SYMPHONIE CONCERTANTE
Choreography: George Balanchine
Music: Wolfgang Amadeus Mozart
(Symphonie Concertante in E flat, K.364)
Decor and costumes: James Stewart Morcom
Premiere: November 12, 1947, City Center of Music and Drama, New York. (Prior to the official premiere, SYMPHONIE CONCERTANTE was presented November 5, 1945, at Carnegie Hall, New York, on a program "Adventure in Ballet" by pupils of the School of American Ballet.)
Principal dancers: Maria Tallchief, Tanaquil LeClercq, Dorothy Dushok, Ruth Gilbert, Georgia Hiden, Rita Karlin, Pat McBride, Irma Sandre, Todd Bolender.

THE TRIUMPH OF BACCHUS AND ARIADNE
(BALLET CANTATA)
Choreography: George Balanchine
Music: Vittorio Rieti
Decor and costumes: Corrado Cagli
Premiere: February 9, 1948, City Center of Music and Drama, New York.
Principal dancers: Lew Christensen (Major-domo), Nicholas Magallanes (Bacchus), Tanaquil LeClercq (Ariadne), Herbert Bliss (First Satyr), Marie Jeanne (First Nymph), Charles Laskey (Silenus), Francisco Moncion (Midas), Claudia Hall (The Little Girl), Pat McBride (The Young Girl).

CAPRICORN CONCERTO
Choreography: Todd Bolender
Music: Samuel Barber
Decor and costumes: Esteban Francés
Premiere: March 22, 1948, City Center of Music and Drama, New York.
Principal dancers: Maria Tallchief, Herbert Bliss, Francisco Moncion.

SYMPHONY IN C
Choreography: George Balanchine
Music: Georges Bizet
Premiere: March 22, 1948, City Center of Music and Drama, New York. (Revival of LE PALAIS DE CRISTAL, first produced for the Paris Opéra, July 28, 1947.)
Principal dancers: First Movement, Maria Tallchief, Nicholas Magallanes; Second Movement, Tanaquil LeClercq, Francisco Moncion; Third Movement, Beatrice Tompkins, Herbert Bliss; Fourth Movement, Elise Reiman, Lew Christensen.

ÉLÉGIE
Choreography: George Balanchine
Music: Igor Stravinsky
Premiere: April 28, 1948, City Center of Music and Drama, New York. (Prior to the official premiere, ÉLÉGIE was presented November 5, 1945, at Carnegie Hall, New York, on a program "Adventure in Ballet" by pupils of the School of American Ballet.)
Dancers: Tanaquil LeClercq and Pat McBride.

ORPHEUS
Choreography: George Balanchine
Music: Igor Stravinsky
Decor and costumes: Isamu Noguchi
Premiere: April 28, 1948, City Center of Music and Drama, New York.
Principal dancers: Nicholas Magallanes (Orpheus), Francisco Moncion (Dark Angel), Maria Tallchief (Eurydice), Herbert Bliss (Apollo), Edward Bigelow (Pluto), Job Sanders (Satyr), Tanaquil LeClercq (Leader of the Bacchantes), Beatrice Tompkins (Leader of the Furies).

THE NEW YORK CITY BALLET

MOTHER GOOSE SUITE
Choreography: Todd Bolender
Music: Maurice Ravel
Premiere: November 1, 1948, City Center of Music and Drama, New York. (Revival from American Concert Ballet, 1941.)
Principal dancers: Beatrice Tompkins (Spectator), Marie Jeanne (Young Girl), Todd Bolender (Hop o' My Thumb), Una Kai (Bird), Dick Beard (Prince), Francisco Moncion (Beast).

THE GUESTS
Choreography: Jerome Robbins
Music: Marc Blitzstein
Premiere: January 20, 1949, City Center of Music and Drama, New York.
Principal dancers: Maria Tallchief, Francisco Moncion, Nicholas Magallanes.

JINX
Choreography: Lew Christensen
Music: Benjamin Britten
(Variations on a Theme by Frank Bridge)
Decor and costumes: George Bockman
Book: Lew Christensen
Premiere: November 24, 1949, City Center of Music and Drama, New York. (Revival from Dance Players, 1942.)
Principal dancers: Francisco Moncion (Jinx, a Clown); Janet Reed, Ruth Sobotka, Frank Hobi (Wire-Walkers); Herbert Bliss, Barbara Milberg, Barbara Walczak (Equestrians); Beatrice Tompkins (Bearded Lady); George Hiden (Strong Lady); Dorothy Dushok (Tattooed Lady); Val Buttignol (Ringmaster).

FIREBIRD
Choreography: George Balanchine
Music: Igor Stravinsky
Decor and costumes: Marc Chagall
Premiere: November 27, 1949, City Center of Music and Drama, New York.
Principal dancers: Maria Tallchief (Firebird), Francisco Moncion (Prince Ivan), Pat McBride (Prince's Bride), Edward Bigelow (Kastchei).

BOURRÉE FANTASQUE
Choreography: George Balanchine
Music: Emmanuel Chabrier
Costumes: Karinska
Premiere: December 1, 1949, City Center of Music and Drama, New York.
Principal dancers: Bourrée Fantasque, Tanaquil LeClercq, Jerome Robbins; Prelude, Maria Tallchief, Nicholas Magallanes, Edwina Fontaine, Yvonne Mounsey; Fête Polonaise, Janet Reed, Herbert Bliss.

ONDINE
Choreography: William Dollar
Music: Antonio Vivaldi
(Violin Concertos)
Decor and costumes: Horace Armistead
Premiere: December 9, 1949, City Center of Music and Drama, New York.
Principal dancers: Tanaquil LeClercq (Ondine), Francisco Moncion (Matteo), Melissa Hayden (Giannina), Yvonne Mounsey (Hydrola).

THE PRODIGAL SON
Choreography: George Balanchine
Music: Serge Prokofiev
Decor and costumes: Georges Rouault
Premiere: February 23, 1950, City Center of Music and Drama, New York. (Revival from the Diaghilev Ballets Russes, 1929.)
Principal dancers: Jerome Robbins (The Prodigal Son); Maria Tallchief (The Siren); Michael Arshansky (The Father); Frank Hobi, Herbert Bliss (Servants of the Prodigal Son); Jillana, Francesca Mosarra (The Two Sisters).

THE DUEL
Choreography: William Dollar
Music: Raffaello de Banfield
Costumes: Robert Stevenson
Premiere: February 24, 1950, City Center of Music and Drama, New York. (Revision of Dollar's LE COMBAT, which premiered February 24, 1949, London.)
Dancers: Melissa Hayden, William Dollar, Val Buttignol, Walter Georgov, Shaun O'Brien.

THE AGE OF ANXIETY
Choreography: Jerome Robbins (based on the poem The Age of Anxiety by W. H. Auden)
Music: Leonard Bernstein (Symphony No. 2)
Decor: Oliver Smith
Costumes: Irene Sharaff
Premiere: February 26, 1950, City Center of Music and Drama, New York.
Principal dancers: Tanaquil LeClercq, Todd Bolender, Francisco Moncion, Jerome Robbins, Melissa Hayden, Pat McBride, Yvonne Mounsey, Beatrice Tompkins, Edward Bigelow, Herbert Bliss.

ILLUMINATIONS
Choreography: Frederick Ashton (based on poems by Arthur Rimbaud)
Music: Benjamin Britten
(Les Illuminations, ten pieces for tenor or high voice and string orchestra, 1939)
Decor and costumes: Cecil Beaton
Premiere: March 2, 1950, City Center of Music and Drama, New York.
Principal dancers: Nicholas Magallanes (Poet), Tanaquil LeClercq (Sacred Love), Melissa Hayden (Profane Love).

PAS DE DEUX ROMANTIQUE
Choreography: George Balanchine
Music: Carl Maria von Weber (Clarinet Concerto)
Costumes: Robert Stevenson
Premiere: March 3, 1950, City Center of Music and Drama, New York.
Dancers: Janet Reed and Herbert Bliss.

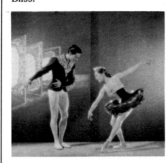

JONES BEACH
Choreography: George Balanchine and Jerome Robbins
Music: Jurriaan Andriessen (Berkshire Symphonies)
Premiere: March 9, 1950, City Center of Music and Drama, New York.
Principal dancers: Melissa Hayden, Tanaquil LeClercq, Yvonne Mounsey, Maria Tallchief, Beatrice Tompkins, Herbert Bliss, Todd Bolender, William Dollar, Frank Hobi, Nicholas Magallanes, Jerome Robbins, Roy Tobias.

THE WITCH
Choreography: John Cranko
Music: Maurice Ravel (Piano Concerto No. 2)
Decor and costumes: Dorothea Tanning
Premiere: August 18, 1950, Royal Opera House, Covent Garden, London.
Principal dancers: Melissa Hayden, Francisco Moncion.

MAZURKA FROM "A LIFE FOR THE TSAR"
Choreography: George Balanchine
Music: Mikhail Glinka (from his opera A LIFE FOR THE TSAR)
Premiere: November 30, 1950, City Center of Music and Drama, New York.
Dancers: Janet Reed and Yurek Lazowski; Vida Brown and George Balanchine; Barbara Walczak and Harold Lang; Dorothy Dushok and Frank Hobi.

SYLVIA: PAS DE DEUX
Choreography: George Balanchine
Music: Léo Delibes
Costumes: Karinska
Premiere: December 1, 1950, City Center of Music and Drama, New York.
Dancers: Maria Tallchief and Nicholas Magallanes.

PAS DE TROIS (I)
Choreography: George Balanchine
Music: Leon Minkus
(from his score for the ballet DON QUIXOTE, 1869)
Costumes: Karinska
Premiere: February 18, 1951, City Center of Music and Drama, New York. (Revival from Grand Ballet du Marquis de Cuevas, 1948.)
Dancers: Maria Tallchief, Nora Kaye, André Eglevsky.

LA VALSE
Choreography: George Balanchine
Music: Maurice Ravel
(Valses nobles et sentimentales and La Valse)
Costumes: Karinska
Premiere: February 20, 1951, City Center of Music and Drama, New York.
Principal dancers: Diana Adams, Tanaquil LeClercq, Yvonne Mounsey, Patricia Wilde, Herbert Bliss, Frank Hobi, Nicholas Magallanes, Francisco Moncion.

LADY OF THE CAMELLIAS
Choreography: Antony Tudor
Music: Giuseppe Verdi
Decor and costumes: Cecil Beaton
Book: after the novel by Alexandre Dumas fils.
Premiere: February 28, 1951, City Center of Music and Drama, New York.
Principal dancers: Vida Brown (Prudence), Diana Adams (Marguerite Gautier), Brooks Jackson (M. le Comte de N.), Hugh Laing (Armand Duval), John Earle (Armand's Father).

CAPRICCIO BRILLANTE
Choreography: George Balanchine
Music: Felix Mendelssohn
Costumes: Karinska
Premiere: June 7, 1951, City Center of Music and Drama, New York.
Dancers: Maria Tallchief and André Eglevsky; Barbara Bocher, Constance Garfield, Jillana, Irene Larsson.

CAKEWALK
Choreography: Ruthanna Boris
Music: Louis Moreau Gottschalk (arrangement and orchestration by Hershy Kay)
Decor and costumes: Robert Drew
Premiere: June 12, 1951, City Center of Music and Drama, New York.
Principal dancers: Tanaquil LeClercq, Yvonne Mounsey, Janet Reed, Beatrice Tompkins, Patricia Wilde, Herbert Bliss, Frank Hobi.

THE CAGE
Choreography: Jerome Robbins
Music: Igor Stravinsky (String Concerto in D)
Costumes: Ruth Sobotka
Premiere: June 14, 1951, City Center of Music and Drama, New York.
Principal dancers: Nora Kaye (The Novice); Yvonne Mounsey (The Queen); Nicholas Magallanes, Michael Maule (The Intruders).

THE MIRACULOUS MANDARIN
Choreography: Todd Bolender
Music: Béla Bartók
Decor and costumes: Alvin Colt
Book: Melchior Langyel
Premiere: September 6, 1951, City Center of Music and Drama, New York.
Principal dancers: Robert Barnett, Edward Bigelow, Jacques d'Amboise, Walter Georgov, Michael Maule (The Men); Melissa Hayden (The Woman); Frank Hobi (An Old Man); Roy Tobias (A Young Man); Beatrice Tompkins (A Blind Girl); Hugh Laing (The Mandarin).

À LA FRANÇAIX
Choreography: George Balanchine
Music: Jean Françaix
(Serenade for Small Orchestra)
Premiere: September 11, 1951, City Center of Music and Drama, New York.
Dancers: Janet Reed, Maria Tallchief, André Eglevsky, Frank Hobi, Roy Tobias.

TYL ULENSPIEGEL
Choreography: George Balanchine
Music: Richard Strauss
(from Tyl Eulenspiegel)
Decor and costumes: by Esteban Francés
Premiere: November 14, 1951, City Center of Music and Drama, New York.
Principal dancers: Alberta Grant (Tyl Ulenspiegel as a Child), Susan Kovnat (Philip II as a Child), Jerome Robbins (Tyl Ulenspiegel), Ruth Sobotka (Nell, His Wife), Brooks Jackson (Philip II, King of Spain), Frank Hobi (Duke), Beatrice Tompkins (Duchess), Tomi Wortham (Woman).

SWAN LAKE
Choreography: George Balanchine (after Lev Ivanov)
Music: Peter Ilyich Tchaikovsky
Decor and costumes: Cecil Beaton
Premiere: November 20, 1951, City Center of Music and Drama, New York.
Principal dancers: Maria Tallchief (Odette); André Eglevsky (Prince Siegfried); Frank Hobi (Benno); Patricia Wilde and Yvonne Mounsey (Leading Swans); Doris Breckenridge, Kaye Sargent, Ruth Sobotka, Gloria Vauges (Cygnets); Edward Bigelow (Rothbart, a Sorcerer).

LILAC GARDEN

Choreography: Antony Tudor
Music: Ernest Chausson (Poème for violin and orchestra, Opus 25)
Decor: Horace Armistead
Costumes: Karinska

Premiere: November 30, 1951, City Center of Music and Drama, New York. (Revival from Ballet Rambert, 1936, when it was presented under the title JARDIN AUX LILAS.)
Principal dancers: Nora Kaye (Caroline), Hugh Laing (Her Lover), Antony Tudor (The Man She Must Marry), Tanaquil LeClercq (The Woman in His Past).

THE PIED PIPER

Choreography: Jerome Robbins
Music: Aaron Copland (Concerto for Clarinet and String Orchestra)

Premiere: December 4, 1951, City Center of Music and Drama, New York.
Principal dancers: Diana Adams, Melissa Hayden, Jillana, Tanaquil LeClercq, Janet Reed, Barbara Bocher, Herbert Bliss, Todd Bolender, Nicholas Magallanes, Jerome Robbins, Roy Tobias.

BALLADE

Choreography: Jerome Robbins
Music: Claude Debussy (Six Épigraphes antiques and Syrinx)
Decor and costumes: Boris Aronson

Premiere: February 14, 1952, City Center of Music and Drama, New York.
Dancers: Nora Kaye, Tanaquil LeClercq, Janet Reed, Robert Barnett, Brooks Jackson, Louis Johnson, John Mandia, Roy Tobias.

CARACOLE

Choreography: George Balanchine
Music: Wolfgang Amadeus Mozart (Divertimento No. 15 in B flat major, K. 287)
Costumes: Christian Bérard

Premiere: February 19, 1952, City Center of Music and Drama, New York.
Principal dancers: Diana Adams, Melissa Hayden, Tanaquil LeClercq, Maria Tallchief, Patricia Wilde, André Eglevsky, Nicholas Magallanes, Jerome Robbins.

BAYOU

Choreography: George Balanchine
Music: Virgil Thomson (Acadian Songs and Dances)
Decor and costumes: Dorothea Tanning

Premiere: February 21, 1952, City Center of Music and Drama, New York.
Principal dancers: Francisco Moncion (Boy of the Bayou); Doris Breckenridge (Girl of the Bayou); Melissa Hayden, Hugh Laing, Irene Larsson, Barbara Walczak, Walter Georgov, Stanley Zompakos (Leaves and Flowers); Diana Adams, Herbert Bliss, Una Kai, Marilyn Poudrier, Brooks Jackson, Shaun O'Brien (Starched White People).

LA GLOIRE

Choreography: Antony Tudor
Music: Ludwig van Beethoven (Egmont, Coriolanus, Leonora III overtures)
Decor: Gaston Longchamp
Costumes: Robert Fletcher

Premiere: February 26, 1952, City Center of Music and Drama, New York.
Principal dancers: Nora Kaye (La Gloire), Francisco Moncion (Sextus Tarquinius and Hamlet's Stepfather), Hugh Laing (Hippolytus and Laertes), Doris Breckenridge (Ophelia), Beatrice Tompkins (Hamlet's Mother), Diana Adams (The Dancer in Gray).

PICNIC AT TINTAGEL

Choreography: Frederick Ashton
Music: Sir Arnold Bax (The Garden of Fand)
Decor and costumes: Cecil Beaton

Premiere: February 28, 1952, City Center of Music and Drama, New York.
Dancers: Francisco Moncion (The Husband—King Mark); Diana Adams (The Wife—Iseult); Yvonne Mounsey (Her Maid—Brangaene); Jacques d'Amboise (Her Lover—Tristram); Stanley Zompakos, Brooks Jackson (His Rivals—The False Knights); Alan Baker, John Mandia (Her Chauffeur and Footman—Heralds); Robert Barnett (The Caretaker—Merlin).

SCOTCH SYMPHONY

Choreography: George Balanchine
Music: Felix Mendelssohn (Scotch Symphony, 2nd, 3rd, and 4th movements)
Decor: Horace Armistead
Costumes: Karinska and David Ffolkes

Premiere: November 11, 1952, City Center of Music and Drama, New York.
Principal dancers: Maria Tallchief, Patricia Wilde, André Eglevsky, Michael Maule, Frank Hobi.

METAMORPHOSES

Choreography: George Balanchine
Music: Paul Hindemith (Symphonic Metamorphoses on Themes by Carl Maria von Weber, 1943)
Costumes: Karinska

Premiere: November 25, 1952, City Center of Music and Drama, New York.
Principal dancers: Tanaquil LeClercq, Nicholas Magallanes, Todd Bolender.

HARLEQUINADE PAS DE DEUX

Choreography: George Balanchine
Music: Riccardo Drigo
Costumes: Karinska

Premiere: December 16, 1952, City Center of Music and Drama, New York.
Dancers: Maria Tallchief and André Eglevsky.

KALEIDOSCOPE

Choreography: Ruthanna Boris
Music: Dimitri Kabalevsky
Costumes: Alvin Colt

Premiere: December 18, 1952, City Center of Music and Drama, New York.
Principal dancers: Melissa Hayden, Patricia Wilde, Herbert Bliss, Todd Bolender, Frank Hobi.

INTERPLAY

Choreography: Jerome Robbins
Music: Morton Gould (American Concertette)
Decor and costumes: Irene Sharaff

Premiere: December 23, 1952, City Center of Music and Drama, New York. (Revival from Ballet Theater, 1945. First performed in a Billy Rose show, CONCERT VARIETIES, June, 1945, Ziegfeld Theater, New York.)
Dancers: Carolyn George, Jillana, Irene Larsson, Janet Reed, Robert Barnett, Todd Bolender, Jacques d'Amboise, Michael Maule.

CONCERTINO

Choreography: George Balanchine
Music: Jean Françaix
Costumes: Karinska

Premiere: December 30, 1952, City Center of Music and Drama, New York.
Dancers: Diana Adams, Tanaquil LeClercq, André Eglevsky.

VALSE-FANTAISIE

Choreography: George Balanchine
Music: Mikhail Glinka
Costumes: Karinska

Premiere: January 6, 1953, City Center of Music and Drama, New York.
Dancers: Tanaquil LeClercq, Diana Adams, Melissa Hayden, Nicholas Magallanes.

WILL O' THE WISP

Choreography: Ruthanna Boris
Music: Virgil Thomson
Decor and costumes: Dorothea Tanning

Premiere: January 13, 1953, City Center of Music and Drama, New York.
Principal dancers: Ruthanna Boris, Frank Hobi.

THE FIVE GIFTS

Choreography: William Dollar
Music: Ernest Dohnanyi (Variations on a Nursery Tune)
Costumes: Esteban Francés
Book: after a story by Mark Twain

Premiere: January 20, 1953, City Center of Music and Drama, New York. (Revival from American Concert Ballet, 1943.)
Principal dancers: Todd Bolender (The Youth), Melissa Hayden (The Fairy), Carolyn George (Pleasure), Yvonne Mounsey (Death), Jillana (Fame), Irene Larsson (Love), Jacques d'Amboise (Another Youth).

AFTERNOON OF A FAUN

Choreography: Jerome Robbins
Music: Claude Debussy
Decor: Jean Rosenthal
Costumes: Irene Sharaff

Premiere: May 14, 1953, City Center of Music and Drama, New York.
Dancers: Tanaquil LeClercq and Francisco Moncion.

THE FILLY

(or A STABLEBOY'S DREAM)
Choreography: Todd Bolender
Music: John Colman
Decor and costumes: Peter Larkin

Premiere: May 19, 1953, City Center of Music and Drama, New York.
Principal dancers: Roy Tobias (Stableboy), Diana Adams (The Mare), Nicholas Magallanes (The Stallion), Ellen Gottesman (The Foal), Maria Tallchief (The Filly).

FANFARE

Choreography: Jerome Robbins
Music: Benjamin Britten (The Young Person's Guide to the Orchestra)
Decor and costumes: Irene Sharaff

Premiere: June 2, 1953, City Center of Music and Drama, New York.
Dancers: The entire company.

CON AMORE

Choreography: Lew Christensen
Music: Gioacchino Rossini (LA GAZZA LADRA, IL SIGNOR BRUSCHINO and LA SCALA DI SETA overtures)
Decor and costumes: James Bodrero
Book: James Graham-Lujan

Premiere: June 9, 1953, City Center of Music and Drama, New York. (Revival from the San Francisco Ballet, 1953.)
Principal dancers: Sally Bailey, Nancy Johnson, Jacques d'Amboise.

OPUS 34

Choreography: George Balanchine
Music: Arnold Schoenberg (Begleitmusik, 1930)
Decor and costumes: Esteban Francés

Premiere: January 19, 1954, City Center of Music and Drama, New York.
Principal dancers: Diana Adams, Patricia Wilde, Tanaquil LeClercq, Nicholas Magallanes, Francisco Moncion, Herbert Bliss.

THE NUTCRACKER

Choreography: George Balanchine (after Lev Ivanov)
Music: Peter Ilyich Tchaikovsky
Decor: Horace Armistead
Costumes: Karinska

Premiere: February 2, 1954, City Center of Music and Drama, New York.
Principal dancers: Maria Tallchief, Tanaquil LeClercq, Yvonne Mounsey, Janet Reed, Jillana, Irene Larsson, Alberta Grant, Nicholas Magallanes, Herbert Bliss, Francisco Moncion, Robert Barnett, Edward Bigelow, George Li, Michael Arshansky, Paul Nickel.

QUARTET

Choreography: Jerome Robbins
Music: Serge Prokofiev (String Quartet No. 2, Opus 92)
Costumes: Karinska

Premiere: February 18, 1954, City Center of Music and Drama, New York.
Principal dancers: Patricia Wilde, Jillana, Yvonne Mounsey, Herbert Bliss, Jacques d'Amboise, Todd Bolender.

WESTERN SYMPHONY

Choreography: George Balanchine
Music: Hershy Kay

Premiere: September 7, 1954, City Center of Music and Drama, New York.
Principal dancers: First Movement, Diana Adams, Herbert Bliss; Second Movement, Janet Reed, Nicholas Magallanes; Third Movement, Patricia Wilde, André Eglevsky; Fourth Movement, Tanaquil LeClercq, Jacques d'Amboise.

IVESIANA

Choreography: George Balanchine
Music: Charles Ives

Premiere: September 14, 1954, City Center of Music and Drama, New York.
Principal dancers: Janet Reed, Patricia Wilde, Allegra Kent, Diana Adams, Tanaquil LeClercq, Francisco Moncion, Jacques d'Amboise, Todd Bolender, Herbert Bliss.

the New York City Ballet

ROMA
Choreography: George Balanchine
Music: Georges Bizet
Decor and costumes: Eugene Berman
Premiere: February 23, 1955, City Center of Music and Drama, New York.
Principal dancers: Tanaquil LeClercq and André Eglevsky; Barbara Milberg, Barbara Walczak, Roy Tobias, John Mandia.

PAS DE TROIS (II)
Choreography: George Balanchine
Music: Mikhail Glinka
Costumes: Karinska
Premiere: March 1, 1955, City Center of Music and Drama, New York.
Dancers: Patricia Wilde, Melissa Hayden, André Eglevsky.

PAS DE DIX
Choreography: George Balanchine
Music: Alexander Glazounov (from RAYMONDA)
Costumes: Esteban Francés
Premiere: November 9, 1955, City Center of Music and Drama, New York.
Dancers: Maria Tallchief and André Eglevsky; Barbara Fallis, Constance Garfield, Jane Mason, Barbara Walczak, Shaun O'Brien, Roy Tobias, Roland Vazquez, Jonathan Watts.

SOUVENIRS
Choreography: Todd Bolender
Music: Samuel Barber
Decor and costumes: Rouben Ter-Arutunian
Premiere: November 15, 1955, City Center of Music and Drama, New York.
Principal dancers: Irene Larsson, Jillana, Carolyn George, Todd Bolender, Roy Tobias, Jonathan Watts, John Mandia, Herbert Bliss.

JEUX D'ENFANTS
Choreography: George Balanchine, Barbara Milberg, Francisco Moncion
Music: Georges Bizet
Decor and costumes: Esteban Francés
Premiere: November 22, 1955, City Center of Music and Drama, New York.
Principal dancers: Melissa Hayden, Barbara Fallis, Barbara Walczak, Roy Tobias, Robert Barnett, Richard Thomas, Jonathan Watts.

ALLEGRO BRILLANTE
Choreography: George Balanchine
Music: Peter Ilyich Tchaikovsky (Third Piano Concerto)
Premiere: March 1, 1956, City Center of Music and Drama, New York.
Dancers: Maria Tallchief and Nicholas Magallanes; with Barbara Fallis, Carolyn George, Barbara Milberg, Barbara Walczak, Arthur Mitchell, Richard Rapp, Roland Vazquez, Jonathan Watts.

THE CONCERT
(or THE PERILS OF EVERYBODY)
Choreography: Jerome Robbins
Music: Frédéric Chopin
Decor: Jean Rosenthal
Costumes: Irene Sharaff
Premiere: March 6, 1956, City Center of Music and Drama, New York.
Principal dancers: Tanaquil LeClercq, Yvonne Mounsey, Wilma Curley, Patricia Savoia, Todd Bolender, Robert Barnett, John Mandia, Richard Thomas.

THE STILL POINT
Choreography: Todd Bolender
Music: Claude Debussy, (transcription for orchestra by Frank Black)
Premiere: March 13, 1956, City Center of Music and Drama, New York. (Originally arranged for the Emily Frankel–Frank Ryder modern dance group.)
Dancers: Melissa Hayden, Irene Larsson, Jillana, Jacques d'Amboise, Roy Tobias, John Mandia.

DIVERTIMENTO NO. 15 (I)
Choreography: George Balanchine
Music: Wolfgang Amadeus Mozart (Divertimento No. 15 in B flat major, K. 287)
Decor: James Stewart Morcom
Costumes: Karinska
Premiere: December 19, 1956, City Center of Music and Drama, New York. (Prior to the official premiere, DIVERTIMENTO NO. 15—a revival of CARACOLE of 1952—was presented May 31, 1956, at the Mozart Festival in Stratford, Connecticut.)
Principal dancers: Diana Adams, Melissa Hayden, Yvonne Mounsey, Patricia Wilde, Barbara Milberg, Nicholas Magallanes, Roy Tobias, Jonathan Watts.

THE UNICORN, THE GORGON, AND THE MANTICORE
(A MADRIGAL FABLE)
Choreography: John Butler
Music and book: Gian Carlo Menotti
Decor: Jean Rosenthal
Costumes: Robert Fletcher
Premiere: January 15, 1957, City Center of Music and Drama, New York. (Commissioned by the Elizabeth Sprague Coolidge Foundation in the Library of Congress, and first presented October 21, 1956, in the Coolidge Auditorium, Washington, D.C.)

Dancers: Janet Reed (The Countess), Roy Tobias (The Count), Nicholas Magallanes (Man in the Castle—the Poet), Arthur Mitchell (The Unicorn), Eugene Tanner (The Gorgon), Richard Thomas (The Manticore), John Mandia (The Mayor), Wilma Curley (The Mayor's Wife), Jonathan Watts (The Doctor), Lee Becker (The Doctor's Wife).

THE MASQUERS
Choreography: Todd Bolender
Music: Francis Poulenc
Decor and costumes: David Hays
Premiere: January 29, 1957, City Center of Music and Drama, New York.
Principal dancers: Melissa Hayden (A Young Woman), Jacques d'Amboise (A Soldier), Yvonne Mounsey (The Passerby), Charlotte Ray (A Friend of the Young Woman), Robert Barnett (The Boy She Meets), Jonathan Watts (Another Soldier).

PASTORALE
Choreography: Francisco Moncion
Music: Charles Turner
Decor: David Hays
Costumes: Ruth Sobotka
Premiere: February 14, 1957, City Center of Music and Drama, New York.
Dancers: Allegra Kent, Francisco Moncion, Roy Tobias, Geralyn Donald, Barbara Fallis, Ruth Sobotka, Anthony Blum, Richard Rapp, Shaun O'Brien.

SQUARE DANCE
Choreography: George Balanchine
Music: Arcangelo Corelli and Antonio Vivaldi
Premiere: November 21, 1957, City Center of Music and Drama, New York.
Principal dancers: Patricia Wilde and Nicholas Magallanes.

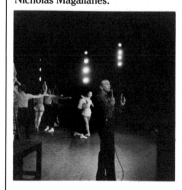

AGON
Choreography: George Balanchine
Music: Igor Stravinsky
Premiere: November 27, 1957, City Center of Music and Drama, New York.
Dancers: Diana Adams, Melissa Hayden, Barbara Milberg, Barbara Walczak, Todd Bolender, Arthur Mitchell, Roy Tobias, Jonathan Watts, Roberta Lubell, Francia Russell, Dido Sayers, Ruth Sobotka.

GOUNOD SYMPHONY
Choreography: George Balanchine
Music: Charles Gounod (Symphony No. 1 in D major)
Decor: Horace Armistead
Costumes: Karinska
Premiere: January 8, 1958, City Center of Music and Drama, New York.
Principal dancers: Maria Tallchief and Jacques d'Amboise.

STARS AND STRIPES
Choreography: George Balanchine
Music: Hershy Kay (after music by John Philip Sousa)
Decor: David Hays
Costumes: Karinska
Premiere: January 17, 1958, City Center of Music and Drama, New York.
Principal dancers: Allegra Kent, Diana Adams, Robert Barnett, Melissa Hayden, Jacques d'Amboise.

WALTZ SCHERZO
Choreography: George Balanchine
Music: Peter Ilyich Tchaikovsky
Costumes: Karinska
Premiere: September 9, 1958, City Center of Music and Drama, New York.
Dancers: Patricia Wilde and André Eglevsky.

MEDEA
Choreography: Birgit Cullberg
Music: Béla Bartók (orchestration by Herbert Sandberg)
Costumes: Lewis Brown
Premiere: November 26, 1958, City Center of Music and Drama, New York. (Revival from the Royal Swedish Opera Ballet, Stockholm, 1954.)
Principal dancers: Melissa Hayden (Medea); Jacques d'Amboise (Jason); Delia Peters, Susan Pillersdorf (Their Children); Shaun O'Brien (Creon, King of Corinth); Violette Verdy (Creusa, His Daughter).

OCTET
Choreography: Willam Christensen
Music: Igor Stravinsky
Premiere: December 2, 1958, City Center of Music and Drama, New York.
Dancers: Barbara Walczak, Dido Sayers, Roberta Lubell, Judith Green, Edward Villela, William Weslow, Robert Lindgren, Richard Rapp.

THE SEVEN DEADLY SINS
Choreography: George Balanchine
Music: Kurt Weill
Decor and costumes: Rouben Ter-Arutunian
Book: Bertholt Brecht, translated by W. H. Auden and Chester Kallman
Premiere: December 4, 1958, City Center of Music and Drama, New York. (Revival from Les Ballets 1933.)

Principal dancer: Allegra Kent (Anna II).
Principal singers: Lotte Lenya (Anna I); Stanley Carlson, bass (Mother); Gene Hollman, bass (Father); Frank Porretta, tenor (Brother I); Grant Williams, tenor (Brother II).

NATIVE DANCERS
Choreography: George Balanchine
Music: Vittorio Rieti (Symphony No. 5)
Decor: David Hays
Girls' costumes: Peter Larkin
Jockey silks: H. Kauffman & Sons, Saddlery Co.
Premiere: January 14, 1959, City Center of Music and Drama, New York.
Principal dancers: Patricia Wilde and Jacques d'Amboise.

EPISODES (I)
Choreography: Martha Graham
Music: Anton von Webern (Passacaglia, Opus 1; and Six Pieces for Orchestra, Opus 6; both 1909)
Decor: David Hays
Costume design and execution: Karinska
Premiere: May 14, 1959, City Center of Music and Drama, New York.
Principal dancers: Martha Graham (Mary, Queen of Scots), Bertram Ross (Bothwell), Sallie Wilson (Elizabeth, Queen of England).

EPISODES (II)
Choreography: George Balanchine
Music: Anton von Webern (Symphony, Opus 21; Five Pieces, Opus 10; Concerto, Opus 24; Variations for Orchestra, Opus 30; "Ricercata for Six Voices from Bach's Musical Offering")
Decor: David Hays
Costume design and execution: Karinska
Premiere: May 14, 1959, City Center of Music and Drama, New York.
Principal dancers: Violette Verdy, Jonathan Watts, Diana Adams, Jacques d'Amboise, Allegra Kent, Nicholas Magallanes, Paul Taylor, Melissa Hayden, Francisco Moncion.

NIGHT SHADOW
(Later called LA SONNAMBULA)
Choreography: George Balanchine
Music: Vittorio Rieti (after themes by Vincenzo Bellini)
Decor and costumes: André Levasseur
Premiere: January 6, 1960, City Center of Music and Drama, New York. (Revived for this company by John Taras; world premiere by Ballets Russes de Monte Carlo, February 27, 1946, City Center of Music and Drama.)
Principal dancers: Allegra Kent, Erik Bruhn, Jillana, John Taras, Suki Schorer, Edward Villella, and William Weslow.

PANAMERICA
Choreography: George Balanchine, Gloria Contreras, Jacques d'Amboise, Francisco Moncion, John Taras
Music: A series of short works by Latin-American composers Carlos Chávez, Luis Escobar, Alberto Ginastera, Julian Orbón, Juan Orrego Salas, Sivestre Revueltas, Hector Tosa, Heitor Villa-Lobos
Decor: David Hays
Costumes: Karinska and Esteban Francés
Premiere: January 20, 1960, City Center of Music and Drama, New York.
Principal dancers: Violette Verdy, Erik Bruhn, Patricia Wilde, Jillana, Edward Villella, Diana Adams, Nicholas Magallanes, Francisco Moncion, Maria Tallchief, Arthur Mitchell, Conrad Ludlow, Allegra Kent, Jonathan Watts, Roy Tobias.

THEME AND VARIATIONS
Choreography: George Balanchine
Music: Peter Ilyich Tchaikovsky (Suite No. 3 in G)
Costumes: Karinska
Premiere: February 5, 1960, City Center of Music and Drama, New York. (World premiere by Ballet Theater, September 27, 1947.)
Principal Dancers: Violette Verdy and Edward Villella.

PAS DE DEUX (I)
Choreography: George Balanchine
Music: Peter Ilyich Tchaikovsky
Costumes: Karinska
Premiere: March 29, 1960, City Center of Music and Drama, New York.
Dancers: Violette Verdy, Conrad Ludlow.

THE FIGURE IN THE CARPET
Choreography: George Balanchine
Music: George Frederic Handel (Water Music and Royal Fireworks Music)
Book: George Lewis
Decor and costumes: Esteban Francés
Premiere: April 13, 1960, City Center of Music and Drama, New York.
Principal dancers: Violette Verdy, Melissa Hayden, Jillana, Diana Adams, Patricia McBride, Mary Hinkson, Jacques d'Amboise, Edward Villella, Francisco Moncion, Arthur Mitchell, Nicholas Magallanes.

MONUMENTUM PRO GESUALDO
Choreography: George Balanchine
Music: Igor Stravinsky (an arrangement for orchestra of three madrigals by Don Carlo Gesualdo)
Decor: David Hays
Premiere: November 16, 1960, City Center of Music and Drama, New York.
Principal dancers: Diana Adams and Conrad Ludlow.

VARIATIONS FROM DON SEBASTIAN
(Later called DONIZETTI VARIATIONS)
Choreography: George Balanchine
Music: Gaetano Donizetti
Decor: David Hays
Women's costumes: Karinska
Men's costumes: Esteban Francés
Premiere: November 16, 1960, City Center of Music and Drama, New York.
Principal dancers: Melissa Hayden and Jonathan Watts.

LIEBESLIEDER WALZER
Choreography: George Balanchine
Music: Johannes Brahms (Opus 52 and Opus 65).
Decor: David Hays
Costumes: Karinska
Premiere: November 22, 1960, City Center of Music and Drama, New York.
Dancers: Diana Adams and Bill Carter, Melissa Hayden and Jonathan Watts, Jillana and Conrad Ludlow, Violette Verdy and Nicholas Magallanes.

JAZZ CONCERT
(a four-part program consisting of the ballets CREATION OF THE WORLD, RAGTIME, LES BICHES, and EBONY CONCERTO):

CREATION OF THE WORLD
Choreography: Todd Bolender
Music: Darius Milhaud
Premiere: December 7, 1960, City Center of Music and Drama, New York.
Dancers: Patricia McBride, Conrad Ludlow, Janet Reed, Lois Bewley, Arthur Mitchell, Edward Villella.

RAGTIME
Choreography: George Balanchine
Music: Igor Stravinsky
Premiere: December 7, 1960, City Center of Music and Drama, New York.
Dancers: Diana Adams and Bill Carter.

LES BICHES
Choreography: Francisco Moncion
Music: Francis Poulenc
Premiere: December 7, 1960, City Center of Music and Drama, New York.
Principal dancers: Sara Leland and Anthony Blum.

EBONY CONCERTO
Choreography: John Taras
Music: Igor Stravinsky
Premiere: December 7, 1960, City Center of Music and Drama, New York.
Dancers: Patricia McBride and Arthur Mitchell.

MODERN JAZZ:

VARIANTS
Choreography: George Balanchine
Music: Gunther Schuller (arrangement for orchestra, playing in the pit, and for the Modern Jazz Quartet, playing onstage)
Premiere: January 4, 1961, City Center of Music and Drama, New York.
Principal dancers: John Jones (guest artist), Diana Adams, Melissa Hayden, Arthur Mitchell.

ELECTRONICS
Choreography: George Balanchine
Music: Remi Gassmann (electronic work by Oskar Sala and the composer)
Decor: David Hays
Premiere: March 22, 1961, City Center for Music and Drama, New York.
Principal dancers: Diana Adams, Violette Verdy, Jacques d'Amboise, Edward Villella.

VALSE ET VARIATIONS
(Later called RAYMONDA VARIATIONS)
Choreography: George Balanchine
Music: Alexander Glazounov (a score compiled from the ballet RAYMONDA)
Decor: Horace Armistead
Costumes: Karinska
Premiere: December 7, 1961, City Center of Music and Drama, New York.
Dancers: Patricia Wilde, Jacques d'Amboise; with Victoria Simon, Suki Schorer, Gloria Govrin, Carol Sumner, Patricia Neary; and Susan Keniff, Marlene Mesavage, Marnee Morris, Ellen Shire, Bettijane Sills, Lynda Yourth.

A MIDSUMMER NIGHT'S DREAM
Choreography: George Balanchine
Music: Felix Mendelssohn (all incidental music composed for the several productions of the play, among them Opus 20 and Opus 61; as well as the following pieces: Overture to Athalie, Opus 74; Overture to The Fair Melusine, Opus 32; Overture to The First Walpurgis Night, Opus 60; Symphony No. 9 for Strings; and Overture to Son and Stranger, Opus 89)
Decor: David Hays
Costumes: Karinska
Premiere: January 17, 1962, City Center of Music and Drama, New York.
Principal dancers: Melissa Hayden (Titania), Conrad Ludlow (Cavalier to Titania), Edward Villella (Oberon), Arthur Mitchell (Puck), Patricia McBride (Hermia), Jillana (Helena), Nicholas Magallanes (Lysander), Bill Carter (Demetrius), Gloria Govrin (Hippolyta), Francisco Moncion (Theseus), Roland Vazquez (Bottom), Violette Verdy and Conrad Ludlow (pas de deux in Act 2).

BUGAKU
Choreography: George Balanchine
Music: Toshiro Mayuzumi
Decor: David Hays
Costumes: Karinska
Premiere: March 20, 1963, City Center of Music and Drama, New York.
Principal dancers: Allegra Kent, Edward Villella.

ARCADE
Choreography: John Taras
Music: Igor Stravinsky (Concerto for Piano and Wind Instruments)
Decor: David Hays
Costumes: Ruth Sobotka
Premiere: March 28, 1963, City Center of Music and Drama, New York.
Principal dancers: Suzanne Farrell, Arthur Mitchell.

MOVEMENTS FOR PIANO AND ORCHESTRA
Choreography: George Balanchine
Music: Igor Stravinsky (Movements for Piano and Orchestra, 1958–59)
Premiere: April 9, 1963, City Center of Music and Drama, New York.
Principal dancers: Suzanne Farrell, Jacques d'Amboise.

THE CHASE
(THE VIXEN'S CHOICE)
Choreography: Jacques d'Amboise
Music: Wolfgang Amadeus Mozart (Horn Concerto No. 3 in E Flat, K. 447)
Decor: David Hays
Costumes: Karinska
Premiere: September 18, 1963, City Center of Music and Drama, New York.
Principal dancers: Allegra Kent (The Vixen), André Prokovsky (The Duke), Shaun O'Brien (A Wealthy Friend).

FANTASY
Choreography: John Taras
Music: Franz Schubert (Fantasy Piano Duet, Opus 103, orchestrated by Felix Mottl)
Premiere: September 24, 1963, City Center of Music and Drama, New York.
Principal dancers: Patricia McBride and Edward Villella; Carol Sumner, Marlene Mesavage, Robert Rodham, Earle Sieveling.

MEDITATION
Choreography: George Balanchine
Music: Peter Ilyich Tchaikovsky (from Souvenir d'un lieu cher, a set of three pieces for violin and piano, Opus 42, orchestrated by Alexander Glazounov)
Premiere: December 10, 1963, City Center of Music and Drama, New York.
Dancers: Suzanne Farrell, Jacques d'Amboise.

TARANTELLA
Choreography: George Balanchine
Music: Louis Gottschalk (Grande Tarantelle, reconstructed and orchestrated by Hershy Kay)
Costumes: Karinska
Premiere: January 7, 1964, City Center of Music and Drama, New York.
Dancers: Patricia McBride, Edward Villella.

QUATUOR
Choreography: Jacques d'Amboise
Music: Dimitri Shostakovich (String Quartet No. 1)
Premiere: January 16, 1964, City Center of Music and Drama, New York.
Dancers: Mimi Paul and Jacques d'Amboise; Roland Vazquez and Robert Maiorano.

CLARINADE
Choreography: George Balanchine
Music: Morton Gould (Derivations for Clarinet and Jazz Band, 1954–55)
Premiere: April 29, 1964, New York State Theater. (The music, composed for Benny Goodman, was played by him in the orchestra pit on opening night. CLARINADE was the first new ballet staged at the New York State Theater, Lincoln Center.)
Dancers: Gloria Govrin and Arthur Mitchell, Suzanne Farrell and Anthony Blum, with Bettijane Sills and Richard Rapp, Carol Sumner and Robert Rodham, and corps de ballet.

DIM LUSTRE
Choreography: Antony Tudor
Music: Richard Strauss (Burleske for Piano and Orchestra)
Decor and costumes: Beni Montresor
Premiere: May 6, 1964, New York State Theater. (This ballet was originally created by Tudor for Ballet Theater, October 20, 1943.)
Principal dancers: Patricia McBride (The Lady with Him), Edward Villella (The Gentleman with Her), Robert Rodham (It Was Spring), Patricia Neary (She Wore Perfume), Richard Rapp (He Wore a White Tie).

IRISH FANTASY
Choreography: Jacques d'Amboise
Music: Camille Saint-Saëns
(from incidental ballet music
for the opera HENRY VIII)
Decor: David Hays
Costumes: Karinska
Premiere: August 12, 1964, Greek
Theater, Los Angeles. (New York
premiere: October 8, 1964, New
York State Theater.)
Principal dancers: Melissa Hayden,
André Prokovsky, and Anthony Blum,
Frank Ohman.

PIÈGE DE LUMIÈRE
Choreography: John Taras
Music: Jean-Michel Damase
Decor: Felix Labisse
Costumes: André Levasseur
Book: Philippe Hériat
Supervision: David Hays
Premiere: October 1, 1964, New
York State Theater. (This ballet was
originally created by Taras for Grand
Ballet du Marquis de Cuevas,
December 23, 1952.)
Principal dancers: Maria Tallchief
(Queen of the Morphides), André
Prokovsky (Iphias), Arthur Mitchell
(Young Convict).

BALLET IMPERIAL (II)
Choreography: George Balanchine
Staging: Frederic Franklin
Music: Peter Ilyich Tchaikovsky
(Piano Concerto No. 2 in G major)
Decor: Rouben Ter-Arutunian
Costumes: Karinska
Premiere: October 15, 1964, New
York State Theater. (This ballet was
originally created by Balanchine for
American Ballet Caravan,
May 29, 1941.)
Principal dancers: Suzanne Farrell,
Patricia Neary, Jacques d'Amboise.

PAS DE DEUX AND DIVERTISSEMENT
Choreography: George Balanchine
Music: Léo Delibes
(from SYLVIA, LA SOURCE, and NAÏLA)
Costumes: Karinska
Premiere: January 14, 1965, New
York State Theater.
Principal dancers: Melissa Hayden,
André Prokovsky, Suki Schorer.

SHADOW'D GROUND
Choreography: John Taras
Music: Aaron Copland
(Dance Panels, 1962)
Book: Scott Burton
Production (with photographic projections):
designed by John Braden
Premiere: January 21, 1965, New
York State Theater.
Principal dancers: Kay Mazzo, Robert
Maiorano, Suki Schorer, Richard Rapp,
Jillana, Roland Vazquez.

HARLEQUINADE
Choreography: George Balanchine
Music: Riccardo Drigo
Decor and costumes: Rouben Ter-Arutunian
Premiere: February 4, 1965, New
York State Theater.
Principal dancers: Patricia McBride,
Edward Villella, Suki Schorer, Deni
Lamont, Gloria Govrin, Carol Sumner.

DON QUIXOTE
Choreography: George Balanchine
Music: Nicolas Nabokov
Decor and costumes: Esteban Francés
(costumes executed by Karinska)
Premiere: May 28, 1965, New York
State Theater. (Gala Benefit Preview,
May 27, 1965, with George
Balanchine in title role.)
Principal dancers: Richard Rapp,
Suzanne Farrell, Deni Lamont, Mimi
Paul, Marnee Morris.

VARIATIONS
Choreography: George Balanchine
Music: Igor Stravinsky
(Variations for Orchestra, dedicated to the
memory of Aldous Huxley)
Premiere: March 31, 1966, New
York State Theater.
Principal dancer: Suzanne Farrell.

SUMMERSPACE
Choreography: Merce Cunningham
Music: Morton Feldman
Decor and costumes: Robert Rauschenberg
Supervision of New York
production: John Braden
Premiere: April 14, 1966, New York
State Theater. (Revival from Merce
Cunningham and his Dance Company,
premiere, August 17, 1958, at the
American Dance Festival, Connecticut
College, New London, Connecticut.)
Dancers: Anthony Blum, Kay Mazzo,
Patricia Neary, Sara Leland, Deni
Lamont, Carol Sumner.

BRAHMS-SCHOENBERG QUARTET
Choreography: George Balanchine
Music: Johannes Brahms
(First Piano Quartet in G Minor,
Opus 25, orchestrated by
Arnold Schoenberg)
Decor: Peter Harvey
Costumes: Karinska
Premiere: April 21, 1966, New York
State Theater. (Gala Benefit Premiere:
April 19, 1966)
Principal dancers: Melissa Hayden,
André Prokovsky, Gloria Govrin,
Patricia McBride, Kent Stowell, Allegra
Kent, Edward Villella, Suzanne Farrell,
Jacques d'Amboise.

DIVERTIMENTO NO. 15 (II)
Choreography: George Balanchine
Music: Wolfgang Amadeus Mozart
(K. 287)
Decor: David Hays
Costumes: Karinska
Premiere: April 27, 1966, New York
State Theater. (Revival of Balanchine's
1956 ballet of the same name.)
Principal dancers: Melissa Hayden,
Bettijane Sills, Sara Leland, Mimi Paul,
Suki Schorer, Arthur Mitchell, Richard
Rapp, Kent Stowell.

JEUX
Choreography: John Taras
Music: Claude Debussy
Decor and costumes: Raoul Pène DuBois
(costumes executed by Karinska)
Premiere: April 28, 1966, New York
State Theater.
Dancers: Melissa Hayden, Allegra
Kent, Edward Villella.

NARKISSOS
Choreography: Edward Villella
Music: Robert Prince
Decor and costumes: John Braden
Premiere: July 21, 1966, Saratoga
Springs Performing Arts Center. (New
York premiere: November 24, 1966,
New York State Theater.)
Principal dancers: Edward Villella
(Narkissos), Patricia McBride (Echo
Figure), Michael Steele (Image-
Nemesis Figure).

LA GUIRLANDE DE CAMPRA
Choreography: John Taras
Music: Georges Auric, Arthur Honegger,
Francis Poulenc, Germaine Tailleferre,
Daniel Lesur, Alexis Roland-Manuel,
and Henri Sauguet, after a theme by
André Campra (written in 1717)
Decor: Peter Harvey
Costumes: Peter Harvey and
Esteban Francés (the latter some
costumes taken from Balanchine's
THE FIGURE IN THE CARPET)
Premiere: December 1, 1966, New
York State Theater. (A private benefit
performance was presented April 19,
1966 at the same theater.)
Principal dancers: Violette Verdy,
Melissa Hayden, Conrad Ludlow, Mimi
Paul, Patricia Neary, Marnee Morris,
Sara Leland, Suki Schorer, Carol
Sumner.

PROLOGUE
Choreography: Jacques d'Amboise
Music: selected from keyboard works
of William Byrd, Giles Farnaby,
and others (arrangement and orchestration
by Robert Irving)
Decor and costumes: Peter Larkin (costumes
executed by Karinska)
Premiere: January 12, 1967, New
York State Theater.
Principal dancers: Arthur Mitchell
(Othello), John Prinz (Iago), Frank
Ohman (Cassio), Mimi Paul
(Desdemona), Kay Mazzo (Emilia),
Marnee Morris (Allegra).

TROIS VALSES ROMANTIQUES
Choreography: George Balanchine
Music: Emmanuel Chabrier
Costumes: Karinska
Premiere: April 6, 1967, New York
State Theater.
Principal dancers: Melissa Hayden,
Arthur Mitchell, and Gloria Govrin,
Marnee Morris, Frank Ohman, and
Kent Stowell.

JEWELS
(a three-part program consisting of
Emeralds, Rubies, and Diamonds)
Choreography: George Balanchine
Music: Gabriel Fauré, from
PELLÉAS ET MÉLISANDE and SHYLOCK
(Emeralds); Igor Stravinsky,
Capriccio for Piano and Orchestra
(Rubies); and Peter Ilyich Tchaikovsky,
from Symphony No. 3 in D major
(Diamonds)
Scenery: Peter Harvey
Costumes: Karinska
Premiere: April 13, 1967, New York
State Theater.
Principal dancers: Violette Verdy,
Mimi Paul, Conrad Ludlow, Francisco
Moncion, Sara Leland, Suki Schorer,
and John Prinz (Emeralds);
Patricia McBride, Edward Villella,
and Patricia Neary (Rubies); Suzanne
Farrell and Jacques d'Amboise
(Diamonds).

GLINKAIANA
Choreography: George Balanchine
Music: Mikhail Glinka
Scenery and costumes: Esteban Francés
Premiere: November 23, 1967, New
York State Theater.
Principal dancers: Violette Verdy,
Paul Mejia; Mimi Paul, John Clifford;
Melissa Hayden; and Patricia
McBride, Edward Villella.

METASTASEIS AND PITHOPRAKTA
Choreography: George Balanchine
Music: Iannis Xenakis
Premiere: January 18, 1968, New
York State Theater.
Principal dancers: Suzanne Farrell
and Arthur Mitchell.

HAYDN CONCERTO
Choreography: John Taras
Music: Franz Joseph Haydn
(Concerto for Flute and Oboe)
Scenery and costumes: Raoul Pène DuBois
(costumes executed by Karinska)
Premiere: January 25, 1968, New
York State Theater.
Principal dancers: Kay Mazzo, Patricia
McBride, John Prinz, Earle Sieveling.

SLAUGHTER ON TENTH AVENUE
Choreography: George Balanchine
Music: Richard Rodgers
(from the musical ON YOUR TOES)
New orchestration: Hershy Kay
Scenery: Jo Mielziner
Costumes: Irene Sharaff
Premiere: May 2, 1968, New York
State Theater.
Principal dancers: Suzanne Farrell
and Arthur Mitchell.

STRAVINSKY: SYMPHONY IN C
Choreography: John Clifford
Music: Igor Stravinsky
Costumes: John Braden
Premiere: May 9, 1968, New York
State Theater.
Principal dancers: Kay Mazzo, Marnee
Morris, Renee Estópinal, Anthony
Blum, John Prinz.

TCHAIKOVSKY SUITE NO. 2
Choreography: Jacques d'Amboise
Music: Peter Ilyich Tchaikovsky
(Suite No. 2 for Orchestra)
Production design: John Braden
Premiere: January 9, 1969, New York
State Theater.
Principal dancers: Marnee Morris,
John Prinz; Allegra Kent, Francisco
Moncion; and Linda Merrill, John
Clifford.

FANTASIES
Choreography: John Clifford
Music: Ralph Vaughan Williams
(Fantasia on a Theme by Thomas Tallis)
Costumes: Robert O'Hearn
Premiere: January 23, 1969, New
York State Theater.
Principal dancers: Sara Leland, Kay
Mazzo, Anthony Blum, Conrad
Ludlow.

LA SOURCE
Choreography: George Balanchine
Music: Léo Delibes
(from LA SOURCE and NAÏLA)
Costumes: Karinska
Premiere: February 5, 1969, New
York State Theater.
Principal dancers: Violette Verdy,
John Prinz, and Suki Schorer.

PRELUDE, FUGUE, AND RIFFS
Choreography: John Clifford
Music: Leonard Bernstein
Premiere: May 15, 1969, New York State Theater. (Gala Benefit Preview: May 8, 1969.)
Principal dancers: Linda Merrill and John Clifford.

DANCES AT A GATHERING
Choreography: Jerome Robbins
Music: Frederic Chopin (Mazurka Op. 63, No. 3; Waltz Op. 69, No. 2; Mazurka Op. 33, No. 3; Mazurka Op. 6, No. 2 and No. 4; Mazurka Op. 7, No. 4 and No. 5; Mazurka Op. 24, No. 2; Waltz Op. 42; Waltz Op. 34, No. 2; Mazurka Op. 56, No. 2; Etude Op. 25, No. 4; Waltz Op. 34, No. 1; Waltz Op. 70, No. 2; Etude Op. 25, No. 5; Etude Op. 10, No. 2; Scherzo Op. 20, No. 1; Nocturne Op. 15, No. 1.—for solo piano)
Costumes: Joe Eula
Premiere: May 22, 1969, New York State Theater. (Gala Benefit Preview: May 8, 1969.)
Principal dancers: Allegra Kent, Sara Leland, Kay Mazzo, Patricia McBride, Violette Verdy, Anthony Blum, John Clifford, Robert Maiorano, John Prinz, and Edward Villella.
Pianist: Gordon Boelzner.

PAS DE DEUX (II)
Choreography: Jacques d'Amboise
Music: Anton von Webern (Six Pieces for Orchestra)
Production design: John Braden
Premiere: May 29, 1969, New York State Theater.
Principal dancers: Deborah Flomine and Jacques d'Amboise.

REVERIES
Choreography: John Clifford
Music: Peter Ilyich Tchaikovsky (Suite No. 1, movements 1, 3, 4, and 6)
Costumes: Joe Eula
Premiere: December 4, 1969, New York State Theater.
Principal dancers: Gelsey Kirkland, Johnna Kirkland, Anthony Blum, Conrad Ludlow, and Gloria Govrin.

IN THE NIGHT
Choreography: Jerome Robbins
Music: Frederic Chopin (Nocturnes: Op. 27, No. 1; Op. 55, No. 1 and No. 2; and Op. 9, No. 2.—for solo piano)
Costumes: Joe Eula
Premiere: January 29, 1970, New York State Theater.
Principal dancers: Kay Mazzo and Anthony Blum; Violette Verdy and Peter Martins; and Patricia McBride and Francisco Moncion.
Pianist: Gordon Boelzner.

WHO CARES?
Choreography: George Balanchine
Music: George Gershwin (Lyrics: Ira Gershwin)
Orchestration: Hershy Kay
Decor: Jo Mielziner
Costumes: Karinska
Premiere: February 5, 1970, New York State Theater.
Principal dancers: Karin von Aroldingen, Patricia McBride, Marnee Morris, and Jacques d'Amboise.

SARABANDE AND DANSE
Choreography: John Clifford
Music: Claude Debussy (orchestration by Maurice Ravel)
Costumes: Joe Eula
Premiere: May 21, 1970, New York State Theater.
Principal dancers: Johnna Kirkland, Violette Verdy, John Clifford, Earle Sieveling.

SUITE NO. 3
Choreography: George Balanchine
Music: Peter Ilyich Tchaikovsky
Scenery and costumes: Nicolas Benois
Premiere: December 3, 1970, New York State Theater. (Including a revival of Balanchine's THEME AND VARIATIONS of 1960.)
Principal dancers: Karin von Aroldingen, Anthony Blum; Kay Mazzo, Conrad Ludlow; Marnee Morris, John Clifford; and Gelsey Kirkland, Edward Villella.

KODÁLY DANCES
Choreography: John Clifford
Music: Zoltán Kodály (Dances of Galanta and Dances of Marosszék)
Costumes: Stanley Simmons
Premiere: January 14, 1971, New York State Theater.
Principal dancers: Johnna Kirkland, Anthony Blum, and Colleen Neary.

FOUR LAST SONGS
Choreography: Lorca Massine
Music: Richard Strauss
Decor: John Braden
Costumes: Joe Eula
Premiere: January 21, 1971, New York State Theater.
Dancers: Robert Maiorano, Susan Pilarre, Bonnie Moore, Meg Gordon, Johnna Kirkland, Bryan Pitts, Lisa de Ribere, Bonita Borne, Nolan T'Sani.

CONCERTO FOR TWO SOLO PIANOS
Choreography: Richard Tanner
Music: Igor Stravinsky
Costumes: Stanley Simmons
Premiere: January 21, 1971, New York State Theater.
Principal dancers: Gelsey Kirkland, Colleen Neary, James Bogan, John Clifford, David Richardson, and Christine Redpath, Giselle Roberge.

CONCERTO FOR JAZZ BAND AND ORCHESTRA
Choreography: George Balanchine and Arthur Mitchell
Music: Rolf Lieberman
Premiere: May 6, 1971, New York State Theater. (One performance only for the Benefit of the New York City Ballet.)
Dancers: The Dance Theater of Harlem and the New York City Ballet.

OCTANDRE
Choreography: Richard Tanner
Music: Edgar Varèse (Octandre, 1924, and Intégrales, 1925)
Premiere: May 13, 1971, New York State Theater.
Principal dancers: Johnna Kirkland, Bryan Pitts, and Christine Redpath.

THE GOLDBERG VARIATIONS
Choreography: Jerome Robbins
Music: Johann Sebastian Bach (For solo piano)
Costumes: Joe Eula
Premiere: May 27, 1971, New York State Theater.
Dancers: Karin von Aroldingen, Renee Estópinal, Susan Hendl, Gelsey Kirkland, Sara Leland, Patricia McBride, Anthony Blum, John Clifford, Peter Martins, Robert Maiorano, Michael Steele, Helgi Tomasson, Robert Weiss, Bruce Wells.
Pianist: Gordon Boelzner.

PAMTGG
Choreography: George Balanchine
Music: Roger Kellaway (based on themes by Stan Applebaum and Sid Woloshin)
Decor: Jo Mielziner
Costume design: Irene Sharaff
Premiere: June 17, 1971, New York State Theater.
Principal dancers: Kay Mazzo, Victor Castelli; Karin von Aroldingen, Frank Ohman; and Sara Leland, John Clifford.

PRINTEMPS
Choreography: Lorca Massine
Music: Claude Debussy
Costume design: Irene Sharaff
Premiere: January 13, 1972, New York State Theater.
Principal dancers: Violette Verdy and Christine Redpath, Virginia Stuart.

CHOPINIANA
Staging: Alexandra Danilova, after Michel Fokine
Music: Frederic Chopin (Prelude Op. 28, No. 7; Nocturne Op. 32, No. 2; Waltz Op. 70, No. 1; Mazurka Op. 33, No. 3; Mazurka Op. 67, No. 3; repeat of Prelude Op. 28, No. 7; Waltz Op. 64, No. 2; Waltz Op. 18, No. 1.—for solo piano)
Premiere: January 20, 1972, New York State Theater.
Principal dancers: Kay Mazzo, Peter Martins, Karin von Aroldingen, Susan Hendl.
Pianist: Gordon Boelzner.

WATERMILL
Choreography: Jerome Robbins
Music: Teiji Ito
Decor: Jerome Robbins in association with David Reppa
Costumes: Patricia Zipprodt
Premiere: February 3, 1972, New York State Theater.
Dancers: Edward Villella and Penny Dudleston, Hermes Conde, Jean-Pierre Frohlich, Bart Cook, Tracy Bennett, Victor Castelli, Deni Lamont, Colleen Neary, Robert Maiorano.

SONATA
Choreography: George Balanchine
Music: Igor Stravinsky (a fragment of his first sonata for solo piano)
Premiere: June 18, 1972, New York State Theater.
Dancers: Sara Leland, John Clifford.
Pianist: Madeleine Malraux.

SCHERZO FANTASTIQUE
Choreography: Jerome Robbins
Music: Igor Stravinsky
Premiere: June 18, 1972, New York State Theater.
Principal dancers: Gelsey Kirkland, Bart Cook, and Bryan Pitts, Stephen Caras, Victor Castelli.

SYMPHONY IN THREE MOVEMENTS
Choreography: George Balanchine
Music: Igor Stravinsky
Premiere: June 18, 1972, New York State Theater.
Principal dancers: Sara Leland, Marnee Morris, Lynda Yourth, Helgi Tomasson, Edward Villella, Robert Weiss, and Deborah Flomine, Johnna Kirkland, Delia Peters, Susan Pilarre, Giselle Roberge, Deni Lamont, Robert Maiorano, Frank Ohman, Earle Sieveling, Bruce Wells.

VIOLIN CONCERTO
(later called STRAVINSKY VIOLIN CONCERTO)
Choreography: George Balanchine
Music: Igor Stravinsky
Premiere: June 18, 1972, New York State Theater. (The music was first used for dancing by Balanchine, in a wholly different version, for the original Ballets Russes in 1941, under the title BALUSTRADE, with costumes and scenery by Pavel Tchelitchev.)
Principal dancers: Karin von Aroldingen, Kay Mazzo, Jean-Pierre Bonnefous, Peter Martins.
Violinist: Joseph Silverstein

SYMPHONY IN E FLAT
Choreography: John Clifford
Music: Igor Stravinsky (Opus 1)
Costumes: Stanley Simmons
Premiere: June 20, 1972, New York State Theater.
Principal dancers: Gelsey Kirkland and Peter Martins.

CONCERTO FOR PIANO AND WINDS
Choreography: John Taras
Music: Igor Stravinsky
(For piano, wind instruments,
timpani, and string bass)
Costumes: Rouben Ter-Arutunian
Premiere: June 20, 1972, New York
State Theater. (The music was first
used for dancing by Taras, in a wholly
different version, for the New York
City Ballet in 1963, under the title
ARCADE.)
Principal dancers: Bruce Wells, Robert
Maiorano, Frank Ohman, Tracy
Bennett, Victor Castelli, Peter
Naumann.

DANSES CONCERTANTES
Choreography: George Balanchine
Music: Igor Stravinsky
Decor and costumes: Eugene Berman
(originally produced for the
Ballets Russes de Monte Carlo)
Premiere: June 20, 1972, New York
State Theater.
Principal dancers: Lynda Yourth and
John Clifford.

OCTUOR
Choreography: Richard Tanner
Music: Igor Stravinsky
(For wind instruments)
Premiere: June 21, 1972, New York
State Theater.
Dancers: Elise Flagg, Deborah
Flomine, Delia Peters, Lisa de Ribere,
Tracy Bennett, James Bogan,
Daniel Duell, Jean-Pierre Frohlich.

SERENADE IN A
Choreography: Todd Bolender
Music: Igor Stravinsky
(For solo piano)
Costumes: Stanley Simmons
Premiere: June 21, 1972, New York
State Theater.
Principal dancers: Susan Hendl,
Robert Maiorano, Robert Weiss.
Pianist: Madeleine Malraux.

**DIVERTIMENTO FROM
"LE BAISER DE LA FÉE"**
Choreography: George Balanchine
Music: Igor Stravinsky
Premiere: June 21, 1972, New York
State Theater.
Principal dancers: Patricia McBride,
Helgi Tomasson, and Bettijane Sills,
Carol Sumner.

SCHERZO À LA RUSSE
Choreography: George Balanchine
Music: Igor Stravinsky
Costumes: Karinska
Premiere: June 21, 1972, New York
State Theater.
Principal dancers: Karin von
Aroldingen and Kay Mazzo.

CIRCUS POLKA
Choreography: Jerome Robbins
Music: Igor Stravinsky
Premiere: June 21, 1972, New York
State Theater.
Dancers: Jerome Robbins (Ring
Master) and children from the School
of American Ballet.

SCÈNES DE BALLET
Choreography: John Taras
Music: Igor Stravinsky
Costumes: Karinska
Premiere: June 22, 1972, New York
State Theater.
Principal dancers: Patricia McBride
and Jean-Pierre Bonnefous.

DUO CONCERTANT
Choreography: George Balanchine
Music: Igor Stravinsky
(For violin and piano)
Premiere: June 22, 1972, New York
State Theater.
Principal dancers: Kay Mazzo and
Peter Martins.
Violinist: Lamar Alsop.
Pianist: Gordon Boelzner.

THE SONG OF THE NIGHTINGALE
Choreography: John Taras
Music: Igor Stravinsky
Costume and prop design: Rouben
Ter-Arutunian
Premiere: June 22, 1972, New York
State Theater.
Principal dancers: Gelsey Kirkland,
Elise Flagg, Penny Dudleston,
Francisco Moncion, Peter Naumann.

PIANO-RAG-MUSIC
Choreography: Todd Bolender
Music: Igor Stravinsky
Costumes: Stanley Simmons
Premiere: June 23, 1972, New York
State Theater.
Principal dancers: Gloria Govrin and
John Clifford.
Pianist: Madeleine Malraux.

DUMBARTON OAKS
Choreography: Jerome Robbins
Music: Igor Stravinsky
Costumes: Patricia Zipprodt
Premiere: June 23, 1972, New York
State Theater.
Principal dancers: Allegra Kent and
Anthony Blum.

ODE
Choreography: Lorca Massine
Music: Igor Stravinsky
(Elegiacal Chant in Three Parts
for Orchestra, 1943)
Premiere: June 23, 1972, New York
State Theater.
Principal dancers: Colleen Neary,
Christine Redpath, Robert Maiorano,
Earle Sieveling.

PULCINELLA
Choreography: George Balanchine
and Jerome Robbins
Music: Igor Stravinsky
(after Giambattista Pergolesi)
Scenery and costumes: Eugene Berman
Premiere: June 23, 1972, New York
State Theater.
Principal dancers: Violette Verdy,
Edward Villella; Francisco Moncion,
Michael Arshansky, Shaun O'Brien;
George Balanchine, Jerome Robbins.

**CHORAL VARIATIONS ON BACH'S
"VOM HIMMEL HOCH"**
Choreography: George Balanchine
Music: Igor Stravinsky
(For mixed chorus and orchestra)
Scenery: Rouben Ter-Arutunian
Premiere: June 25, 1972, New York
State Theater.
Principal dancers: Karin von
Aroldingen, Melissa Hayden, Sara
Leland, Violette Verdy, Anthony
Blum, Peter Martins.

REQUIEM CANTICLES
Choreography: Jerome Robbins
Music: Igor Stravinsky
(For contralto, bass soloists,
chorus, and orchestra)
Premiere: June 25, 1972, New York
State Theater.
Principal dancers: Merrill Ashley,
Susan Hendl, Robert Maiorano,
Bruce Wells.

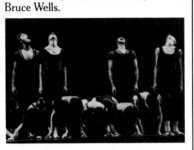

CONCERTO NO. 2
(later called TCHAIKOVSKY CONCERTO NO.2)
Choreography: George Balanchine
Music: Peter Ilyich Tchaikovsky
(For solo piano)
Premiere: January 12, 1973, New
York State Theater. (This ballet is a
reworking of Balanchine's BALLET
IMPERIAL of 1964.)
Principal dancers: Patricia McBride,
Peter Martins, Colleen Neary, Tracy
Bennett, Victor Castelli, Suzanne Erlon,
Marjorie Spohn.
Pianist: Gordon Boelzner.

A BEETHOVEN PAS DE DEUX
Choreography: Jerome Robbins
Music: Ludwig van Beethoven
(Four Bagatelles for solo piano)
Costumes: Florence Klotz
Gala Benefit Preview: May 16, 1973,
New York State Theater. (For one
performance only; premiere scheduled
for the fall of 1973.)
Dancers: Violette Verdy and Jean-
Pierre Bonnefous.
Pianist: Jerry Zimmerman

CORTÈGE HONGROIS
Choreography: George Balanchine
Music: Alexander Glazounov
(from RAYMONDA)
Decor and costumes: Rouben Ter-Arutunian
Premiere: May 17, 1973, New York
State Theater. (Gala Benefit Preview:
May 16.)
Dancers: Melissa Hayden and Jacques
d'Amboise; Karin von Aroldingen and
Jean-Pierre Bonnefous.

AN EVENING'S WALTZES
Choreography: Jerome Robbins
Music: Serge Prokofiev (from Suite of
Waltzes)
Decor and costumes: Rouben Ter-Arutunian
Premiere: May 24, 1973, New York
Theater.
Dancers: Patricia McBride and Jean-
Pierre Bonnefous; Christine Redpath
and John Clifford; Sara Leland and
Bart Cook.

GRAPHIC CREDITS

This book was photo-composed in film by University Graphics, Shrewsbury, N.J., and Typographic Innovations, Inc., New York, N.Y.; the four-color and Stonetone Process reproduction was carried out by Rapoport Printing Corporation, New York, N.Y. The full-color process separations were supplied by Chanticleer Press, New York, N.Y. The binding was done by Sendor Bindery, New York, N.Y.

The text type, Cheltenham, was designed by Bertram Grosvenor Goodhue specifically for Ingalls Kimball, Cheltenham Press of New York. The Cheltenham face appeared in 1902; it owes little or nothing to historical inspiration, and in that sense it is truly a twentieth-century type design.

The display type, ITC Serif Gothic is an original typeface designed by Herb Lubalin and Tony DiSpigna. It combines gothic simplicity with traditional roman elegance.

Production and manufacturing coordination was directed by Ellen McNeilly.

Manuscript and proof coordination was handled by Neal T. Jones.

Design and graphics were directed by R. D. Scudellari.

PHOTO CREDITS

The dance photographs on the following pages are by George Platt Lynes: 5, 21, 22, 24, 28, 32-9, 41, 42, 45, 48, 51, 70, 79-81, 83-5, 86 (right), 87, 88, 97-100, 101 (right), 102, 104, 105 (left), 106-7, 108, 113-24, 154 (right), 248 (all but top, col. 1), 249 (col. 2), 250 (all but bottom, col. 5), 251 (top, col. 1; col. 2), 257. All other dance photographs are by Martha Swope.